Splintered Malice

By

H G Tudor

Splintered Malice

By

H G Tudor

Published by Insight Books

A Brilliant Mind

My mind is brilliant. It is a masterpiece of intellect and memory. Most people have a mind that is prevented from achieving magnificence because it is spread too thin. The phrase 'jack of all trades and master of none' is one that is certainly applicable here. Other people must use their minds to do their jobs, care for their children, operate a home, socialise with their friends and so forth. At the outset a mind is charged with absorbing knowledge about so many things. In an academic setting it is obliged to learn about mathematics, English, geography, history, physics and all the other subjects that pupils are forced to engage in. How can the mind become honed and sharpened when it is expected to demonstrate such elasticity. Who could function effectively when there is pushed and pulled in such a manner? Your minds are sent one way and the dragged in a different direction as you switch between so many differing and competing things. My mind is not like this.

My mind has been created to do one thing. It has been created to gather fuel. It exists for no other purpose. Everything else that happens is simply a by-product or collateral damage of the everlasting quest for fuel. Sometimes great things may happen as a consequence of what my kind and I do but that is just a happy coincidence. We never intended for that invention or that report to be made so that it would be brilliant in itself. No, we did it because we knew that it would provide us with fuel. This single-minded purpose for which our minds have been designed means that we are ultra-effective. Nothing else gets in the way as our mind channels all its energies to securing fuel. Our minds are engineered to be masters of manipulation and memory banks that store away the tiniest of details from way back to enable us to call on that fact or instance so that we may better discharge our obligation to find fuel. Every firing synapse inside our minds, every electric current that races across and through it has only one aim and that is to bring about fuel.

Why are machines so efficient? It is because they are designed with one purpose in mind. The washing machine will wash your clothes, the coffee maker will dispense a coffee for you and the television set will show your pictures and generate sound. You may suggest that a machine does several things but that is merely separate machines placed within a composite. Machines are not troubled by decisions as what to have to eat for dinner or where a new picture should be placed. They have one aim and they discharge it with sleek and admirable effectiveness. The mind of the narcissist is similarly designed. It is a triumph of engineering. It can carry out different tasks, naturally, but each of these has only one outcome. The outcome is the provision and securing of fuel.

Compare it to your mind. You may paint a marvellous picture as the artistic part of your mind applies itself to such a creation. You did that to exercise your artistic skills, to make you happy and perhaps to make someone else happy when you give or sell them that painting. You read a book to enjoy the content. You sing a song because it makes you feel uplifted. You cook a meal because you need to feed others. All of these applications of your mind achieve different outcomes but that is not the case with our minds.

We are superior and our superiority is based on the single application for which our minds have been created. It stands to reason that if you specialise in one thing and one thing alone you will be the best at it by far. That is what has happened with our minds. They are programmed to act with a single purpose and in doing so they achieve brilliance.

Triple Track

One of the key elements to my success in achieving my aims is through my brilliant mind. This is because my mind engages in something called triple tracking. This first arose when I was engaged in discussion with Dr O. For those of you who are not familiar with Dr O, she is the immaculately presented doctor charged with providing me with enlightenment about whom I am and why I do as I do. She is always pristine and I often reflect on how clean I imagine that she will taste. Dr O works with Dr E as well and I have been subjected to their repeated consultations and observations as we have developed our relationships. Accordingly, I was discussing with Dr O the issue of how I went about planning my harvesting of fuel.

"I am always planning," I explained to Dr O.

"Always?" she asked.

"Indeed. Even as we are talking now I am speaking to you and considering the impact of my words. Another part of my mind is analysing what I am saying and what you are responding with whilst another part of my mind is considering what is to be said or done next. I call it triple tracking."

"I see," remarked Dr O and she made a note in her book that rested on one of her elegant knees.

"And you do this all of the time?" she asked.

"Absolutely. I may be sat talking to somebody. I am explaining something to them as my mind is considering how best I might extract fuel from them as it is also considering who else I might garner my fuel from. I am dealing with the present, reflecting on the present and then thinking about the future. Three stages are in play and I am addressing all three stages at once. I have always been able to do this. It provides for a greater degree of efficiency and effectiveness."

"Give me an example."

"Okay. Let us say that I am asking a person questions about their past. I am asking the questions as I am also considering the best questions to ask, having regard to the way that the conversation is going and also in order to provoke the most interesting responses. At the same time I will be making a note of those responses with a view to considering how best to utilise them in the future. Thus, making it more specific, my target and I might be discussing how this person had been bullied as a child. I consider which questions I should ask to draw out more detail of how and when the bullying took place. When the person tells me that the bullying was premised on excluding that person from playing with other children then I make a note in the future to use isolation and exclusion as an excellent method for drawing an emotional reaction from him or her and thus gain fuel."

Dr O nodded and continued to make notes.

"Do you think everybody has this capacity to triple track, as you describe it?"

"No," I answered firmly, "I have not come across anyone else who has done this. Admittedly, it is not something that I ask people about, but I can tell that people do not do this and certainly not those who are of my kind. It is difficult to explain but ordinary people would have no real cause for it and therefore would not develop this skill of their mind. They are too busy caught up in the here and now. They operate on a single track. If they are paying attention to what is being said and I mean they are really paying attention, then they will hesitate before they speak because they need time to think about what they are going to say. If they respond straight away then it is clear that they have not been listening to what has been said to them because they have not been focussed on listening and have been able to respond immediately. There is no chance that they have even been considering how they might use the information or situation for a future benefit."

"Might they double track. For instance, I am listening to you and at the same time I am reflecting on what you are saying in order to formulate my response."

"But are you really doctor? Can you honestly say that you hear everything I have said when your mind is focussed on what you are going to ask me next? Are you not preoccupied by what is about to happen so that you lose something of what is actually happening now?"

"I understand your point but I think I am able to listen to you and think about my response and do both fully."

"Well you are an intelligent woman, Dr O, so perhaps you can double track but I bet you cannot triple track."

She did not respond to this and by her silence I judged that she evidently agreed with me.

"And this triple tracking that you engage in, its use is purely for fuel?"

I nodded.

"Might you apply it in another way? For example, what if you were a barrister and you were asking a witness a question, anticipating and analysing the response and then considering how it would impact on evidence further down the line. I should imagine that many barristers and of course they are intelligent people, will do this regularly."

"The difference is that the barrister will have prepared his questions or a skeleton of what they will be. He or she has already applied his or her mind to the questions that are to be asked."

"Surely that is not the case all the time, there will be occasions where a witness does not answer in a way that is to be expected and therefore the barrister will have to alter his tack and frame new questions. Surely the same applies to you when you are speaking to one of your targets?" she asked.

"Ah but he is trained to be prepared for that and he will have already formulated in his preparation where to go to next if a different answer has been provided," I countered.

"But," began Dr O but I interrupted her.

"But aren't you trained to be prepared?" I said.

"Sorry?"

"You were about to say 'but aren't you trained to be prepared' weren't you?" I asked.

"Yes, yes I was."

"That wasn't training, that was me thinking ahead and anticipating what you were going to ask next. It is an innate ability that I have and this is what sets me apart from the others. They may appear to triple track but they do so from rigorous training and also doing the same thing over and over again."

Dr O said nothing and wrote in her notebook.

I knew as well what she was writing even though she was sat across from me, her notebook tilted away from me.

It is this knowledge which makes me so effective and sets my mind apart from the minds of others.

The Eyes Are My Sanctuary

When I first meet you and I look into your eyes I find a certain sanctuary. Your optimistic eyes seem like paradise to me. I can see the hope, the desire and the adoration burning in your eyes. Be they brown, blue, green or grey I can see the promise of salvation. That is why I try so hard to win you over. I apply everything I can think of to ensure that you stay with me so I can gaze deep into your eyes and drink the delight, trust and admiration that flow from them. You have no idea how much I need to see those things. The more I show you love, affection and how interested I am in you, the greater the radiance that shines towards me and the sanctuary that you have created for me remains in place. It surrounds and protects me, keeping the pain and the hurt at bay. It is a simple formula; I shower you with affection and attention and you return to me that magical protection in the form of how you look at me. The admiring glance across the restaurant table, the wide-eyed desire when we are in bed together, the simmering passion as I undress you and the sheer adoration as you quicken your pace to cross a room or a road to meet me. I need that place of safety and respite. A sanctuary where I know that the whispering, taunting voices will be silenced. A place of salvation where that cold-fingered dread cannot grip my throat and silence my scream of terror. Those draining shades that manifest from a past which I try to consign into oblivion cannot reach me in this place. That is what I hope for and believe every time somebody new enters my life. If I can just keep you sending me the power and the protection arising from those magnificent eyes then I will be safe. I apply my every effort to maintaining that gaze which will keep the darkness and the foul creatures lurking amongst it at bay. Everything I do is geared around making you feel happy, loved and wanted so that you will keep looking at me in that way and preserving my sanctuary.

Yet, no matter how hard I try, notwithstanding every effort I apply to maintaining your state of joy and happiness, you let me down. Each time someone new appears I am given renewed hope that this time the sanctuary will be permanently preserved and each time you fail me. Why do you do this to me when I try so damn hard for you? The burning admiration that you exhibited towards me suddenly dims. The adoration that blazed across the room has lost its intensity. The shining lustre of desire has become dulled. You do this to me and in so doing you turn the key of the gates, lift the heavy bar and push them open. You do this on purpose don't you? You breach the citadel so that the screeching, moaning and howling tormentors that have gathered beyond its walls are admitted to assault me once again as they try to pull me into the abyss of insanity. The craven creatures slither forward, their mucus-covered tendrils slipping and sliding as they seek me out, determined to coil about me and drag me silent with terror into that place I must not go. Why do you do this to me? What have I done to deserve this treatment? All I have ever done is love you with a perfect love to cause you to generate that sanctuary and now, with no warning or help, you allow the paradise to be violated by those that seek to harm me.

I am left with no option but to fight them. I need to muster my strength and seek to defeat these agents of darkness by gathering my rage and anger. I must lash out in all directions, often and without restraint in order to stop my tormentors from destroying me. It matters not who is caught up in this frenzy it is incidental whether you or anyone else finds themselves collateral damage from my necessary defence of my being. I fight and fight and fight, it is exhausting but it must be done. I have to survive until the next promise of sanctuary is identified and drifts my way. There I will find peace and a place to restore my waning strength. Is it you? Perhaps this time the sanctuary will remain intact.

Impervious to Penetration

You should consider that you are rather fortunate to be given these glimpses into the workings of my mind through this book and the others that I have written. Ordinarily you are unable to peer into the dark mind of my kind and I. As an empathic individual you do cultivate an ability to understand the way that other people are thinking and how they are feeling. It provides you with a degree of intuition and this is applicable to many of the people that you meet. You apply this ability for the purposes of doing good things and I understand why you do that. Notwithstanding this ability however it does not work with us. You are unable to establish what is going through our minds or what we might be thinking, no matter how desperate you are to be able to do this. This is because we do not abide by the normal rules and conventions of everyone else. We do not travel on the well-worn path but instead we take those routes which are from the beaten path. These routes are tangled, unmapped and dangerous and they are so designed to prevent others from following us down them. We do not want you to know what we are thinking.

This is because we have no desire to convey you any advantage in seeking to escape our effects and make it harder for us to obtain fuel from you. We must cloak our minds and make them impervious to your attempts to read them. We must operate through secrecy and covert behaviours so that you never see us coming, so that you never know what will happen next and so that you have no opportunity to evade us. Not only do we shroud our minds in this manner through our rejection of logic and the adoption of behaviours which are outside those considered normal we also ensure you cannot read us through our eyes.

Many people look to the eyes as a device for gauging what someone might be thinking or perhaps more accurately feeling. If we are explaining something to somebody and we confusion in that person's eyes we know we must adopt a clearer method in our explanation. If we are conveying some news and see a pained expression in those eyes we know (if it was you making the comment) to alter the manner in which it is expressed to make it less painful or to do or say something to offer support. Of course, when we see it, we merely increase the pain in order to extract a reaction from you.

This weakness of the eyes in allowing another person to gauge how someone is feeling and therefore ascertain what they are thinking is not something that we can countenance. This is vulnerability and we do not like vulnerabilities at all. We have enough to contend with without allowing you to see what they are. Accordingly, in order to ensure that our mind is impervious to your inspection we will either adopt a cold, dead look in our eyes which renders them impenetrable or we will simply reflect back at you what you are feeling and mislead you. When we adopt that cold stare, it may be designed to induce a sense of dread in you but it has a primary purpose. This purpose is to create a shield so that you are unable to ascertain what we are thinking and thus our plotting mind is secure from external influence and can proceed in its scheming. Should we reflect back to you what you are showing to us we are doing this to mislead you but also again to prevent you from having any chance of understanding what is going on in our dark minds. Our minds are the core of our operations. Our minds control everything in order to achieve our aim of securing fuel and as such, this most precious of devices must not be compromised in any way by people like you and your meddling.

We must ensure that our minds are ring-fenced, cut-off and protected from your attempts to read us. Should you be able to do that then you will be taking away one of our advantages. We know what you are thinking and we know what you are going to do next because you are an empath and you not only wear your heart on your sleeve but you wear your mind there as well. Your eyes allow us straight into what you are thinking and feeling. Your mind may as well be transparent or broadcast its thoughts onto a flat screen for all to see. You are easy to work out and study, hence why we choose you. A similar fate must not befall us and this is why we ensure at all times that our minds are impervious to your penetration.

Kiss Me

The kiss is probably the pinnacle of romanticism from everything that I have observed. The couple who flirt with one another throughout the film in an attempt to create a will they or won't they scenario, finally kiss and everybody smiles. The kidnapped child is finally reunited with his parents and is smothered in relieved kisses. The power of seduction that exists in that first kiss between a passionate couple which then leads to their love making. A kiss good bye on a steam filled railway platform. As ever, books and films have played their part in elevating the status of the kiss to near legendary status.

Like so much of what I do, the kiss is a weapon which I use to maximise the impact of my machinations. At the outset I shall use it to overpower you. You are unlikely to have much resistance to my overtures following my campaign of love-bombing but if there is any it will be obliterated the first time I kiss you. I have studied a thousand kisses. From Burt Lancaster and Deborah Kerr in From Here to Eternity to Clark Gable and Vivien Leigh in Gone With the Wind through to Demi Moore and Patrick Swayze in Ghost. I have viewed Audrey Hepburn jump from her taxi to kiss George Peppard in the rain in the film, Breakfast at Tiffany's and the post-nuptial kiss between Prince Charles and Princess Diana. It is not just the famous kisses that have been subjected to my scrutiny. I have sat at railway stations and watched the greeting kiss, full of excitement and passion or the departure kiss which encapsulates longing. I have watched the almost frenzied and desperate embrace that arises from a man finally ensnaring his quarry in a nightclub after spending a couple of hours chatting her up. Whilst sipping from my drink in a restaurant I see hundreds of kisses between spouses, lovers, friends and acquaintances all delivered in different styles with varying emphasises. All of this knowledge is collated and stored ready for my use.

I have been told many times how good a kisser I am. I am blessed with full lips and therefore do not suffer the sometimes dispassionate affliction that can befall those who have lips of a thinner nature. From my observations I have learned to make my advance slowly, lingering just in front of the other person's lips as I reach a hand up to cradle their neck and let my fingers lightly caress the back of their neck. My soft lips press gently against theirs and then I retreat slightly before advancing again and then retreating. I do this several times before allowing my mouth to press on to theirs and remain there as we lock our embrace, lips moving slowly together, each time moving a little wider until a tentative tongue gently probes and touches against hers. My tongue flicks back and forth as the embrace grows stronger. I can hear her low moan of delight and know that this approach is working. I reach another arm around her and pull her closer to me, bodies pressed against one another and now her mouth has opened wider, her own tongue almost battling with mine. I know that the tingle will be racing up and down her spine; I know that she will feel the churning in her stomach and that light headedness will be sweeping across her. I am well practised in the art of the seductive kiss and during our golden period I shall allow you to experience it often. I shall do it when we meet in my house at the end of the day, I will embrace you in that fashion when I lead you by the hand to our bedroom and I shall surprise you by grabbing hold of you in the lift and kissing you in this way.

What of course is all the sweeter about being able to embrace you in such a scintillating fashion is the fact that I will withdraw this marvellous kiss. You will take hold of me and push your mouth against mine only to find that my lips are set rigid and do not respond in the way you have been used to. There is no warmth or passion. You wonder where it has gone. The truth is that there was never any there to begin with. Like so much of what I do, it is an artifice purely designed to capture you and make the inevitable denigration all the more contrasting. I can see the confusion in your eyes as you try again to kiss me but the effect is the same. You look at me, eyes searching for an answer but I do not offer one. You ask me what is wrong and I look away and say that there is nothing wrong. I have a variety of responses which confuse you when you try to kiss me or expect to be kissed. When once I kissed you often and repeatedly I will reduce it to next to nothing. This reduction coupled with a lack of explanation has you flailing around for some kind of reason. You end up blaming yourself of course that is to be expected. I will do any or all of the following:-

1. Remain tight-lipped when we kiss;

2. Move my head so you kiss my cheek rather than my mouth;

3. Put my hand up and block your advance;

4. Hug you instead so that your kiss flies into thin air over my shoulder

5. Just walk away

Where once my kiss was magical and uplifting, now it is cold or non-existent. You relished our passionate embraces and now you find yourself remarking how it is like kissing an automaton or a mannequin. I do not care. All I wish to achieve is your pained and hurt reaction to the cold front that I exhibit where once there was heat and passion.

The Power of Pain

My mind has always applied itself to how I can exert control over other people. By applying control I get them to do what I want and this will enable me to obtain fuel from them. I witnessed at an early stage the power of pain and this formed in my mind an indelible reason to utilise it in order to gain and maintain control.

I do not recall precisely how old I was but I do recall that I had not yet started secondary school so I must have been under the age of twelve. There was a group of us children that played together and it was during a particular summer that we had been engaged in some kind of game in the fields near to where we all lived. The fields and the small river which ran through them with the occasional copse made for an exciting environment in which we could play out invented games. From battles between armies, to tales of fantasy involving orcs and elves through to pretending to be astronauts on an undiscovered planet, we made full use of the space that we were afforded.

I recall that one hot afternoon we had been engaged in a game which involved a battle and one of our group, a boy called Jonathan had been the general. He was not very good and he had made a series of stupid decisions that meant our side lost the battle. I was determined not to lose the war and I proposed that I should now be the general and it should be me who organised our troops. He was a whiny child who began to bleat about how I was often the general and it was his turn today. He explained his turn was to last all day. I grew irritated by his desire to remain in place as the general and a calamitous one at that. How dare he assume the mantle of greatness when it was patently clear that he was not up to the task? How dare he lead us to slaughter and defeat? I was not happy but despite my protests he would not stand down. The other side had long since departed across the other side of the fields and were awaiting the shot for battle to be joined. Our troops had been dispatched to various locations leaving just Jonathan and I at the rear. I was furious with him. My rage at his idiocy was burning inside of me and as he stood on the rock from which the general always directed our troops, since it afforded a good view across the meadow I moved besides him. With a violent shove I pushed him from the rock and he fell into a clump of stinging nettles that had grown next to the rock. He howled in pain as the first stings took effect and wearing a t-shirt and shorts, his exposed limbs and face fell prey to the vicious stings of the nettles. He cried out and jumped up trying to move free of the nettles but as he neared the edge I gave him another shove and sent him tumbling back into the midst of them causing him to cry out again. With tears streaming down his face and arms showing the welts from the repeated stings he tried to emerge again and once more I pushed him back into the stinging nettles. I did this again and then once again until with face red and swollen he decided against trying to get past me and stumbled through the nettles, wincing and whimpering as he took another route. I watched him leave until all that could be heard was his juddering sobbing. I climbed onto the rock and from there took control of our troops and directed them to a stunning victory.

Jonathan's father later attended at our house. I saw him striding up the path with Jonathan in tow, his father incandescent with anger. I stood at the top of the stairs and listened as he thundered and shouted but he did not breach our porch. My mother barred his way and I could not hear her voice but I knew that she would be keeping him in his place with her steely tones and flinty looks. Eventually Jonathan and his father walked away back down the path and I watched their family retreat for the second time that day.

There was no punishment from my mother. Nothing was said to me at all. In her usual fashion she had dealt with the matter. I know not what she said but she made no mention of it to me. This was her way of dealing with such matters.

I continued to play with the group and with Jonathan. Every time he looked at me I could see the pain in his eyes just as I had that day when I had pushed him repeatedly into the stinging nettles. He never asked to be general again and was always the first to suggest that I be appointed as leader of our troops. He had experienced pain doled out by me and he knew what to do thereafter. I also knew what power could be derived from such pain. It was a lesson in learning an instrument of manipulation.

Acting Up

I recall one occasion when a particularly upset girlfriend of mine, Hannah, descended into one of her typical fits of hysteria. Hannah was an actress. She had been involved in acting since she was a teenager and had also appeared in a Royal Shakespeare Company production of Hamlet. She played Ophelia. I found this rather apt. She loses her mind over the Prince of Denmark and drowns. Typical self-centred response. Poor Hamlet. His father dies and his mother shacks up with his uncle. Not only this but his uncle murdered his father and has taken the throne of Denmark leaving Hamlet cast adrift and mired in woe. His girlfriend Ophelia is meant to support him but what does she do? She gets all worked up about Hamlet telling her "Get thee to a nunnery" and climbs a willow tree and falls in the water below and drowns. I found Hannah to be prone to such similar histrionics. I put it down to her being an actress and her desire for everything to be achieved in one take. She was meticulous in her preparation for her acting. At first, I would help her and play the other parts to help her learn her lines. She was so grateful for my support in this regard, remarking how hard it was to find someone willing to do this and so often. If truth be told, I revelled in it. Not only was her gratitude all good fuel, I am of course something of the actor myself and the opportunity to grab the script and play a part was something I enjoyed. I did not pay much attention to Hannah's delivery, only listening to what she was saying so I knew when to speak my lines. I was too concerned with ensuring I delivered a masterful performance. This would often draw praise from Hannah and she commented on a number of occasions that I appeared to have missed my calling. I was in agreement.

Of course, over time I grew tired of her repeated declarations of how good my deliver was and I began to look for ways to irritate and annoy her. I knew she put so much effort into her rehearsals and preparation because she wanted the final performance to be outstanding. Whether it was filming for a TV show (she has appeared in a couple of rather good British television dramas) or a stage production of a famous play, her performance had to be the best. I often gained the impression that she was doing this in order to outshine me. I may not be recognised as much as Hannah but that did not mean that what she did was better or more important than what I did. Quite the opposite. She needed to be reminded who was the leader and superior mind in our coupling. I began at first to fluff lines or speak when it was her turn to say her line which drew sighs of exasperation. I delighted in her irritation as I knew that it would soon become annoyance and she would erupt into one of her tirades. I would jump places in the script, says words incorrectly, use the wrong tone for questions and statements and then I began to hide her scripts so she could not practise. A meltdown was inevitable and foolishly she aimed all of this at me. I just continued to make comments that would keep her in frenzy. You would be surprised to see this waif-like lady who usually is the picture of serenity on television react in the way she did. My goodness, did she have a foul mouth on her.

I rarely got angry with her. Her performances were so gratifying and amusing that I just could not generate a spark, even when she was blaming me. It was actually easier to keep trying to get it right and purposefully messing it up again. Several times I had to exit the room under the pretence of being upset so I could lock myself in the bathroom and stuff my hand into my mouth as I collapsed in paroxysms of mirth, her shrill voice echoing through the house.

The occasion that entertained me the most and which I began this post by recalling was when she was rehearsing her part for a six part dark drama that was part of a major channel's autumn drama selection. It was a fantastic piece of writing and Hannah had a chunky part. I got her so worked up and histrionic as I messed about, murmured the lines, said sections incorrectly and so on that she erupted into one of her fits. As the insults flowed I drank the fuel she poured over me and then she made a strange croak and gripped her throat. Feigning interest, I went to her side and she pointed at her throat, eyes filling with tears. It transpired that she had badly strained her vocal chords and a doctor instructed her to rest them completely. She could not rehearse and was unlikely to be ready for filming. The producers replaced her with another actress and dismayed by her fall from such a prestigious production, I sought out somebody else to entertain me.

A Modern Little Black Book

Once upon a time the names and numbers of conquests and potential conquests all nestled on the pages of a little black book. This pocket-sized companion contained a veritable goldmine of fuel which enabled me to draw on it as and when required. The advance of technology has rendered this tome obsolete but it lives on in spirit contained in my mobile telephone. There the contact list provides me with a ream of individuals who I can turn on and off at will in order to provide me with fuel. Each name is entered into this electronic address book and beside each name I place in brackets the code which denotes their ranking in proximity of supply. The letter F stands for family, A for acquaintance, ICF for inner circle friend and IP for intimate partner. You may think it odd that I have to use such letters for people that I ought to know what category they fall into, but the reality is that there are so many of them I can lose track. Does it matter? Absolutely it does. The ranking of that individual determines how potent the fuel they supply will be and I have to take this into account when I am aiming to elicit their method of delivery of that fuel. The response of an intimate partner always ranks higher than an acquaintance and therefore the distinction and the recording of the same remains important.

One of my favourite actions to perform using my modern little black book is to issue a blanket text message to many of those contained with my list of contacts. I will usually do this when I am with someone else, perhaps sat at a bar or across a table at dinner. My repeated tinkering with my phone as I compose the message and then begin to add the recipients to a growing list always rankles with my companion and causes them to react. That begins the torrent of fuel that will flow. I detail a message and then send it to a raft of people and then sit back and await the responses. I deliberately leave my phone on the table or the bar or the arm of the chair so the flash of the light and the screen illuminates as the responses begin to flood in. You try and ignore the responses at first but I can see from your frequent glances towards the device that it has caught your attention. You may try and pass comment in an innocent fashion by remarking,

"Somebody is popular" or

"You are getting a lot of messages."

I smile and nod and it is when I start to pick up the phone to read them that I receive your expressions of irritation and annoyance which please me all the more. The fuel is truly flowing now. Your sighs, comments and noisy placing down of glasses and cutlery provide me with fuel and the declarations of admiration and affection that stream from my phone adds to it all the more. Each time I pick up the phone your annoyance increases and this will cause me to begin to reply to some of the messages to heighten your reaction. This results in yet more supply from the additional messages and the fuel continues to flow.

I keep all the messages that I send and receive. I have no concern that you will be able to dip into my little black book as you are not allowed any admittance to it and naturally it is pass code protected. Not that you would even be allowed to touch my phone. Those that attempt to do so are met with an instant and scathing rebuke. If I could lop off their offending hand which has touched my library of appliances I would. I like to scroll through these messages from time to time and drink on the residual fuel that still emanates from them. This exercise also allows me to create my chart where I detail those who respond the fastest and with the most appreciative messages. I band those in my little black book into different categories based on this exercise, bronze, silver, gold and platinum. Once that has been done I create a group for each banding on my phone so that I can later send a message to all the platinum members knowing that the responses will be swift and full of admiration. That is always useful when a quick and instant fix of fuel is required. Should I decide that I would prefer a slower delivery of fuel, possibly over the course of an evening knowing that I will be with somebody, I decide to message those people in the silver banding. This organisation and preparation is worthwhile and should underline how ruthlessly efficient we are in our harvesting of my fuel. This is why my modern little black book is so important to me and should you ever go near it or, heaven forbid, I misplace it, you will understand why my reaction is both fierce and furious.

Going Round in My Mind

I was engaged in a discussion with Dr E. We had happened on the subject of relaxation and rest.

"When would you say that you relax?" he asked me as he adjusted his spectacles.

"I don't."

"You do not relax." Dr E said it more as a statement as opposed to a question.

"That's right. How can I relax when there is so much to do, so much to be done and I have a mind like mine?"

"Tell me, what is your mind like?" he asked.

"What do you think it is like?" I responded. I always like to try and get Dr E to pin his colours to mast the early on. That way I am in a better position to manipulate the conversation.

"If I knew that there would be no need for all of these sessions as I try to understand your mind," he replied.

"But I thought you told me that you know all about my kind and me?" I responded.

"I know about the condition that it is suggested is applicable to the way that you behave, but it would be arrogant of me to assume that I knew the way that your mind works. That is part of the work I must do with you, to know your mind and to enable you to know your mind also."

"Oh I know my mind, doctor, don't trouble your thoughts with that," I smiled.

"I am pleased to hear that. Do tell me about it then?"

"Well where do I start? It is a formidable thing my mind."

"Well, let's return to what was being said in the earlier part of this conversation shall we? You explained to me that your mind does not allow you to relax."

"I actually said 'how can I relax when I have a mind like mine'."

"Of course, please, explain that to me in more detail."

"My mind is like an engine. It is like a supercomputer. From the moment I switch it on until the moment I disengage it when I go to sleep it is whirring, formulating and computing."

"So you engage your mind, switch it on?" asked Dr E.

"Absolutely. It fires into life once I wake and from that moment onwards it is always working things out, plotting, scheming and manipulating."

"I see. You mentioned that you disengage it when you go to sleep. Tell me more about that."

"It is pretty simple really. I lay my head on the pillow and decide that it is time for it to be switched off. It is like pulling the plug. As soon as it is done then my mind goes blank and I am straight to sleep."

"You do not lie awake contemplating what has happened during the day or what you have done or what might need to be done the next day?" asked Dr E.

"No. I have worked all of that already. There is little point in contemplating what has already happened. It cannot be changed and cannot be altered. It has already served its purpose. There is nothing to be gained in returning to it."

"But do you not like to sit and recall your memories?"

"Sometimes but I only do so when I know that I can use them in some way. For example, I will recall memories for the purpose of telling a story to someone of for the sake of explaining something. In those situations they serve a purpose to me. Otherwise a memory is just a spent and useless thing."

Dr E remained silent as he scribbled away in his black and red notebook.

"What about feeling worried about what might need to be done or feeling regret at something that has happened? Those are the types of thing that can keep a person from sleeping as their mind pores over and analyses such things."

"No. That is redundant and a waste of time. I do not worry about things. I get on and control them. I have nothing to regret. Every decision I made was the right one at the time," I explain.

"But what if it is not the right one in retrospect?"

"I do not look back on what I have done and ascribe any judgement to it. That serves no purpose."

"I see. So your mind is devoid of anything when you go to sleep?"

"Correct. The machine has been switched off and thus I go straight to sleep and I always sleep well."

"Do you dream?" asked Dr E.

"Could you be more specific? Do I dream or do I have dreams when I sleep?"

"Tell me about both," suggested Dr E.

"I do not dream I do. Dreaming is for the romantic and the fantasists, I create and do."

"Very well and what about dreaming when you are asleep?"

"Never."

"You may do but fail to recall them?" suggested Dr E.

I shrugged.

"I never dream."

"Okay. So between waking and sleeping your mind is always racing yes? Tell me, what causes it to race?"

"Fuel. Where will my fuel come from, who will provide it, how much, how can I get more, will there be enough, who else do I need to provide me with fuel, what will be the best way of getting fuel from this person or situation, who can I rely on to be a near constant supply of fuel, why has the fuel dropped, why has this fuel stopped, why can I not obtain the fuel, how can I increase the fuel?"

"Do you think of anything else? For example, how a view across some hills might be beautiful or how you are looking forward to going to a football match with a friend?" asked Dr E.

"I will think how beautiful the view is to tell someone later to make them jealous that I saw it and not them so they react and provide me with fuel. I look forward to the football match to spend time with someone who will provide me with fuel and to enable me to study how they behave at this match so I can harvest more fuel."

"So your mind is focussed on fuel all the time?" Dr E asked.

"Yes."

"Do you find this tiring?"

"Sometimes but once I gather the fuel it makes me feel powerful and this dispels my fatigue."

"And if you cannot obtain the fuel, I suppose the tiredness becomes greater?" suggested the doctor.

"There can never be a time when I cannot obtain fuel. That is why my mind works so hard and is always racing."

Dr E nodded and made more notes as he did I thought about how my last text message to Kim will have upset her and I felt a surge of power as I began to consider where I would take Samantha this evening in order to show her off at a suitably impressive venue and then I recalled that I needed to send out some more e-mails to continue my campaign against Andrea and there would be an opportunity tomorrow at work to show off with the presentation that I was making and I knew that I needed to make a couple of unpleasant telephone calls to a colleague in order to keep him on his toes and in awe of my power.

"Yes, it is always racing," I added as Dr E continued with his writing.

A Sense of Purpose

In one exchange with hissy fit Hannah, she of the perfectly poised potty mouth I was blundering my way through the Madness of King George and my off kilter timing was causing her to explode once again. Her script had been thrown to the ground and the papers lay scattered. She was ramrod stiff and her tiny feet seemed nailed to the floor as they did not move. Instead, she seemed to move only from the ankle, the rest of her body in perfect alignment as she jolted from side to side. Her caustic tongue went into overtime and I stood with a false perplexed look on my face conveying that I was mystified as to what was causing her such concern.

"You do this on purpose don't you?" she accused. Those small round brown eyes glinted with the fury that coursed through her. I must admit, other than my own rage, I do not think that anybody who I have ever met has come anywhere near to the seething outrage that Hannah used to feel. Were it not for her magnanimous nature and her ability to take an interest in people you might have thought that she was one of my kind. She was very good at making people feel wanted. Notwithstanding her degree of fame, she made time for people and welcomed listening to them and asking about them. She actually preferred for people to talk about themselves rather her having to speak about herself. She took pride in the calibre of her performance, enjoyed the decent money she commanded as well but ultimately it was all about the performance. Something I could identify with.

"It is not difficult to do HG, it really is not," she ranted "You used to be so damn good at doing this, much like everything else in our relationship. I don't know what has happened to you, but you seem to have lost your sense of purpose. I admired you because you tackle everything head on and you are usually brilliant at everything you turn your hand to, but I am beginning to wonder if your power has peaked. Are you losing it? This is shambolic; you are useless, absolutely useless."

She then descended into combining a thesaurus with profanity as she found every synonym she could for incompetence and interspersed these descriptions with a heavy serving of swear words. Her breath was coming in staccato bursts as she built herself into frenzy, her cheeks reddening as her voice rose and rose.

"I really do have to ask, for what purpose God put you on this earth?"

Finally she stopped and she held my gaze. I could feel the fire ignite inside me as for once she had created the spark. The flames leapt into life, the heat surging upwards through me. She had questioned my purpose. She was challenging my existence. Who did she think she was? My eyes narrowed as I savoured the vitriol that now pumped through my body, the rising malice giving me power and reminding me that I am the supreme authority and she is but dust on the wind. Already the schemes of manipulation flickered through my racing my mind like a thousand screens showing trailers for the malevolence that would be unleashed on this thespian for her audacity in questioning my purpose.

I felt the words form in my throat and the anger soared with them as I strode up to her. She remained defiant, still in that strange stiff pose and she did not shirk despite the clear intent signalled by my rapid walk towards her. I thrust my face into hers, eyeball to eyeball and with incandescent rage burning through me I yelled into her face,

"I was invented by God to test your belief in him."

She blinked once and then again. The edifice immediately cracked and came crashing down as she let out a howl of upset and her eyes filled with tears.

Nobody does rage like me.

Nobody delivers the final line like me.

Nobody questions my purpose.

Minder

I was once again in consultation with Dr E. This time he had decided that he wanted to discuss with me the question of empathy. I rolled my eyes when he said this to me.

"That is not a topic you want to discuss?" he asked.

"No, it is a topic you want to discuss."

"Yes I do. Perhaps you will indulge me?"

I hesitated and decided to apply the use of silence for a few seconds. He continued to look at me as I considered whether I should say no in order to provoke a reaction from him. He did his best to always appear implacable but I knew that I could get to him. It had happened from time to time.

"Very well, let us discuss it although there is nothing to discuss."

"What makes you say that?"

"I am not a practitioner of empathy."

"Why not?"

"It serves no purpose."

"Why do you say that?"

"Because being empathic is not something which is natural to me. It is not natural to me because if I went around being empathic, as opposed to pretending to be when it suited me, then I would have to use up too much energy being this way and this would leave me drained and without the resources I need to gather my fuel."

"I see. Do you not think that you would feel, let us say 'good' for want of a better word, inside, if you cared for other people?"

"Good God no. I would feel awful. I would be denied my fuel and this makes me feel weak. I do not like to feel weak because I am not weak."

"I see," commented Dr E and set about writing once again. I waited and ran through seven different ways I was going to provoke my girlfriend this evening which included hiding some jewellery she had just had bought for her by her mother.

"Have you ever felt empathy towards another person?"

"No."

"Is that no you have never felt it or no you do not recall doing so?"

"I have never felt it."

"Even as a child? Did you care about your parents? Your siblings? Your friends?"

I hated it when Dr E started talking about my childhood. I wished he would not do that. That was then and this was now. That past served no purpose. It had happened and was done and I chose not to remember much of it but he had this habit of dredging it up. I suppose it was a deliberate ploy of his and he wanted me to acknowledge and confront the things that had happened when I was younger. I

35

remember the time in one session that I say down and the first thing that Dr E did was produce a plastic bag. The fear that took hold of that instant had me paralysed and my heart felt like it would burst from my chest. I watched him with wide eyes as he moved the plastic bag from beneath his sit and onto his lap. He had not looked at me and he did not notice the relief flood across my face when he pulled one of his new black and red notebooks from the plastic bag, before he folded the bag up and placed it in the pocket of his jacket that was across the back of his chair. I do not like plastic bags. I thought someone had told him something about the use of the plastic bag and he was going to use it for the purposes of taking me back to my childhood. Thank God he did not. I would have tried to flee the consultation, if my legs had worked of course. I had to become argumentative after that in order to exasperate Dr E and gather some fuel to compose myself. I would have ordinarily picked up my phone and texted some of my acolytes to obtain a fix but after two sessions where I had done this it was made a condition of my treatment that I surrendered the phone to his secretary. I only agreed on the basis of it being placed in a box with had a lock on it and I retained the key. Nobody else goes near my phone.

"Did you care about anyone when you were a child?" asked Dr E craning forward.

"Yes I heard you," I snapped in irritation, "I was thinking."

"Please do take your time."

"No I did not."

"Why?"

"There was no point?"

"What makes you say this?" asked Dr E.

"Must we do this?"

"Would you rather not?"

"Yes."

"Why?" pressed Dr E. Jesus, always why, always fucking why.

"Because I find it boring," I lied although I knew what was coming next.

"Why do you find it boring?"

"I find it boring because it happened ages ago. I find it boring because it serves no purpose."

"I see. Would you not agree however that past behaviour is the best indicator of future behaviour?"

"Depends who you are making reference to," I answered shifting in my seat.

"Well to you, naturally."

"No it isn't."

"Why do you say that?" asked Dr E rolling out his favourite word once again.

"It might work for ordinary people because they do not change but I can change. I can be anything I want to be. I may act one way yesterday and a different way today because I have that level of control over my life. Other people do not but I am different from them."

"Very well, so thinking about the ways that you have behaved in the past towards, let us say, your girlfriends, have you not always repeated those behaviours with other girlfriends?"

"Yes because that was the best way of achieving the result which I required."

"So does it not follow that since you have always adopted a similar modus operandi with regard to those people then you will do the same in the future?"

"I may but if I decide not to I will not. You see the difference is I know my mind and I know that I have control of my situation. I am not at the behest of anyone else. I am not dictated to."

"I understand but would you not agree that we must all give and taken in order to get along, there must be yielding and compromise in order to achieve an aim, so that we can all rub along as it is?" pressed Dr E.

"No. I do not give. I do not compromise. That is why I am not, going back to the point which you raised some time ago, someone who engages in empathy. It serves no purpose to me. "

"So you are not someone who will take care of someone else and by that I mean you do it instinctively as opposed to doing it to achieve some other aim?" added Dr E.

"I am not minded to care for others because my mind is not that way inclined."

Dr E nodded and resumed his note taking. I glanced at the clock and saw that the time was nearly up. I did not show it but I felt powerful since I had escaped his attempt to plunge me into my childhood once again. That is a part of my mind that I rarely wished to visit.

The Asylum of the Grotesque

"Why don't you try to love me the way that I love you?" - Paula

"Perhaps if you just tried you could find a better way to something deeper and more substantial." - Kate

"I know it is within you, it has to be, all you need is to embrace it and place your trust in me." - Alex

"I know you flirt with all kinds of dirt, but beneath the sin, I know you want to love me like I love you." - Karen

"If you let me I will show you how to love without condition or cruelty, it can be done by all of us. Just let me try." - Caroline

I still hear these words from these women (and more besides) as I sit late at night in the large living room to the rear of my house. It is on the first floor and provides me with a commanding view of the fields to the rear of the property, the occasional copse breaking up the undulating countryside. I had two bedrooms knocked together and created this living room where I like to sit and look out across the view as the sun vanishes and the cool, calmness of the night arrives. The sky shifts from the medley of flaming oranges, reds and yellows to a soothing azure and then the darkness descends. Karen and I enjoyed sitting in the large elbow chairs that faced the window. Often we would say nothing as around us the lamps would switch on, a gentle click signifying their creation of a pool of light as the timer activated them one by one.

I will often leave the city behind and come out here so I can sit in this house which I regard as my castle and with a glass of Chablis in hand, watch the sky change colour. The occasional noise of a distant animal might be heard but largely there is silence. There is the enveloping stillness of a calm world until I hear their words. All of them meant what they said and did so with the best of their intentions. I know that because I could see it in their eyes. Whether it was the earnest green, the heart-felt hazel, the beseeching blue or the inspiring grey, I still see them as they tried to make me see a different way. They wanted me to change. They wanted to make me something else.

Now Karen no longer sits beside me, I rarely bring the girlfriends that I acquire out here. I prefer the solitude, only for a few days. I will periodically check my electronic devices and the winking displays, lists of messages and e-mails sustain me as so many seek my attention. Without Karen, I decide against having the lamps gently bloom and instead prefer the gathering darkness. It is here that I can sit and plan. It is in this quiet that I can marshal my resources, mark my targets and organise my machinations. It is also when I resist those pleas to become that which I regard as impossible to achieve. I prefer to walk amongst my trophies. I stride amidst the frozen tributes to my brilliance as I picture each and every of my conquests as if they are beautifully crafted statues each in a pose denoting my victory over them. There is Siobhan, on her knees looking up at me as she begs me not to go, her pretty features contorted by the pain she is experiencing. Paula sits at a table, her hands clamped over her mouth, her eyes wide with fear as she fights to say nothing, terrified that a word might slip from her lips. Becky dangles limps, the strings rising upwards attached to her hands, her feet, her head, her hips and other places. She is the broken puppet.

Kate stands on tip toe, her face a mask of anguish as with one hand raised above her eyes she peers into the distance as if searching for something, an empty dog lead in her hand. I let my hands glide over the smooth stone that has captured their defeat and embodied it in an eternal stance. My fingers drift over open mouths, curled lips, tear-filled eyes and flared nostrils. I savour the misery, anger and dejection that have been injected into these statues. I regularly walk amongst them and it reminds me of my power, the hold that I have over these people who sought to change me but could only ever disappoint me. Why would I ever want to do what they would have me do? Why would I embrace their suggestions when I can create these monuments to my omnipotence? These masterpieces of misery always reinforce that I am destined to do this for this is what I do best. I am reassured, validated and comforted that my way is the right way when I take a stroll in my asylum of the grotesque.

The Tallest of Poppies

I am well used to suffering the jealous behaviour of others as a consequence of their resentment arising from my brilliance. No matter how inclusive and charming I may be there are always some who suffer from the politics of envy. If I understood what sympathy really was I suppose I might have some for these people. It must be horrendous never achieving anything of note and being mired in mediocrity. Thankfully, not all those who are not blessed with the talents that my kind and I have are prone to this behaviour. If that was the case then surely we would face anarchy. Many of them realise their status as an epsilon semi-moron to borrow Aldous Huxley's description from Brave New World and they are content to fulfil that role. There is much to be said for knowing your place. Few are destined to greatness and one will lead a much more satisfying life if one accepts that at an early stage and you leave the important stuff to those of us who occupy the rarefied stratosphere of superb achievement.

It is a regrettable trait that certain people, envious and jealous of my achievements feel the need to attack me. It is puzzling since so often I have exhibited nothing but pleasantness and compliments towards them and have enabled them to benefit from my largesse, but still they feel the need to attack me and pour scorn on what I do. Admittedly, they are in the minority and that is a helpful indicator and confirmation (if it were needed) that their stance is both unpleasant and erroneous. They might catcall my kind and me, attempting to attribute our success to underhand and devious methods, but they are merely fuming that they did not think of driving forward in such a manner themselves. Whenever I have to deal with one of these idiots who tries to denigrate me then I must always remind them that you cannot add to the stature of a dwarf by cutting off the leg of a giant. That usually sends them away with a flea in their ear.

No, I have no sympathy for these fools, only contempt. Perhaps if they had tried harder at school, worked harder in their occupations and applied their minds with the singularity of vision and purpose that my kind and me are famed for, then and only then, these people might have achieved something.

I resist all attempts to cut me down. I am the tallest of poppies and you must crane your neck, look upwards and admire me for what I am. Of course, it is entirely appropriate that I maintain my stature by removing those who might unseat me. Should anyone else grow close to where I am and have the audacity to cast a shadow over my progress and achievements then I am left with no choice but to wield my scythe and cut them down. I must do it to them before they do it to me. It is the law of the jungle and you do not grow as tall and as fine as me without being able to eradicate the aspirers, the false climbers and the clambering imposters. Threaten my superiority and I will cut you down without hesitation or regret. I am compelled to ensure that the glow of sunny admiration falls on me and that there is no shadow from any other that might impinge my steady advance upwards.

Fuel is the Rule

Fuel is the very thing that I must have. It is through fuel that I function and exist. I regard all emotional energy as sustenance. A lack of emotion causes me considerable concern and this will ultimately result in my detachment and me seeking the same from an alternative and more reliable source. There are those that suggest that I derive fuel from certain inanimate objects, for instance, status symbols. I drive an expensive car, wear the tailor-made suit and live in a large house and all of that apparently provides me with fuel. It is true that we covet these things as they accord with our sense of entitlement. They also enable us to demonstrate to the wider world our success and achievement. We crave such materialistic representations of success. However, my kind and I do not desire the Rolex watch, IPad or diamond encrusted mobile telephone in themselves. We want those items because of the responses that they create in other people.

Those who see us drive by in a Bentley convertible invariably stand and stare open-mouthed. That reaction to our prestige provides us with the fuel we need. The admiring glances that we draw when we walk through the department at work in one of our excellent suits provide us with fuel. The compliments we receive for the style of shoes, the holiday cottage we own and the extravagant party that he have laid on are all sources of fuel to us. Inanimate objects are the platforms for the provision of our fuel. Whilst some people will marvel at our choice of motor vehicle, there are others who will express jealousy and envy. Those reactions are most welcome as well. The cutting comments that accompany a green-eyed stare are lost on us. The words evaporate because it is the emotion that is bundled up inside those words and the baleful stare that we want.

Our fascination and reliance on the inanimate object and the part it plays in the provision of fuel does not end however with what you may regard as traditional inanimate objects. The most effective inanimate object which provides us with fuel is you. How can we regard a person as an inanimate object? In the same way that the words in a scathing comment dissipate as we seize on the emotion, the identity of those providing us with fuel, slips to one side as we savour the fuel that we can extract. Those of you who we seduce and draw into our world where we can draw deep on your fuel will stand to be regarded as nothing more than an appliance. We see no person. We recognise no identity. We see a machine that has one purpose and one purpose alone. That purpose is the provision of fuel for us.

Chaos, Chaos Everywhere

One of the defining features of our behaviour is the association with chaos. Our arrival into somebody's life is described as a whirlwind. We are regarded as tempestuous, a tornado and a flailing dervish. People describe how we leave a trail of destruction behind us. Reference is made to the drama and the rollercoaster ride that people experience when they become sucked into our sphere of influence. The honest amongst them admit that at the time they found this intoxicating, the excitement of wondering what was going to happen next, the thrill of the unpredictable and the allure of the heightened activity that surrounds us. Others bemoan the mayhem that occurs, the random behaviour and the lack of certainty, never mind from one day to the next, but hour to hour. People conclude that we are creatures of chaos. That conclusion is wrong.

We are ordered and methodical in everything that we do. We ascertain on a daily basis our need for fuel. We establish which sources will provide that fuel and how this will be achieved. We regulate our network of supply like a technician overseeing the electricity grid of a country. Where there is a risk of disruption to that supply we organise a contingency. Should we apply our energies to solving the disruption or should we replace it as quickly as possible? We monitor and observe to ensure that our lifeblood is supplied effectively and efficiently. We identify our fresh targets and then assiduously plan how that person will be seduced. We gather intelligence about that individual, what they like and dislike, who they socialise with, how strong their family connections are as we build up a dossier all about them. There is no random selection of our targets. We cannot leave such important matters to chance. We must undertake keen preparatory work so that when we strike we succeed and our target is ensnared. Once that person has been lured into our grasp we then structure our treatment of him or her. How might we best extract the juiciest fuel from them during the golden period? How long do we anticipate that period will last? Where else should we be obtaining fuel from during this time? What threats exist to affecting or interrupting the supply of fuel from this appliance? These thoughts and many others filter through our minds as we plan, plot and scheme.

You may think that we suddenly flip from pleasant to nasty. Yes, I will admit that that is the appearance we give when we engage such a volte face. The reality is that such a change has been carefully considered and orchestrated to achieve the maximum impact. The apparent sudden shift from calm to volcanic eruption has been calculated to bring about the assertion of our superiority, control and the provision of fuel. Our rage will spiral out of control but the unleashing of that rage was a considered act. Once the spark has ignited the flames it however there may be no telling how hot the flames will burn and for how long, but we decided to create the spark. Each word and gesture has been considered and reflected upon in order to ascertain how effective it will be in furthering our aims. We plan an onslaught of affection which appears like a sudden storm, yet we planned this dizzying and disorientating display. The sudden appearance of silent treatment and its duration has all been worked out beforehand.

The difference is that we plan everything we do before we unleash the chaos that exists inside us. The effect of our careful scheming is chaotic in nature that is entirely true. The outcome of our love bombing is a torrent of whirling and tumbling affection. Our campaigns of mistreatment seem to burst out of nowhere, assailing you from random directions like staccato machine gun fire. We lift you up, spin you around, turn you upside down and shake you all about. It is a chaotic process but it is the outcome that contains the chaos as we unleash it from within. As Friedrich Nietzsche put it, "One must still have chaos in oneself to be able to give birth to a dancing star."

The Devil's Toolkit

You may not realise this but my kind and me are always prepared. We carry with us at all times a toolkit which is stocked with many useful tools and instruments to assist us in our day-to-day machinations. These tools enable us to carry out our quest to obtain fuel. Sometimes you may not realise that we are actually using these tools and on other occasions you cannot help but notice. Every one of our kind comes equipped with this toolkit. Not all of the tools are used by every member of our brethren and we are always on the lookout for additions that can be made to it. It can be tiring lugging it around with us but it is a necessary burden if we are to achieve our aims. Luckily for you, I am going to provide you with an insight into what lies inside the Devil's Toolkit.

Saw of Interruption - this is regularly used to cut you off when you are speaking.

Chisel of Misery - a very handy instrument which is used on a frequent basis to chip away at your self-esteem

Hammer of Intimidation - a blunt instrument that is used to bludgeon you into submission

Screwdrivers of Diversion - this flexible tool comes with two adjustable ends. The **Denial** and the **Blame-Shift.** Either of these ends can be fitted to twist the truth

Pliers of Manipulation - these are used to push and pull, turn and wrench until we get what we want.

Unlimited Tape Measure - this is used to see if you come up to standard but unsurprisingly you never measure up

Stanley Knife - a diverse blade which is used for figuratively making small yet painful cuts or if need be slicing you open

Spanner of Disruption - I have plenty of these in the toolkit and use them to throw into the works on a repeated basis to mess things up for you and others

Fuse Wire - I know you keep blowing yours so this is often used

Insulation Tape - for keeping you insulated from everyone else. It is a large roll and never runs out

Torch of Illumination - this does not work as there are never any batteries in them. Well they are fuel aren't they?

Power Drill of Inferiority - this is used to drill into you over and over again how useless and pathetic you are

Charming Sander - very handy for smoothing everything over in an instant

Snare - always handy for trapping the unwary empath

Immobility Clamps- used for keeping you right where I want you

Blowtorch of Rage - I may need to take this back to Lucifer since it seems to blow hot and cold

Goggles of Reflection - I don't want to get anyone, I mean anything, in my eyes do I?

Sugar-coated Knuckleduster of Attrition - wears you down but you don't realise it

Laser Tape Measure - projects brilliantly

Ear Defenders - always necessary when doling out the silent treatment

Scissors of Snipping - all-purpose tool for cutting through any barriers or boundaries

Gas Lamp - prone to going on and off without rhyme or reason

Circular Conversation Saw - I think this one is faulty as well as it goes round and round but never actually does anything

Pot of Fairy Dust - we sprinkle this liberally and everything sparkles and shines. Shame they could not make some that lasted longer though.

Quite the collection isn't it and I am sure you will recognise some personal favourites of the narcissist in your life.

Pedalling the Myth

"Someday my prince will come."

"I need a knight in shining armour to come and rescue me."

"Where is my Prince Charming?"

These are familiar comments and they all arise as a consequence of the myth that has been created and perpetuated. It is well established that my kind and me create an illusion. Have you considered the fact that we are just giving you what you expect? We are saying what you want to hear, doing what you want to see and complying with a pre-conceived notion of how relationships ought to be? How has this idea been formulated? Who created the concept of the happy ever after? Was it the Brothers Grimm or Hans Christian Andersen through the fairy tales that they wrote or were they just recording something which had existed orally for centuries before as they added a new gloss to the fairy tale? Maybe we should blame Hollywood for its depiction of how love conquers all and the hero saves the day by dashing to aid the stereotypical damsel in distress. The number of films in which that happens is numerous. Richard Gere appears in his limousine to woo Julia Roberts in Pretty Woman, in Love Actually, Hugh Grant goes door to door in search of the tea lady Martine McCutcheon and in The Matrix Trilogy even the kick-ass feisty Trinity is masterfully caught by Neo to prevent her falling. In Rear Window, James Stewart rescues Grace Kelly, in the unusual Wild At Heart, Nicholas Cage (playing Nicholas Cage) comes to the assistance of Laura Dern at a metal gig and who can forget Shrek where an ogre goes hell for leather to beat Prince Charming of all people and gain the hand of Princess Fiona. I am sure you can think of many more examples. There are thousands of instances of this stylised concept of romance and love. Certain films dedicate the entirety of the production to it. Others have a different subject matter but still the concept remains. Luke Skywalker went to rescue the Princess trapped in the Death Star. Clint Eastwood helped the young lady in Pale Rider and she fell in love with him although he left her (was that a cowboy discard perhaps?) and even uber narcissist James Bond gives the Bond Girl her slice of heaven for a few screen minutes. Everywhere you look the idea of romance and the knight in shining armour is reinforced. Pop songs, advertisements (once upon a time a man would go to great lengths just to deliver a box of chocolates to his paramour in the Milk Tray ad) , greetings cards, magazines, newspapers, sitcoms, novels and so on and so forth. The airbrushed, photo shopped, sweeping sound tracked and every sense heightened message is driven at you each and every day. There is a dashing hero (or heroine) out there who will save you and treat you like a princess (or prince).

This is the message that is all around you. This is what you have been raised to expect. Someone will save the day and sweep you off your feet. Everything is going to be alright. You will have your happy ever after. It is hardly surprising that you have bought into this master illusion. Who would not? It is all pervading and virtually impossible to resist. It appeals to that deep-seated desire to be cared for and protected and this is done by maintaining a myth that someone should arrive on a white charger, armour gleaming to pull you from the clutches of the evil troll or moustachioed villain.

"I need a hero" sang Bonnie Tyler and then she laid down the criteria required for said hero to attain. I do not recall her mentioning a steady income, being handy with a paintbrush and making a nice cup of tea. Instead she, along with countless others, generates an ideal and you bought into it. You want the fairy tale. I understand it. Why would you not when all around you, you are being told that this is the way it should be. Who would not want that sensation of being swept off their feet, romanced and made to feel wonderful? And who says we do not provide it? There is no denying that when our kind come along we invariably pick you up in a marvellous whirlwind of love, attention and affection as we suck you into an illusion. Where does the fault lie? Is it us that are to blame for creating this construct to draw you in? Is it your fault for falling for the myth and casting common sense aside for wanting the unattainable? Or does the blame lie elsewhere? Is it those that created and not maintain this illusion? If it is those in this latter category that have created this monster that you believe in and we merely comply with, then the question becomes this. Who are they? Are they your kind or our kind?

Contrariwise

Contrariwise,' continued Tweedledee, 'if it was so, it might be; and if it were so, it would be; but as it isn't, it ain't. That's logic."

Makes perfect sense to me but I should imagine it will not to you. Welcome to the logic of my world. The penchant that our kind and I exhibit for telling you that the colour black is actually white and when you eventually agree (and you will no matter how ridiculous this may appear) we will tell you that it was black all along. Or it is orange. Or it is azure.

Our ability to deploy contrariwise must rank amongst one of the most confusing, infuriating and draining manipulative techniques that we possess. Well, judging by your reactions when we wheel this out it is. In all honesty, it is used so often it may as well be a default setting. No matter what you say to us we will automatically adopt a contrary position even if that contrary position appears to you as untenable and that it flies in the face of logic. We will always find ways of undermining, denying and deflecting what you are saying to us, most particularly if you are trying to make us look bad, prove we are wrong or you are challenging us in some way. We cannot allow those things to happen. We have a number of standard phrases that we will use in furtherance of this ability.

"Why must you always exaggerate?"

"No, I have never done that."

"You are over-reacting. Again."

"I think you will find that you are being sensitive, I did not mean it the way you are interpreting it."

"You always look at it the wrong way."

"I didn't say that."

"Your memory is playing tricks on you."

"You/he/she/the world is making things up."

"If you say so but you have got it wrong."

"I never do that."

"You always have to make a scene don't you?"

Do any of these sound familiar to you? Our capacity to be presented with evidence of something and then in the next breath deny the existence of that evidence is staggering. We will reject what you say, deny we ever said anything (even though we actually said it just ten minutes ago) and twist our position so many times we appear to turn into a corkscrew.

Why do we do this? It serves three purposes. The first is because we are never wrong then we must never be shown to be wrong. You seem to have a fascination for trying to demonstrate to us that we are wrong about the things we say and do. That is nonsense. We cannot be wrong and you must accept that. Our use of contrariwise enables us to ensure that we remain right and you remain wrong. It is entirely logical to us. If it is not so to you then that is your problem. You wanted to come into our world so now you must accept its rules. Do not try and argue that you did not agree to this. When you embraced our illusion you consented to this state of affairs. Do not try and deny that it is the case otherwise we will just have to provide you with some more contrariwise.

The second reason that we do this is that we have to have you in a state of confusion. This means that being a creature of order and logic you will try and make sense of our contrariwise which will merely serve to put your head in a spin. Furthermore, you cannot help yourself but want to show us that we are wrong. You cannot accept that we are unable to see the point that you are making. That is entirely the point. You are subjected to our rules now and logic, reason and sense rode out of town many moons ago. This confusion will leave you susceptible to our other manipulations and drain you of your resistance and resolve making it harder for you to escape our grip.

The third reason is down to our lifeblood, yes fuel. Your evident frustration, curses and desperation as you try to make us see that we are wrong provides us with delicious dollops of fuel. You tear your hair out, repeat yourself, and raise your voice and collapse sobbing in frustration. It is all good fuel to us. No matter if you argued the point with the forensic precision of a top barrister we would twist the words so they achieve what we want and not what you want. To borrow from Lewis Carrol's fantastic writing I leave you with the words of humpty dumpty, who was clearly a pioneer of our kind.

"When I use a word it means just what I choose it to mean."

Like a Motorway

When I come along in my luxurious and expensive motor vehicle it is too difficult to resist that open passenger door and you hop in without hesitation. I won't be taking you for a gentle drive through undulating countryside or for a meandering excursion along the coast. No. It is straight to the motorway. You are pinned back in your seat by the sudden acceleration as we speed away. You let out a laugh, delighted by the surge of excitement as I move straight into the fast lane and the speedometer needle climbs as we go faster and faster. It is exhilarating to be driven along by such a confident and masterful driver.

The motorway I take you on has been purpose built for me. It cuts through the landscape, not going around or under or over but straight through. There are no obstacles for my motorway. It is direct and effective. Its construction bludgeoned everything else out of the way as it made its mark on everything around it. Nothing could stop it as mile after mile it stretched across the land. Nothing gets in the way of my motorway.

You marvel at how quickly it takes you to so many different places. You smile as you press your nose to the glass and watch the signs flash past 'Desire','Heaven','Excitement' and 'Delight' are all signposted. My motorway takes you to these places in a matter of moments and no sooner have we visited one place then we are back on my motorway, speeding through the night to the next location. The motorway takes us direct to the best restaurants, the most exotic destinations, and the concerts where it enables us to drive right up to the front of the stage and the hitherto exclusive and difficult places you always tried to reach are suddenly in front of you, all courtesy of this expansive motorway network.

My motorway never has traffic jams, is free of roadworks and always takes the most direct route to the destination. It is breath-taking how fast we travel along it, yet you always feel safe, content in the knowledge that I am taking care of you on this modern and well-maintained transport route.

Occasionally you see people that you recognise stood on the hard shoulder. You notice some of your family who watch as we speed by. You see your friends who are parked to one side as we race along. You raise a hand to wave to them but it is too late. We have already rushed by them leaving them far behind, just a passing blur. You are not concerned however as you see the next sign detailing our destination and the anticipation rises as you await your arrival at this glamorous place. All thoughts of family, friends and supporters have been left behind, as quickly as we drove past them.

Sometimes you think you see a warning sign flash on one of the overhead gantries but I am driving so fast along this wide motorway that you cannot be sure.

"Did that say danger ahead?" you ask as we zip underneath another illuminated sign.

"Oh it just a routine test, you do not need to worry about that," I smile and you are instantly reassured. You settle back in your seat as the world and your life flashes by but you are too focussed on what lies ahead at the next destination to worry about what is passing you by. This is the ride of your life and you never want it to stop.

The car suddenly brakes to a halt. Tyres squeal and smoke drifts past as the vehicle violently stops. You lurch forward in your seat and almost bang your head on the dashboard. Disorientated you right yourself as the passenger door opens.

"Out you get," I instruct. The smile is gone and is now replaced by a face you barely recognise as I stare ahead.

"Sorry? What?" you splutter in confusion.

"It is time to go. You need to go that way," I state aggressively and point behind you.

"What do you mean? Why have we stopped? I don't understand," you protest.

"Get out! Out! Out! "I bark and suddenly frightened you scramble out of the car and stand trembling on the tarmac.

"Your life is back that way," I add as the passenger door slams shut and you watch as I roar off up a slip road next to a large sign saying "Fuel this way".

You watch me disappear from view and then turn to face the silent and empty motorway which stretches away into the far distance. You start walking, confused and upset.

The walk back to your life is just like my motorway.

Dark grey and long.

The Harpoon of Seduction

The harpoon. It is not a device you would readily associate with seduction. Indeed, it is not something you would readily link with anything neither pleasant nor subtle since it is usually used in the violent and bloody practice of whaling and sealing. Those who engage in those practices would, I am sure, regard it as a tool of the trade. A device that is used to sink the barbed point into the target and then haul them in by use of the rope or chain attached so that the prey cannot escape. It is a weapon and in our hands is just as deadly.

Our harpoon is effective but subtle. In fact, the harpoon of seduction is one hundred per cent effective in ensnaring our prey. Unlike the barbaric device used at sea, our harpoon does not wound or hurt but instead it makes you feel wonderful as the point is driven deep into your heart and the barbs take hold of you. Once our harpoon has been secured inside of you it is just a question of time before we have hauled you towards us and ensured that you are brought within our sphere of influence.

How does this harpoon work? It must be aimed at a target that will be vulnerable to its sugar-coated tip. If the wrong target has been selected then the harpoon will just bounce off and the intended target will wander away oblivious to what has just happened. This mistake might be made by a Junior Narc as he or she is working out the range and effectiveness of the harpoon. It is not an error that I will commit, nor many like me. We know which targets are susceptible to it. We undertake our preparatory work to ascertain that the target is one that can be speared in this fashion. This groundwork is essential because the nature of the harpoon of seduction is that it is only able to spear a certain type of person.

When the first shot is fired from the harpoon it must be able to pierce the outer defences of the target and then anchor firmly inside that person's heart so that when we pull them towards us, the point remains firmly in place with no risk of slippage or extraction. The shot must be accurate and powerful enough to achieve these two pre-requisites, for if not, there is a risk that a second shot will be needed. This in itself is not disastrous but it expends additional energy, not something we like to do. Furthermore, there is the slight risk of the target realising that a harpoon shot has just been fire so that they shift position and make it more difficult to get that second shot away. If the target is a particularly juicy prospect this is most disconcerting.

The harpoon shot must also be the first shot fired in the attempt to ensnare the target. Yes, the love bombs will follow to ensure that the target has next to no resistance as she or he is pulled towards us. Their resolve will be eroded by a hand grenade of gratuitous affection and the machine gun spitting out flattery bullets, but all of that must come after the harpoon shot. If this is done before hand there is in all likelihood that the target may dodge the onslaught or it will bounce off. The love bombing campaign must always follow the harpoon shot, not the other way around. So, how do you recognise the harpoon shot? Well, ordinarily you do not because the shot is so accurate and with such force it lands home and you have been snared. Now all we need do is pepper you with love and affection to keep you from resisting and realising what is going on and haul you in. Occasionally, a particularly astute target may realise something has happened but they will not be able to place exactly what it is. He or she will sense that something strange has just happened but they cannot put a finger on it. By then it is too late as the first salvo in the love bombing has begun to land.

The harpoon shot has to be powerful and accurate. Accordingly, the way to identify it is as follows:-

1. It must be the first act towards the target. It may be a gesture or words, usually it is the latter, but it must be the first thing we do towards you in terms of drawing you in. I do not mean ordinary friendly conversation and such like, but when we make that first move to draw you in, this must be the harpoon shot ; and

2. To generate the power needed to sink the point deep into your heart the act or gesture must be significant. Indeed, if you look back to when your narcissist ensnared you, you will probably look at the harpoon shot and realise now it stood out a mile. At the time however it was greased with plausibility so it slid right in side of you, even if regarded in the cold light of day, it seemed over the top. A prime example of this would be receiving a text out of the blue from someone you know and may have done for a long time which professes, "I love you and I always have done." That is a harpoon shot. You have known this person, you probably like this person but you never realised that this person felt this way. It seems over-the-top but you feel great as the harpoon shot slams into you and releases its euphoria into your blood stream, so this overrides any caution that might be ringing in your mind.

"I have wanted you for ten years and now this is my chance." Boom! There is another harpoon shot.
"I have admired you from afar for so long but now I need to take this chance to make you happy. It is why I have been put on this earth." Boom! There is another one.
"I was sent by God to look after you." There is another.
 I am sure you can work out which was applicable to you.
Once it is in, the harpoon releases its charm poison, the love bombing begins and you are being pulled straight away into our fantasy. You are going to have a whale of a time aren't you?

The Placebo Effect

It is common for those of you who have done the dance with us to remark once enlightenment has cast its illumination into your mind that,

"It seemed so real, it seemed genuine, in the beginning before it all changed."

Ah yes, the seduction, the love-bombing, the honeymoon or the golden period. Call it what you might, that period of time when everything was wonderful and rosy in the garden certainly seemed to be real enough didn't it? The whispered words of love and affection certainly sounded genuine. The long hugs and hours enveloped in our arms appeared to be real. The ecstatic love-making felt wonderfully intense. Even now as you sit in a state of bewilderment and confusion, your fingers run over the gifts that we bought for you and you can still feel them. Surely they must be real too.

Yet for all the magnificent recall you can apply to the sounds and sensations of that initial period you now know that it was all an illusion. You may not have processed us from your system on an emotional level. Indeed, it is doubtful that you ever will, since that it is the way we are designed so that the Hoover will always remain in play. You have gained understanding though and your mind repeatedly tells you that it was not real, it was not genuine and it was an illusion. You are caught between the two states of knowing it was not real but then knowing what you felt, what you experienced and how your emotions were heightened. Therein lays the answer. It was how you felt. It was your perception that generated such wonderful sensations. You perceived that this acquaintance that you half-knew became the bearer of a perfect of love. You perceived that every text message that was received contained affection and longing. You perceived the burning glances of desire. You saw, heard and felt all of this because you wanted to.

In reality you were fed something that lacked substance and was not genuine. You were told that we would make you feel loved and adored and you therefore felt that you were loved and adored. You were told that we would make you feel special and wanted. You felt special and wanted. The pill that was us contained no potency, no medicine and no effects. It was your perception that created the golden sensations you experienced. Yet again you are no doubt saying to yourself as you read this that it felt so real. Of course it did, because you let it feel so real. You believed in its power so much that you created the feelings that you desperately wanted to experience. You were subjected to the placebo effect. We were no better at tackling depression, high blood pressure or anxiety than a pill made of sugar. Yet, as astounded medical experts have seen time and time again that supplying a patient with what they think is a treatment for pain but is in reality is just a sugar placebo pill produces an improvement in the patient's level of pain. We do the same to you. We make you feel loved, wanted and adored. You are given a placebo however and your desire to experience those wonderful feelings drives you to experience them.

This may sound like it is your fault. In a way you have some culpability for engaging in the thinking that you did which produced such marvellous results. It perhaps now makes more sense as to why this period of wonderful feelings did not last because you were just fed the placebo. However, in the same way that a medical placebo effect takes place; because the good doctor tells you that this pill will lessen your depression so it does, you have been subjected to a similar fraud. We told you how marvellous you would feel and you did. We perpetrated the fraud against you and fed you placebo after placebo with the inevitable effect. The tragedy is that there is not a nocebo effect with us. The downside really was real. Just in case you wondered about that too.

Utopia

Utopia. You want it. We give it to you. What you may not realise is that you are the spark of inspiration for this utopia, we are not. We allow you to design this ideal world. Interestingly, your utopias are strikingly similar. It is a place where you are loved, protected and made to feel safe. For some of you it involves the trappings of comfort and prestige. The impressive residence which has been tastefully furnished inside and is laden with the benefit of society's technological advances. It may manifest as a wardrobe that is bursting with the beautiful and eye-catching. It may hold the sensational from the art world or the most luxurious materials that the world has created over millions of years. In other instances it may be the presentation of a cup of tea on your night stand each morning that forms part of their perfect world.

Some of you reject the material and prefer to build this utopia on a foundation which you regard as more fulfilling, more deep-seated and nourishing. A land where mutual respect is a given, the simple pleasure of a stunning sunset evoking more delight and satisfaction than anything made by Bvlgari or Bentley. You want to be cherished, desired and listened to. For some it might be the intense passion of athletic love-making before the caress of soft hands lulls you into an all-encompassing slumber. Your utopia is a place where there is no anger, no tears and peace of mind. A place where one hand fits perfectly into another and will never let it go, a hand hold that says that it is okay to be frightened but you need not be because I will always be here. It is the knowledge that if you start to fall you will be caught. The wolf will always be kept from the door and nothing lurks in the darkness. It is a halcyon world where the scent of dill onion bread, or bacon or pancakes signifies that we are together and you never want that fragrance to ever diffuse. So many of you offer different interpretations of what constitutes your utopia yet so many themes remain the same. Love, happiness, smiles, warmth, contentment, caring, laughter and passion are recurrent.

You build this utopia. The bricks are in the words that you say when you first meet us. Those sentences over dinner become walls that create these magnificent buildings that rise upwards into the azure sky. Those whispered desires the metal girders that criss cross as the monument to our relationship takes form. The desire in your eyes creates the undulating countryside and crafts the clear rivers that run through the beautiful meadows and fields that form in your utopia. Your touch causes ripples across the landscape, creating and nurturing as the idyll forms. Everything you say and do, every expression and every glance, every thought and act is charged with such massive potential and it is all for the greater good. It is all to build utopia. You provide us with the plans and the materials and we set to, building this perfect world. You direct us and explain what utopia looks like, smells like and feels like. We are beholden to your instruction as we merely reflect what you want. You want to be called sweetheart every time we kiss you on the cheek? We do it. You want to dance through the night to the slowest of ballads? It is done. You want to receive a loving note through your letterbox? Consider it achieved. Each and every constituent part of this utopia is created by you, all we do is take what you want and make it happen. This is what we do. We are the facilitators of your dreams. We pay such close attention to the way you design this world, taking note of what should be excluded, what must be included and ensuring that every detail is executed.

We are so dedicated in our desire to build this perfect world for you that we spend as much time as we can with you, watching and observing, so that even your mannerisms begin to be included in this grand design. We are so skilled that we absorb everything about you, every hope, every desire and every dream and weave them into this utopia so that soon it begins to form and you marvel with an open mouth at how wonderful it is. It as if every breath you exhale creates another segment of this amazing place. Each heart beat thrusts life into it, every step you take transfers energy into this wonderland, your thoughts appear as if they were being written down as we somehow interpret them and cause them to become reality. You are the architect and we are merely the construction workers who endeavour to give you what you want and boy do we deliver. Nobody can create your utopia like us. Nobody has the skill or the dedication to bring this paradise to life. Does it matter that it is a construct, made from thoughts, dreams and wishes? Of course not, it is as real to you as the screen you now stare at and the fluttering sensation in your stomach. You can see it, taste, smell it, hear it and touch it. You are amazed at how perfect it is, it almost seems too incredible but it is not because you inspired it. You provided the drawings and plans and we brought it to life.

This is utopia.

This is all that you have ever wanted.

Now we have built it for you.

Does it matter that it is an illusion?

If so, well, you started it.

A Sense of Detachment

The people that know me and interact with me often remark that I always seem attuned to people and my environment. They remark about how I know so much about certain things, that I have clearly experienced a lot and retained the benefit of this experience. My awareness of matters is high and it is often commented on how I am able to "plug in" to something and instantly understand it, know how it works and what to do. Whether it is a meeting, discussion or event, I always fit in. I am not going to disagree with those comments.

Let us imagine that you are a massive football (soccer for our transatlantic cousins) fan. I listen to how you analyse a forthcoming match and discuss the impact of an expensive new signing. I carefully pay attention as you detail how the opposition centre-half is weak on short passes played into the penalty area. I see your eyes widen and light up with interest as you debate these issues with fellow fans. I make a careful note of what is said by you and the others and store it so that I can regurgitate it later to someone else that is similarly interested in football and pass it off as my own knowledge and observations. I do this with conviction so that nobody recognises that these comments are not my own. I spent the morning before the match that we are attending, reading the sport sections of two quality newspapers and also the satellite broadcaster's webpage for the match, along with other bits and pieces from around the internet in order to assemble my knowledge for this, our first match together. I knew from your social media postings that you are a passionate fan of this team and as I targeted you I pretended I was as well. I managed to recall key trophies the team had won and recent events from the football club's website to enable me to demonstrate I was also a committed fan. In the course of the discussion with you and your friends who are also die-hard fans I trot out a piece I memorised from a football writer, tweaking it here and there to give it a ring of authenticity as I explain how the captain, sorry our captain, needs a holding midfielder alongside him to allow him to venture further forward and play key balls to the lone man up front. You all nod in agreement showing admiration in my knowledge despite it being acquired elsewhere. I feel the fuel flowing.

I attend the match with you and see how excited you are by the occasion. Your conversation speeds up as you talk about the team the manager has selected. The smell of beer and hot dogs and pies mixes together on the concourse, heightening the occasion as the singing from the away fans drifts from inside the stadium. An event like this assails the senses. The press of the crowd as it makes its way inside seems to lend energy to you and your pace quickens, causing me to have to speed up to ensure I am not left behind. Once in our seats your face shows how you are eagerly anticipating the game, the chanting and shouting already loud, bouncing around the stadium and competing with the delivery of the pa announcer. All around me I can see nervous anticipation, bullish enthusiasm and well-founded confidence. I listen to the chants so I learn the words enabling me to join in. I watch you as you crane forward in your seat, eyes fixed on the unfolding match, fists clenched and repeated utterances issued loudly to urge your team on. I mimic your exhortations and body language, leaning towards the pitch and then jumping up as your team, now our team, opens the scoring. You hug me and I return the hug, jumping up and down in a replica of the delight that washes across the home crowd. The taunting chants aimed at the opposition ring out and I readily join in, gesturing towards the disconsolate faces in the adjoining stand. A second goal is scored, this time from the cries of delight and the conjoining of profanity and blasphemy the goal is clearly of both quality and importance.

"That puts us on top of the league on goal difference," you explain as if you are able to see that I am wondering why there is such a heightened reaction to this second goal. I know however that you are not wondering that at all. I know that you are thrilled that I am embracing with such enthusiasm the match, sharing the main passion in your life. I join in with the cheers, the shouting, the cries of frustration and disappointment, the barracking of the referee when he makes a poor decision and ensure I am fully integrated with the experience. I look around me watching the passion, the hope, the fury and the delight etched on the other supporters. The stadium is a cauldron of noise and emotion. I am plugged into this experience along with fifty five thousand other people. I can see the emotions are raw and visceral, even primitive.

I see all of this around me yet I feel none of it. I merely mimic everyone else in order to fit in. I am attached to the experience but I feel nothing. I am completely detached from it. All it does is serve a purpose to enable me to create and build bridges and ties with you. I can see how it all affects you, it is clear to see. I am there yet I am not. I am connected yet removed. This is how it feels, or rather, this is how it does not.

My Pledge to You

I do sincerely and solemnly declare, by almighty God, this pledge to you. I have reduced it to writing so that this shall bear testament to the sincerity by which I have made these promises and so that a record may exist for time eternal to the dedication and commitment contained therein.

I will love and cherish you and be faithful to you. I shall not let thoughts of congress with others trespass upon my mind for it remains pure and devoted to you. I will only ever give you my heart and ask that you have a care for it, for I only have the one and it now belongs to you.

I shall strive each and every day to bring you happiness and joy. Through a dedicated application I will secure your contentment. I will not rest until delight permeates everything around you. I have one purpose and that is to love you with the most perfect love, in every facet of my life.

I will bring you security and solidity, banishing fear and darkness through my unwavering loyalty to you. I shall be that foundation on which we shall build our glorious and everlasting love. I will toil ceaselessly in my endeavours to bring about our togetherness and union.

I will be your angel that spreads his almighty wingspan that shall shield you from harm. No injurious intent or scathing tongue shall ever penetrate the wall that I shall form behind which you will always be assured of shelter.

I promise to make you laugh so that your heart is lifted skywards and no troubles will ever burden you. I will always be there when the forces of darkness seek to hurt you. With my fiery sword I shall smite them into oblivion. Wherever you may tread I will be by your side, ready at a moment's instance to catch you and hold you should the road crumble beneath your feet.

I will never be found wanting when fate conspires against you. You will always be able to look to me and in my eyes find reassurance, hope and optimism. No task shall be too great if at its conclusion your happiness is assured.

I promise that though the winds may howl about us, that although lightning strikes at us and iced rain is driven at us, I will wrap my arms about you and steer you to shelter. I promise that you will always find sanctuary and protection with me.

I will honour your name and join battle with those that besmirch it. I shall only allow truth to pass my lips in all my dealings with you. I shall treat you with respect, reverence and dutiful worship, in recognition of your inner and outer beauty for which I give daily thanks.

I will craft the finest gifts to lay at your feet, toil so that no fruit is forbidden to you; no luxury shall be denied to you and every wish you make I shall deliver.

I shall treat you with deference, patience and compassion. Only the most noble of intentions shall I ever exhibit unto you. My every thought, word and deed will be forged in the furnace of truth and honesty.

I shall keep as watchwords to my burgeoning heart, the lessons of fidelity, humility and grace. I give thanks now and shall each day for the bounty that comes our way. I shall not let petty distractions deter me from my sworn duty to love and honour you.

I swear that I shall listen with an open mind, speak with a true heart and only have eyes for you. I shall fill each of my days with the wonder of you and dedicate myself to the furtherance of our dreams. Each day I shall give thanks for the fact that we have been brought together and I shall treat our love as the most perfect and sacred. Nothing that I shall think, say or do shall ever desecrate what we have.

I shall nurse you through sickness, hold you through sadness and carry you through adversity. My stride will be purposeful and direct as I strive to bring you joy.

I shall only ever lay my hands in sensual delight on you and with my lips kiss no other the way that I shall kiss you. My passion burns for you and you alone. I shall desire you as greatly in the years that come to pass as I do in this moment. Time and age shall not wither or diminish the love that I have for you. With every day that passes I shall find something new to love you for. We may travel over the same route many times but each time I shall make it seem as if it is the first time.

I promise to imbue our lives with magic and wonder. I shall show you the fantastic and the marvellous. I will take pleasure in sharing the simplest delights with you alongside the most extravagant.

I am yours and that is the only ever state I shall maintain. Though temptation may beckon and seduction seeks to lead me astray, I shall, by the grace of God and the fortitude with which I have been blessed, walk only to you.

When the sun sets on our scintillating journey together, as we look back on all that we have created together, all we have achieved together and all we have loved in one another, it is your name that I shall say with my dying breath.

This is my pledge to you. All I ask is that you sign this written pledge and in so doing acknowledge your acceptance of all that is herein contained.

Your Pledge to Me

You signed the pledge. Your tears of joy fell on it and washed away what I had written there revealing instead what has been carved into the stone underneath. It is your pledge to me.

You promise to supply me with the fuel that I need, be it morning, noon or night. You dedicate yourself to loving, cherishing but above all else admiring me. From the moment you wake until the moment you close your eyes and hopefully seek slumber, you will apply your every thought, word and deed to supplying me with the potent fuel that I require.

You swear that you will be cast adrift from everything that you once held dear. You vow that you will raise no complaint nor seek to remedy your splendid isolation and instead you shall give thanks for the opportunity to be beholden to me.

You will agree with me without condition. You will submit to my will and my word. You will be subjugated and dominated and you will allow this to happen with a great gladness in your heart.

You unconditionally accept the dogma of my thinking and you will without demurring or deferring accept my rules even where there are no rules. You shall speak when I demand it and remain silent otherwise. You agree that you will second-guess, anticipate and ascertain all that I require and you shall do so without assistance, hint or help. You will raise no complaint nor identify any contradiction in the diktats that I shall pronounce, no matter how wildly they alter and vacillate.

You agree to remain trapped in the altered reality that shall be created for you and you shall do nothing to seek your escape from it. You agree you shall polish my hall of mirrors and keep the same free from dust, defect or deterioration.

You shall not better anything that I do; you shall diminish anything that you do in deference to my brilliance. You agree to comply with my every wish, demand and command and in so doing recognise that it is for your own good.

You shall recognise that you over-react, forget, fail to remember, blow out of proportion and engage in crazy aberrations of behaviour and you shall give repeated thanks for the tolerance and forgiveness that I allow you in the face of such blatant and sustained provocation.

You willingly and without complaint, claim or seeking redress agree to forgo your self-esteem, your identity and your sense of self. You volunteer to lay your self-worth, reason and confidence as sacrifices on the altar of my greatness.

You will submit to every whim I express, each desire I create and every demand without regard for its depravation, degradation or denigration.

You will with marvellous enthusiasm praise and worship me and with clarion call declare your awe at my almighty brilliance. You shall not suffer others to denigrate my name and instead you swear to defend my honour and reputation irrespective of logic, reason or hypocrisy.

You agree to be coated in confusion, enshrined in bewilderment and driven to demented frustration. You shall willingly strive with every fibre of your being to pander, soothe and placate me save when I do not require such treatment and expect you to realise without indication or clue.

You will go down on your knees and give thanks for the largesse that I exhibit towards you, that you are granted a daily audience with my scintillating superiority and that you are allowed to breathe the air that I breathe.

You shall cast off all notion of self, forgo your relationships and betray your friends and family in order to better dedicate yourself to my greatness. You shall relinquish all interests, hobbies and activities in order to devote your life to me. You shall forgo all assets and chattels, delivering them up for my use, abuse and destruction.

You agree that yes means no, no means yes and yes and no mean whatever I want them to mean. You shall always give thanks for the enlightenment that I shall bring to you and do nothing to evade, dilute, diffuse or ameliorate my greatness.

You agree to become my appliance and an extension of my greater glory. You understand that you have only one role and that is to supply me with my precious fuel. You will not diminish nor interrupt this supply on pain of most terrible retribution.

You swear on pain of damnation that you shall never ignore me, never show indifference towards me and never to fail to react to everything that I say and do.

You will sacrifice everything that you hold dear in recognition of the god that I am and you shall do so whilst smiling despite the trauma you will suffer, the abuse you will endure and the horror visited on you each and every day.

You shall say my name with your dying breath and raise no complaint when I forget who you are.

I note you have already signed this pledge. You are learning already.

The Bolthole

The bolthole is a very important location to my kind. It can come in many forms but the message it sends to you is very clear; you are not welcome. Our kind must always have a bolthole to which we can retreat. This is our sacred territory where you are not allowed to venture. When we first engage with you, you should notice two things which invariably occur. We will spend most of our time where you live. This enables us to stay by your side as often as we can in order to continue our seduction of you. It also means that your resources are the ones that are used up. It is your food, your cable bill and your utilities that we use and since it is your home we will not contribute to those bills. If asked we will point out that we have our own overheads to cover although of course they will be reduced as we are rarely there. We stay at your house and ensure that you provide us with a set of keys so that we may come and go. You are invariably not given a set for our house. When we decide that we want to engage in our methods of gathering fuel and/or we decide to subject you to a period of the effective silent treatment, we return to our house. You cannot enter and we are able to watch you pleading and begging from through a gap in the curtains as you turn up wanting to see us as you try to work out why we have just disappeared.

On the occasions we do allow you to stay at our property then this is little more than a licence which is revocable on a moment's notice. If we want you out of our space then we will turf you out, irrespective of time, weather or convenience. We like to do this to reinforce that it is us who are in control in this relationship and not you.

Even if we properly move in together at one property or buy another one together, we shall manipulate the situation so that your house is sold and the proceeds used towards the joint property whilst we keep our house on. You will be puzzled by such a move but we will find an excuse to do this.

"It represents a useful investment opportunity so I am going to keep it."

"Now is now the right time to sell in that area."

"I need a pied a terre for when I work late in the city."

"I want the market to pick up first before I consider selling the property."

"I don't want to sell it because my ex-wife will come sniffing around for a share of it."

We will find the reason not to sell it. This is of course not the real reason. We want to keep it as our bolthole. We might decide to provide you with a set of keys for this property but then when you try to use them to go inside to find us, the door is bolted so you cannot access the property. Your shouts of frustration prove to be delicious fuel as we sit and listen to you.

Sometimes we will use hotel rooms as boltholes or the office or a bar. As long as it somewhere to which we can retreat and have you guessing as to where we have gone as you frantically telephone and text us, then it serves its purpose.

If there is not another property we will create a bolthole within the house that we share. The study will have a lock fitted and we keep the key on our person all the time. It may be a man-cave in the basement or the garden shed, but there is one simple rule concerning this bolthole. It may be in or around our joint property but you are not to enter it ever. We regard this as our throne room where we sit and plot our schemes. The chosen few will be admitted in order to emphasise to you how you are not special enough to be allowed in and thus prompt a reaction from you. We know it will drive you crazy wondering what we are doing in this place, especially if our guests are of the opposite sex. We will spend hours in this place, secreted away, often sleeping there too. Here we can send our messages and engage in our telephone calls with other sources of fuel, free from interference yet still gaining fuel from you as we know you will be in a spin thinking about what we are doing. We can enter the chat rooms; work our way through the dating sites and blitz social media, all entrenched in our control room. We will delight in sending you a message compelling you to bring us food or a drink and leave it at the door. You of course will comply in order to try and sneak a glimpse of what is going on inside or to try and talk to us, yet the door will be pushed closed in your face.

On occasions the bolt hole will be temporary in nature. Should we decide that we wish to exercise some withdrawal late at night when you are expecting intimacy and love-making, we will move to sleep in the spare room, sliding across the lock we had fitted. We will lie there smiling as we hear you tapping on the door and sobbing for us to come back to the shared bed.

The bolthole is very important to us. It allows us a clear way of reinforcing our control and superiority, it provides a base from which we can engage in our schemes and plotting and it is crucial in the implementation of silent treatment.

If you realise that the person you have a relationship with creates and uses boltholes there is every chance that he or she is one of us. Now you know it to be the case but you are still not coming in.

Born to be Riled

You were predestined to meet me or one of my kind. It was written in the stars and was as likely to happen as the sun rising tomorrow morning. You see, you grew and developed as a healthy and normal person. One of the first gifts that you received was a moral compass and you have always found it to work. You were guided by a decent role model, one that showed you the value of compassion, caring and consideration. You have always prided yourself on being able to step into the shoes of others, see someone else's point of view or imagine what it must be like to be in that other person's position. It is natural for you to take an interest in the person you are talking with, to listen and engage with them. You are a shoulder to cry on, a pillar of support and a rock to others. Others turn to you in their hour of need. You are patient, tender and take great pleasure in helping other people. You might have made a career of it, becoming a doctor or nurse, an aid worker, a social worker, a counsellor or a charity employee. You have been shown the way by others and with your measured view of the world, developed a strong sense of what is right and what is wrong.

You believe in love. Love conquers all. All you need is love. Love changes everything. You believe that we should all show love to one another and in return we will be loved. That is all that you ask for, to be loved.

When you appear on our radar you shine brighter than everything else around you. The empathic radiance that emanates from you is a blazing beacon of benevolence. Our displays flash and light up, alerting us to your presence as the needles and gauges go off the scale. A massive tanker full of fuel has just cruised into view and we are duty bound to hijack it. We follow the path that is all too familiar to you now, of seducing you and dazzling you. You switch off your engines and weigh the anchor, content to dock with us. We have pulled alongside you and scramble over our bow to overwhelm you. It does not take long before we have burst onto the bridge, overpowered your captain and taken control of this tanker full to the brim of fuel. This hijacking is without violence or resistance, in fact your captain is not so much overpowered but rather he readily relinquishes control of the bridge to us, happy to place his trust in us. We have established our credentials through our repeated charm offensive. There can be no doubt that we have passed our mariner's examinations and that we are fully qualified to control this tanker.

Yet this peaceful conquest does not satisfy us. There is no excitement or drama in achieving it so easily. Yes, at first we were content for this state of affairs to be the case. It was easy and pleasant and interesting for we had not been on this vessel before and its cargo, the ever so precious fuel was an unknown variety. Now we have been siphoning off the fuel for quite some time and we need to add a new ingredient to it to increase its potency as we maintain control of this vessel. We want to stir things up in the holds by charting a course through stormy waters. We might purposefully spring a leak, cut away the lifeboats and fire off the flares, before jamming the wheel so the tanker slowly drifts in circles, rolling and yawing through the mountainous waves giving the impression of vast movement but not actually going anywhere.

We have to annoy, provoke, irritate and rile you. This heightens the emotional responses and just like the storm battered tanker, we plough headlong into drama, turmoil and rage. In the same way that you were destined to care and exhibit considerable empathy, you were also damned to be the object of our games and manipulation, all with the aim of provoking you. You were blessed with the skills and traits of an empathic individual, but that blessing came with a price. You were cursed to become a prime target for our kind and to suffer the tortuous examinations of our warped minds that aimed to engender an emotional response from you. This would initially be benign but with that sinking sense of inevitable dread it would become one where you had no choice but to be subjected to manipulation, attack, insult and provocation. Riling you became the key objective. This would not work with those who are not of your stock. They would not be sucked in to begin with, or they would recognise what was happening and walk away and stay away. Not you, your empathic traits force you to try and heal and to fix despite the alarming levels of contemptuous harassment, abuse and demeaning treatment. Your empathy binds you to your tormentor as he or she delights in prodding you each and every day to garner that emotional reaction. You were raised to heal yet destined to be riled and all by our savage tongue and stinging hand.

Tell Tale

We have cast you aside after subjecting you to a litany of abuse, mistreatment and the full horror of our manipulative and disorientating repertoire. You have your absolute all in the pursuit of what you believed to be our perfect love. You have endured humiliation, denigration and belittlement yet you still hung in there, desperate to cure and to heal. You wanted us so much that it hurt and it still does. Not only have we discarded you with a callous disregard for your welfare and sanity, we have added to the pain by parading our latest conquest for the entire world to see. You are no longer the recipient of our burning desire. You have been removed from our grace and favour and a new beneficiary has been installed. The monument to our supposedly everlasting love has been razed to the ground and on that once sacred ground we have erected a new edifice, lauding our new, shinier and much improved interest. What was once promised as lasting forever has been smashed into pieces and erased from the history books.

Your hurt, anger and indignation are tangible. The traitorous behaviour we have subjected to you has torn you apart. It is awful enough that after everything you have done, everything you have given and everything that you have endured, you have been struck from the record. The insult has been magnified and multiplied by reason of our infatuation with your replacement. How dare we do this to you? It is utterly unfair.

Your desire for retribution is immense. You want to cause our come uppance and warn the world about the monster that you see us as. You feel that all must be told about the awful toll that you have taken from our treatment but greater than that, you have that irresistible sense of needing to protect and warn. The empathic nature that made you such an attractive target to us has survived notwithstanding the mauling we have given you. You need to save our conquest from what you have been put through. Not only must you rescue the poor innocent from our toxic touch this will enable you to exact a delicious revenge on us. By taking away the thing that we crave, you know that triumph waits. Our fresh acquisition may work out what has happened, but that will take too long. No, you owe it to her and you owe it yourself to intervene, to educate and warn. It is time to expose us for what you say we are.

You call us for the perfidious behaviour that we have engaged in. You decry our stories of your hysterical and unreasonable behaviour and yet here you are, ready to spread such lies about us to our new love. You hold yourself out as being a person of good nature and compassion yet you are hell bent on ruining our new-found happiness. You were not good enough for us. You let us down and thus you had to be moved to one side replaced. Out with the old and in with the new. That is the natural order of events. The appliance does not work anymore; therefore a new, faster and more effective appliance must be brought to the fore and installed. Why complain about that? Had you been fit for purpose you would still be the object of our affection, but you failed. We gave you every chance and yet you still came up wanting. You are to blame. You only have yourself to blame. Yet, exhibiting the malice that you laughingly accuse us of you go running to our new interest and tell tales about us.

Your poison-laden tongue weaves its malevolent words as you whisper fabricated stories in order to discourage our new love from remaining with us. Do you not understand that this is the very reason why we had to let you go? We tried. We really did, but you would insist on railing against us and not submitting to our will. There was no hope for it other than to remove you from our lives. As people of substance and rigour, we have not gone with our tales of lament to others, seeking to draw sympathy from them. No, that is not for us. We chalked off our time with you as a mistake and we learn from it. Now we have found someone better. So what that we moved with what you regard as unseemly haste, we are entitled to drive forward. You should take heed of our capability in that regard, instead of remaining mired in what might have been. Imprisoning yourself in a tomb of melancholy is not the way of progress. This only underlines our superiority to you. We have moved on. If you cannot, then that is your problem and not ours.

We act with honour and do not stoop to your level. We know that our character speaks for itself with this new person. We allow them to make their own mind up and the extensive groundwork which we put in place has ensured that this person is impervious to your unsavoury behaviour. We know that our impregnable façade of magnificence cannot be pierced by your savage and twisted lies. Run to our new love, run to them and seek to pour your poison in their ears and we shall watch smiling as they turn to you and shake their head. They are immune to your campaign of smears. They know that we are truly wonderful and that you had your chance but you destroyed what we had as a consequence of your quite frankly unhinged conduct. She tells you how magnificently I treat her and you try to explain how it was like that for you in the beginning but your words are lost in translation. You are told that your jealousy has skewed your outlook, that your paranoia has warped your view of the world. Your craziness has been well documented. We have done the protecting. We have done the warning and as always we got in first.

Tell your tales but all you do is reinforce our brilliance and the reason we were oh so right to be rid of you. Nobody likes a tell-tale. Nobody likes you.

Constant Companion

The narcissist in your life may have turned to you and said,

"You are the one true constant in my life," or words to that effect. Of course, when this sentence was said to you with faux sincerity shining in our eyes it was intended as another love bomb that rained down on you from up on high. What we were actually doing was engaging in a rare moment of truth.

We require a constant in our lives for a variety of reasons. To begin with it is because when we are seducing you, you provide us with all that delicious positive fuel and we cannot get enough of it. You are shiny and sparkling and that fuel tastes so glorious. We want to be with you all of the time to drink deep of your fuel but also to ensure that you become addicted to us as we love bomb you. We want you constantly with us so that you are exposed all the time to our charm, our wit and our affection so that as we drink up your fuel, you become addicted to the euphoria you feel by being with someone as wonderful as us. We also want you constantly by our side to isolate you from anyone who may just have the knowledge and temerity to shatter the fantasy world that we have created so you wriggle free from our grip. After expending time and energy in trapping you and clamping our jaws around you, the last thing we want is for you to be able to escape us.

Inevitably you let us down and your supply of positive fuel lessens in quality and quantity. Your dereliction of duty means we must draw fuel from other appliances. A normal and healthy person might think that if a person tire of the other in the relationship one might look at ways of rekindling what first drew those people together. Well, you know what? We do that, only we do it in our skewed manner. We have no interest in working at the relationship that requires too much effort. We will however rekindle the golden period in order to enable our vacillating between devaluing and idealising to have the maximum effect. You may also consider that if someone no longer has any interest in the other person in the relationship and especially if that person is looking elsewhere then he or she would do the decent thing and end the relationship and move on. Not us. We need you. You might question why that should be the case since if we are treating you so badly, why on earth would we want to remain with you? If we are committing acts of infidelity with other people, why do we remain in a relationship with you? The answer is because we need a constant appliance. You are that constant appliance. We have decided that you would supply us with delicious positive fuel and although you would let us down and reduce that supply, we could keep you around as we drew negative fuel from you. You are the mainstay. There is no logic to us in having a relationship then ending it and moving on to another person some time later. That would not provide us with enough fuel, nowhere near enough. We need someone who will always be there so that he or she:-

1. Provides positive fuel to being with;
2. Provides negative fuel thereafter;
3. Represents a good return on our investment (we are not going to throw away such an asset that readily);
4. As a constant enables us to use others in our manipulation to draw more fuel from the constant and the other people (triangulation, smear campaigns and so on)

It is only when we have drained you of most of the fuel that you can supply us with that we shift to a new constant. Usually we have had them lined up for a while. Of course we do not let you go. You still serve a purpose for fuel once you have replenished your levels after a period of time and then it is time to hoover. In some instances we switch back to you as our constant and the most recent person becomes the discarded individual. We will switch back and forth between the two of you, for as long as you allow us to do this. This saves us having to hunt out new supplies as we rotate your roles in your obligation to provide us with fuel.

This is why you are kept despite the many affairs that we have. You are the constant and you may keep that role for years since much of it is dependent on how much you will take before deciding to try and escape us.

We also deploy you as a constant (yes I know you only deploy machines and it should be employ, but you are an appliance remember) because we like to compartmentalise our lives. We are the business ace at work, the champion sportsman on the field, the caring husband and father at home, the wild man on a night out and the sexual Olympian with our mistress. We like to show the world we have a steady wife who does not cause us trouble, one who runs the home and cares for the children. See how successful we are? We can attract someone who wishes to remain with us and provide that visage of stability and domestic bliss. The rest of the world does not need to know about the chaos we unleash on you behind closed doors.

Mentioning chaos identifies a further reason why we like you as our constant. Much of what we do generates chaos - the affairs, the gambling, the driving offences, the cheating and the lying - it is therefore a source of great comfort to us that we can return to you and find you waiting as usual. We have experienced so much upheaval and chaos when we were younger that this constant presence on your part provides us with a degree of reassurance. Of course, we abuse this by unleashing our chaotic nature on you as well, but we know you are not going to go and leave us and that is of great importance to us. Not only does this show the world somebody wants us it also means this appliance will remain and churn out fuel for a good while yet.

For all the other variables we introduce, the other women or men, the threatened departures and the bouts of silent treatment, we need you as our constant companion.

Drive You Around the Bend

I love my car. It is beautiful. Powerful, sleek and impressive. Just like me. The exterior is anthracite black and the windows tinted black which gives it a sinister appearance which is rather apt I suppose. I enjoy driving and especially since I am an excellent driver. My car is a fantastic instrument by which I am able to manipulate you.

To begin with I spend an inordinate amount of time cleaning it. I could of course get someone else to do this for me but I know how much it irritates you when on a glorious sunny afternoon you want to drive out somewhere for the day and all I do is spend it on the drive washing, waxing and polishing my car. You come outside and remonstrate with me, which is all good fuel and only causes me to spend longer cleaning the alloys before moving on to the interior. I manage to provoke an argument with you because you wanted to use the Hoover (you should know by now that only I am allowed to Hoover) inside the house but I have commandeered it for a lengthy period of time as I scrupulously chase after each speck of dust inside my car.

I also engage in long conversations about its performance and how it is running. I know you find this boring and when you are trying to tell me about something, I will continue to dominate the conversation by talking about my car. The irritation you express through your sighs and eye-rolling amuses me no end.

I am naturally a brilliant driver and have demonstrated this on days out on race tracks as I have taken various high performance vehicles out for a spin leaving you stranded on the trackside bored to tears. The occasional temper tantrum you throw when I tell you we are going out for the day, only to arrive at one of the race tracks enables me to demonstrate just how selfish you are and that you have no consideration of the things that I like to do. However, it is when we are in the car together that my vehicle's potential as an instrument of manipulation is truly realised. I drive aggressively; tail gating the car in front, flashing my lights to get that car to move aside and gesticulating at the incompetent buffoons who have the audacity to be driving when I am. The reactions of the other drivers, from fear to anger all provide me with fuel, but it is your pleas for me to slow down as I hurtle along a country lane or your scream as we screech to a halt behind a lorry that really do it for me. The aggression in my driving provides me with an opportunity to demonstrate how superior I am on the roads and motorways. My vehicle is better, faster and more expensive than your scrapheap so move aside right now. At the traffic lights an admiring glance from another driver, especially if she is female, will please me no end and irritate you. I will purposefully drive at the same speed as the other vehicle flashing my winning smile at the other driver as she looks back grinning whilst we drive alongside one another.

Should someone not give way or cut me up I will chase them and do so until they stop, be it at home or their destination. I will leap from the car and berate them at traffic lights whilst they are stationery, smashing my fist on their window and kicking their wing as they grip the steering wheel in terror. How dare they drive like that near me? I return to my car, power raging through my body as I have put them in their place and find you sobbing with fear after I pursued this driver relentlessly. The driver's reaction and your reaction fuelling me deliciously.

I use my car as a bolt hole, often sitting in it and listening to the cricket on the radio or an interesting radio play as you knock on the window trying to get my attention. I ignore you and you stalk around the car, fuming. I know you want to scratch it or dent it but you know better than to do anything like that to my precious car. I will walk away from you and get in the car and drive off leaving you stranded. This is a powerful way of letting you know that you are in the wrong. I park where I want and throw away the parking tickets or abuse the traffic wardens, accusing them of jealousy when they try to give me a ticket. I speed everywhere as I am not to be delayed, it is my time and my journey that are important.

I enjoy suddenly pulling over in the car and demanding you pleasure me. You always comply and as you lower your head I grin at my power over you as I select one of my favourite pieces of music and press down on the accelerator as we drive off. Such is my ability; I can drive at high speed even whilst you attend to me with your mouth. I am truly the king of the road. I will have you over the bonnet and then scold you for leaving hand prints on the polished metal, giving me a wonderful opportunity to criticise you after a seemingly intimate act. Of course, when I have you splayed across the bonnet, skirt hitched up and hair scattered across it, I do not see you beneath me as I thrust and buck. No, I am enjoying congress with my vehicle. We are merging together, two beautiful and powerful creatures that truly complement one another.

You are never allowed to drive my car. It is mine and only I am able to use it to frustrate you, anger you, alarm you and terrify you. It is my black bombshell that is there to draw emotional reactions from you and those around us, to serve my need for fuel. Just like me, my car does not provide many miles to the gallon and needs frequent refuelling, but then anything of quality is always high maintenance isn't it?

Sick to Death

We are strong, powerful and impervious to illness or injury. We are a bastion of invulnerability, a veritable shining example of radiant health and vitality. Our superiority means we stand head and shoulders above everyone else and the weakness that comes with ill health and infirmity is not something that affects us. Except when we decide it must. That is when we play the sickness card. There are three instances, in the main, when we do this.

The first is when we do actually suffer from some illness or an injury. It may just be a fractured eyelash but to us we have been blinded with a red hot poker. The pain, good Lord the pain, it is too great and intense. It wracks us and has us twisted up in agony. Come on empath, do something. Do something now. Soothe our fevered brows, splint our broken limbs and bind our wounds. You must drop anything and everything. Forget being at work today, you must call in and excuse yourself no matter how inconvenient, for you are required to don a nurse's outfit and do your best Florence Nightingale impression for us. This slight snuffle is pneumonia you know and to top it all it is your fault. You insisted on the window of the bedroom being left open; now see what you have done. I may not last the week. You would like that wouldn't you, you ungrateful bitch after everything that I have done for you. You did it on purpose. You wanted me to be ill so you could see me suffer. That is how nasty and selfish you are. Is it any wonder I have been off with other women when this is how I am treated by somebody who is supposed to love me? Yes the smallest spot, minor ache and slight cough are all that is needed to enable us to declare that we are on our death beds. It is good for several uses. First of all, we will use it to avoid doing things such as household chores or attending an event that you wanted to go to. Secondly, it means you must give us plenty of attention by looking after us. Those soothing words and hot water bottles brought to our bedside all provide us with fuel. Thirdly, we are able to provoke you by being demanding and castigating you for not living up to expectations. You didn't bring that hot lemon drink soon enough or those are the wrong pills. We will compare you to others, "My mother would do a better job of looking after me than you." All of which is designed to cause a reaction from you.

The second occasion on which we will play the sickness card is when you are ill or injured. We are not here to look after you. Good Lord, not at all. Why should we? That is not our role. We are too busy looking for fuel and we do not have the time or energy to spend engaged in nursing you. Not only of course are we devoid of the concept of feeling that we should care and that we should feel sorry and compassionate for someone who is unwell, we do not regard it as a task that is worthy of someone as brilliant as us. If you moan enough so that we are compelled to call out a doctor we will pronounce our own diagnosis in order to align ourselves with the brilliance of the medic. When he concludes what ailment it is you are suffering from we will declare,

"Yes, I said to her that that was what was wrong with her, but she won't listen to me doctor, she insisted on getting you out. I am sorry she has wasted your time."

We get to denigrate you and upset you whilst showing off how clever we are because we knew what was wrong with you (even though we did not) and the doctor accords with us. We may as well steal a segment of the doctor's brilliance for our construct whilst he is here mightn't we?

We will then invite the doctor to examine our shoulder or leg as we go to great lengths explaining how much pain we are in. This keeps the spotlight firmly on us and has you annoyed that we have hijacked your consultation. We will look to declare we are far worse off than you. You have a cold, well we have flu. We will use this as an opportunity to accuse you of attention seeking (nice bit of projection there) as we point out how selfish you are for being ill when we are. We have no interest in tending to you and we need to make the situation all about us. Accordingly, we will fake an illness or an injury in order to trump yours.

The third reason as to why we will play the sickness card is when we are low on fuel and low on energy. There may be any number of reasons why this state of affairs has arisen. You may be getting wise to some of our manipulative behaviour and therefore you are not reacting as often so that the level and quality of fuel that you provide is reduced. We may also have a natural dip in our energy levels or feel some degree of vulnerability which means that our resources are being stretched rather thin. This makes it difficult for us to seek out additional sources of fuel. This diminution in fuel reduces our power and this risks the craven creature that lurks within trying to escape and making itself heard. When this happens, the creature's whisperings remind us of our weakened selves. We are not ill. We are not injured. What we are however feeling is weakened, as if we are ill or injured. Accordingly, we play the sickness card in order to obtain an emergency injection of fuel from you or whoever else might be to hand. As an empathic individual you are programmed to respond to this and you cannot resist the opportunity to exhibit your caring nature in order to help us out and nurse us. The attention you lavish on us provides us with fuel and we begin to feel more powerful again. The creature's catcalls fade as he is subsumed within the prison of our constructed edifice once again and our supremacy returns. Our weakness lifts thanks to this provision of fuel from you and this has been instigated by us playing the sickness card. We will do this to garner sympathy from you, from family and friends and also from health professionals. Our favourite ailments of course are of the invisible variety. Depression, a stomach pain or a bad back. We are brilliant actors and ham up our suffering. The portrayal of our poor sick self would please Ferris Bueller. As with most things it is just another fabrication designed to manipulate you and provide us with fuel but you must never dare question us. We of course have researched the symptoms thoroughly and our Munchausen Syndrome is most prevalent. You are duty bound to help us rise from our sick bed or you are a bad person and we will cut you out of our will in the event that this terrible affliction sends us to the reaper. You will be sick to death of our illnesses and injuries but you will be duty bound to attend to them.

Compartment Store

We view our lives as a series of compartments. The compartments are linked and there is an archway from one compartment to another but this archway has been bricked up by us and only we know the secret word that will open up the archway and admit us to the next compartment. You will try and search for an opening so that you may move from one compartment to another but your search will be fruitless. You will rhyme off all the passwords you can think of from 'open sesame' through to 'abracadabra' but none of them will work. There is a simple reason for that. We want you to stay in your compartment until we come back to it. We do not want you interacting with any of our other compartments because then it makes each area harder for us to control. A greater need for control mean more energy expenditure which will mean that there is less available for me to use to gather fuel and that is not something I can allow to happen.

A blissful domestic set-up will be in one compartment where I play the role of doting husband and caring father. To the external observer who looks in on the scene through the Perspex it appears to be a picture of harmony and good relations. Yet the observer cannot hear the shouting nor listen to your sobs as you are on the receiving end of another tirade. The fearful cries and the scathing admonishments fail to air beyond this compartment. You are not able to escape to another place and reveal what is really going on in this compartment. As soon as I depart to the next one then the brickwork closes behind me with lightning quick speed, trapping you where I want you. Of course I will tell you all about what is happening in the other compartments when I return, so that you will be subjected to tales of my magnificence in the work place and anecdotes about the new 'friend' I have in order to create some triangulated jealousy from you.

My work compartment show me as all conquering and masterful yet those that have been subjected to my brutal put downs and suffered from my repeated dumping of work on them as I breeze around town are forbidden from escaping this compartment to pollute the carefully constructed image that I have made for myself.

The members at the golf club who find my boasting odious and have seen me mark down a lower score than that which I had achieved on my score card are unable to blacken my name to my admirers beyond this particular place. Instead I depart the golf club and scurry to the bar where I regale my hangers-on with another story of my five under par round which won the competition. They coo over my success oblivious to what has actually gone on.

Home life, work life, mistress, friends, club, family and more are allotted these compartments. In each one I am a god. I rule supreme able to do as I please so that I can carry forth my stories of heroism into another compartment and there drink deep of their admiring fuel.

I spend much of my time ensuring that the inhabitants of each compartment know about one another, to multiply my fuel of course, but rarely shall I ever allow them to cross paths. This might lead to someone squaring the circle and working out what is behind my carefully orchestrated campaigns of divide and conquer. A must never speak to B who must not be allowed to tell C what really happened. I must maintain my constructed world where these people are little more than dolls in a huge segregated dolls house. I put them in poses and play with them so that I can create a scenario by which I can brag to others in the next room about. If they ever escaped and managed to follow me through these archways so they could compare what I have said with what has actually happened I would be truly finished. Sometimes this happens and then the compartment must be set ablaze, scorched from the record and denied an existence. Next time this compartment will be refurbished, repainted and with new dolls put in place. I must control everything around me. Everyone in their place and a place for everyone.

Tough Decisions

People face tough decisions every day in a wide array of scenarios. It may relate to health, business, relationships or money. Should the aggressive cancer treatment be undertaken despite the risks? How many people should be trimmed now the business has been taken over? Do we send in troops against the enemy on foreign soil? Do I give her another chance despite her infidelity? Does this blue or pink shirt look better? President Obama explained that by the time a matter was referred to him for an outcome there was no easy decision.

This is because people are troubled by conscience. A conscience is that thing which causes you to frame your own decisions as if someone was watching what you are doing or thinking, even though you are alone. People make decisions tougher than they need be because they are worried how people will react, how it will make that person look in front of others, how it will impact on other people and whether they will be damned if they do and damned if they don't. These considerations do not trouble my kind and me.

My kind and I receive a lot of bad press about the things we say and do. Of course you will not be holding your breath in the expectation of some kind of apology because that is just not going to happen. I do know however that you are a reasonable person who looks at matters in a balanced and fair-minded fashion (it is just that I tell everyone else that you are crazy harpy who is out of control). With that in mind, you really ought to give thanks for people like me because we can be relied on to make the tough decisions that have to be made.

For example, imagine there is a redundancy situation in your department and in one particular team four people are at risk of losing their jobs. Two positions have to go and one of your friends is in this pool of individuals at risk. How would you go about deciding who is selected for redundancy and who is not? That part of you that is dedicated to fairness and the correct way of doing things would decide that a prescribed selection criteria should be applied to all four who are at risk. You would apply scores for each person to the criteria and the two lowest would be then selected for redundancy. The empath in you knows however your friend will face serious financial consequences if he lost his job now, notwithstanding the redundancy package. You also fear you will lose your friendship if he is made redundant. You agonise over what you should do. Should you apply the scores fairly and then be beyond reproach in the event of a legal challenge to the decision but risk losing your friend and causing him severe problems? Alternatively, should you massage the scores bumping up a couple of his and reducing a couple of someone else's? Who would know if it is just a few points difference? What about speaking to the head of the department and trying to save one of the jobs so there is only one casualty? In such a scenario you know your friend will be safe as one of the candidates is poor at his job and is nailed on to be chosen. I know that you would face quite a dilemma in trying to make this decision and ultimately you would probably pass it on to someone else citing a conflict of interest.

What about me? What would I do? Would I apply the criteria and the poorest two lose out? After all, surely we want the best employees and if there is dead wood it needs to be cut out irrespective of any friendship that may exist? Would I instead apply my own criteria of who will provide me with the best fuel in this office dynamic and allow that to influence the supposed objective scoring? Would I make the decision that suits me the best and then reverse engineer the situation to give it the veneer of legitimacy? I should imagine that you will be inclined to think that I would do the latter. If so, you would be wrong.

I would fire all four. Their work would be distributed to other people in the department on the basis that they would receive a small bonus if they achieve certain targets. The business makes a greater saving by losing the foursome and four other employees become very grateful to me, thus giving me plenty of fuel, as a consequence of this incentive. I then contact two of the four and explain that if they bide their time I will ensure they can be re-hired in a few months' time, before the pay-off has been depleted and thus they will actually find themselves in a better position. I will recruit those two in the new financial year so the previous year's savings remain good. The re-hired individuals will be eternally grateful to me, ensuring loyalty and further fuel, plus I shall ensure they become my lieutenants as repayment for me looking out for them. The hold I have over my higher-up will ensure the recruitments go through without incident and are done outside of the time allowed for the two who remain out in the cold to bring a tribunal claim.

What about the friend in all of this? Who cares? He should have fuelled me more and he might have been saved. As it is, I have found some new friends who are ever so grateful for my largesse and who are perfectly content to propagate my explanation that the friend was released as a consequence of some behaviour that cannot be expanded on but let us say is outside the range of normative behaviours of decent people in society. When the friend comes calling to vent his spleen at me, well his anger and insults are all good fuel aren't they?

The way you are wired causes you to make decisions tough.

We, by contrast, make the tough decisions.

You really ought to thank us.

Never Let Go

I was engaged in a discussion recently with Dr E. The conversation concerned relationships.

"So, when you end a relationship, tell me how you feel about it?" he began as he unfolded his notebook and found a fresh page.

"I do not end my relationships," I replied.

"I see, so they are always ended by the other person are they?" he asked.

"No."

He waited to see if I was going to say anything else but I remained silent. Come on Dr E; let's see where you are going with this. You cannot outsmart me. He sat looking at me and me at him.

"Those answers suggest to me then that your relationships do not end."

Give Dr E enough time and he always gets there.

"Exactly," I answered.

"I see. We have discussed a number of relationships that you have and have had. With family members, acquaintances, friends and of course lovers. Now, from what you have explained to me I would certainly regard many of those relationships having come to an end, either by your doing or, though admittedly less often, at the hand of the other person."

"Your concept of a relationship evidently differs from mine."

"Please, expand on that point."

"My relationships begin when I determine that they should begin," I started to speak. Dr E frowned but said nothing. I could tell he wanted me to provide clarity to that assertion and I was happy to oblige.

"When I detect somebody who will prove of us to me then our relationship has already begun. It matters not whether we have spoken in person or even made any kind of contact. The decision that the relationship has begun rests with me."

Dr E was making notes as I spoke.

"The nature of the relationship is defined by what use that person is to me in providing me with my fuel. If the fuel they provide is strong and potent then I will be spending a lot of time with that person, others less so. I dictate the pace at which the relationship will develop by such criteria that I understand people like you apply to relationships."

"What criteria are those?" asked Dr E.

"Instances such as familiarity with one another, whether there is a hand shake or a kiss on greeting, the name by which we call one another, whether they can be relied on to provide information, whether they will lend money, whether we go to certain places together and how often, whether we live together, all of these things are what you measure a relationship by."

"And do you regard those criteria as instances that ought to happen over a particular period of time?"

"No. They are all measurements by which I know people like you determine the nature of the relationship. I use them as markers by which the level of fuel can be influenced, accordingly, I will move them along at a pace which suits my demands for fuel."

"But not according to anyone else's input or say a generally accepted norm from society?"

"Well, the other person has to consent to the act, I mean; I haven't imprisoned anyone in my home. Yet." I smiled.

"But if they are to provide their consent surely that means the timescale is taken out of your hands?"

"Not at all. I just make them consent in accordance with my timescale," I said.

"By exerting the influences you have described to me previously?"

"Exactly."

Dr E remained silent as he continued to write.

"So you determine when the relationship begins and the pace at which it proceeds and this relationship never ends?"

"Yes."

"But some of the instances of your intimate relationships that you have described to me certainly fit with the concept that they have ended."

"Not at all. If I have cast someone to one side because, as they always do, they have let me down in some way, then I will not let them walk away. They might think they have been able to do this. Indeed, in certain instances I encourage that train of thought so that the person's defences remain down and thus they are susceptible to me resurrecting our interaction. Nobody leaves me and I do not leave anybody. They will always serve some kind of purpose, at some point and therefore there may be a pause in our interaction but there is never a cessation."

"What if the other person decides they no longer wish to interact with you?"

"Why on earth would they think that?" I asked puzzled.

"Well, your treatment of many of them was harsh and unpleasant."

"But no less than they deserved. People need to know their place and if they step outside of that they must be brought to heel."

"Why?" asked Dr E.

"Because I gave them everything and each time they repay me by letting me down. That is unfair. Each time I give them the world, I really do doctor and no matter how wonderful I am to them they do not do enough in return and they let their affection become dull or they fail to provide me with the adoration that I deserve. It is wrong and they must be made to see how wrong they are punished for their transgressions."

"So you maintain a relationship to punish the other person?"

"In part yes, but it is usually because they still prove of use to me and they have their debt to me to repay."

"I see," remarked Dr E and he continued with his writing.

"And when do they repay this debt?" he asked.

"That's the problem doctor," I said with a sigh," they never do. That is why I never let them go."

A Statement of Intent

I should imagine that most of you have once looked at a picture of a person pushing a boulder up a hill and thought to yourselves,

"Oh yes, that is what life with a narcissist is like."

I know you do as I have had it said to me several times. I always reply,

"Achieving and maintaining brilliance is not meant to be easy. If it was, everyone would be doing it. You have to work hard to keep up with me."

You see there are certain types of empath who really do go above and beyond the call of duty. They may be of a co-dependent nature but it is not necessarily the case. It is more the fact that his person, a super empath, has a near unquenchable desire to do well, to heal, to fix and make things right. They regard anything and everything as a challenge but that no challenge is insurmountable. Their level of optimism is quite frankly baffling but I am not going to complain as I harness it to my advantage. The super empath believes there is good in everyone; it is just a case of finding it. This person believes that good will always triumph, that love will conquer all and no person is a lost cause. Sometimes it is fairly easy to identify these people as they do tend to congregate in the caring professions or if they do not, one can tell that they are a super empath by the way they undertake charity work, care for animals or overly romanticise everything. I have written before about how in the very early stage of our interaction I engage in a systematic and deliberate methodology of ensuring that you are going to supply with me fuel and that you will be drawn into my sphere of influence. This methodology also enables me to spot the super empath. Once I have one on my radar there is an exciting surge of anticipatory power through me as I relish the fuel that will be soon flowing from this hitherto untapped reservoir. When I have a super empath in my sights then I know that this person will go the extra mile, they will put in the hard yards and aim for 110 %. Armed with this knowledge I will issue my statements of intent so they do indeed work hard and supply me with what is amazing fuel.

What do these statements of intent look like? They come in a variety of forms but some examples are as follows:-

"You know I will hurt you so you would be better off staying away from me."

"I don't know what it is but I am on the verge of frenzy and you will get caught up in so you need to steer clear."

"I am difficult to please; I think you should be aware of this."

"Nobody ever meets me expectations."

"I have always been let down in the past and I do not expect you to be any different, so if you want to go now, before it is too hard, then you can."

"I can promise you it will never be dull with me, but I do not know if you could handle it."

"The intensity of my love will be brutal and you will probably be broken by it. It takes a special kind of person to be with me."

"I am giving you the chance to walk away now before it becomes too much for you."

These comments and similar are all the oral equivalent of throwing down the gauntlet. I can say these things utterly safe in the knowledge that you will now walk away. It is against your nature to do so. You hear these words and as a super empath you see a challenge but something that is completely worthwhile. There is a lost soul to be shepherded, a desolate being to make good once more and a wayward person to steer towards the light. You want to rescue me from the dark side, pull me clear of the abyss and save me. No matter how hard I make it sound, how difficult and dangerous it is described I know you want it all the more because you want to prove you can do it. No matter how high the obstacles are raised and how awkward and demoralising the journey, as a super empath you will hang in there.

I do not make these statements of intent for your sake. I am not warning you off out of any sudden sense of guilt or concern. Not a chance. I am doing it to appeal to you all the more. I know it is like turning the after burners on and you will respond by giving you absolute all to try and please me, heal me and fix me.

You never succeed. All you do is provide me with the most wonderful fuel.

The boulder will roll back down the hill, no matter how far you have pushed it and you will be flattened by it. It will happen every time.

Killing With Kindness

I do so enjoy being kind. I want to shower you with acts of generosity, concern and kindness when I first meet you. You are so special and only I can really see that that is the case. Other people have tried to crush the warmth and love inside you, trampling on you like some rare and delicate flower. Not me. I want to pick you and place you inside a jar, shielded from the toxicity of the world. I can nourish you, water you and let you enjoy the warmth from the light than shines from me. I can sense that you have been let down and hurt before. You do not deserve that. Someone as wonderful as you, someone as delicate and giving as you deserves far better. You can rest now though. The search is over. You have found me. I will take care of you now. Nothing will ever trouble you again. I will do so much for you and why not? I am blessed to have found you, but do you know what? We deserve one another. I have been looking for someone like you all my life, someone who I can dedicate myself to. A person I can protect, love and make happy. That is all I have ever wanted. I know I am surrounded by these trappings of success, that I am in demand from many people who want to be involved with me and share my radiance. It is flattering and humbling at the same time. I am not interested in any of that however. I just want to share my life with someone who I can cherish and worship. Now I can.

I know you have walked a hard and winding road. Those scuffed boots you wear, with holes and the sole hanging off bear testament to that. Not once have you complained of course. That is not your way. You need not take another step though because I will carry you. I will lift you up and with one firm foot planted in front of the other I will carry you away and onwards towards our joint destination. It is a wonderful place. I will whisper in your ear as I carry you and tell you all about how I have made this beautiful paradise. I have created it just for you and I.

It is our sanctuary where nobody can find us and nobody can harm us. Sounds idyllic doesn't it?

I want to soothe your fevered brow, I want to hold your hand when you are frightened and I want to see you smile because of me. I want to be the first person you see when you wake up and the last person you see before you fall asleep. I want to love you, care for you, hold you and protect you. I will fetch and carry for you, I will crawl over broken glass just to hand you a cup of water to quench your thirst. I want you to feel bombarded by my innate kindness, swamped by my good nature and overwhelmed by my fair intentions. I want to deliver to you every minute of every day my warmth and kindness so that it becomes all you know. I want you to become dependent on my charity, my largesse and my generosity. I want you to become hopelessly addicted to my love, my desire and my presence. I want to see myself in your eyes and nothing else. I want to hear my words spoken by your tongue. I want you to mimic everything that I do so that when I point, you point and when I nod, you nod. I want my campaign of kindness to obliterate every semblance of what you once were. I want to destroy what once existed and replace it with my design and my desires. I want to murder who you were and resurrect my creation in your place. I want to kill you with kindness.

Never Let Go

I was engaged in a discussion recently with Dr E. The conversation concerned relationships.

"So, when you end a relationship, tell me how you feel about it?" he began as he unfolded his notebook and found a fresh page.

"I do not end my relationships," I replied.

"I see, so they are always ended by the other person are they?" he asked.

"No."

He waited to see if I was going to say anything else but I remained silent. Come on Dr E; let's see where you are going with this. You cannot outsmart me. He sat looking at me and me at him.

"Those answers suggest to me then that your relationships do not end."

Give Dr E enough time and he always gets there.

"Exactly," I answered.

"I see. We have discussed a number of relationships that you have and have had. With family members, acquaintances, friends and of course lovers. Now, from what you have explained to me I would certainly regard many of those relationships having come to an end, either by your doing or, though admittedly less often, at the hand of the other person."

"Your concept of a relationship evidently differs from mine."

"Please, expand on that point."

"My relationships begin when I determine that they should begin," I started to speak. Dr E frowned but said nothing. I could tell he wanted me to provide clarity to that assertion and I was happy to oblige.

"When I detect somebody who will prove of use to me then our relationship has already begun. It matters not whether we have spoken in person or even made any kind of contact. The decision that the relationship has begun rests with me."

Dr E was making notes as I spoke.

"The nature of the relationship is defined by what use that person is to me in providing me with my fuel. If the fuel they provide is strong and potent then I will be spending a lot of time with that person, others less so. I dictate the pace at which the relationship will develop by such criteria that I understand people like you apply to relationships."

"What criteria are those?" asked Dr E.

"Instances such as familiarity with one another, whether there is a hand shake or a kiss on greeting, the name by which we call one another, whether they can be relied on to provide information, whether they will lend money, whether we go to certain places together and how often, whether we live together, all of these things are what you measure a relationship by."

"And do you regard those criteria as instances that ought to happen over a particular period of time?"

"No. They are all measurements by which I know people like you determine the nature of the relationship. I use them as markers by which the level of fuel can be influenced, accordingly, I will move them along at a pace which suits my demands for fuel."

"But not according to anyone else's input or say a generally accepted norm from society?"

"Well, the other person has to consent to the act, I mean; I haven't imprisoned anyone in my home. Yet." I smiled.

"But if they are to provide their consent surely that means the timescale is taken out of your hands?"

"Not at all. I just make them consent in accordance with my timescale," I said.

"By exerting the influences you have described to me previously?"

"Exactly."

Dr E remained silent as he continued to write.

"So you determine when the relationship begins and the pace at which it proceeds and this relationship never ends?"

"Yes."

"But some of the instances of your intimate relationships that you have described to me certainly fit with the concept that they have ended."

"Not at all. If I have cast someone to one side because, as they always do, they have let me down in some way, then I will not let them walk away. They might think they have been able to do this. Indeed, in certain instances I encourage that train of thought so that the person's defences remain down and thus they are susceptible to me resurrecting our interaction. Nobody leaves me and I do not leave anybody. They will always serve some kind of purpose, at some point and therefore there may be a pause in our interaction but there is never a cessation."

"What if the other person decides they no longer wish to interact with you?"

"Why on earth would they think that?" I asked puzzled.

"Well, your treatment of many of them was harsh and unpleasant."

"But no less than they deserved. People need to know their place and if they step outside of that they must be brought to heel."

"Why?" asked Dr E.

"Because I gave them everything and each time they repay me by letting me down. That is unfair. Each time I give them the world, I really do doctor and no matter how wonderful I am to them they do not do enough in return and they let their affection become dull or they fail to provide me with the adoration that I deserve. It is wrong and they must be made to see how wrong they are punished for their transgressions."

"So you maintain a relationship to punish the other person?"

"In part yes, but it is usually because they still prove of use to me and they have their debt to me to repay."

"I see," remarked Dr E and he continued with his writing.

"And when do they repay this debt?" he asked.

"That's the problem doctor," I said with a sigh," they never do. That is why I never let them go."

China Doll

I look on you as my China doll. Petite and unassuming yet containing such allure for me. Everything about you is prim and proper. From the always clean hair which is tied up in a bun to the never scuffed and always shining court shoes that you wear. Your blouses are pristine and that pencil skirt fits you so well. You ooze tidiness and efficiency. If you stand still you do appear to be made from porcelain. Your features are small and refined. Everything is where it should be. Nothing is creased, marked or stained. When you speak your tones are clipped and your diction precise. I watch you and wonder whether you iron the sheets on your bed after you have made love within it. I try and picture your home. Is it some high-rise residence, sleek with chrome and glass? Everything is in the correct place with lots of bare surfaces and minimalism the order of the day. Alternatively, do you seek your sanctuary in a countrified retreat where nothing is out of place? The rooms to that house or cottage may bear testament to the trophies you have collected but there is no display of clutter, dust is always eliminated and it really could be a show home. I enjoy seeing you move since there is a strange clockwork effect to your movements as you shift from one place to another. You do not hesitate or dally but rather you know where you need to be and where you will move to next.

I have peered into your office and it was no surprise to find that it was a temple to order. I was impressed. Your desk is a tribute to the concept of clear desk theory with one tray stacked neatly with incoming mail waiting to be dealt with. You do not have a desk tidy on display as you prefer to keep your pens et al in the top right hand draw. I know, without even looking, that the pens will all face the same way in the drawer. Your keyboard and monitor are just off to the right. I bet if I tipped your keyboard upside down no crumbs or hairs would fall from it. I can see you hoovering that keyboard with a mini device ensuring that it gleams like that open space of desktop. There are no pictures of family on that desk, no scattered files or week old coffee cups. When something lands on your desk it is either addressed immediately or put in an appropriate place to await attention. I daresay your e-mail inbox is the only one in the building that is empty and even your spam inbox will be perused daily and emptied of the bizarre. You never eat at your desk. I know because I have waited and seen you always eat with a friend, colleague or contact at the various cafes and restaurants in a small radius of the office block where you work. You never have anyone waiting for your arrival and you always depart so you return on time to the office. Punctuality runs through you.

Your existence is flawless and I find this so attractive. Everything about your life is pristine and someone so precise and exact both fascinates me and attracts my attention. It is clear that you exert total control over your life for if you were not to do so you would not be able to maintain this appearance. There are no loose ends with you, no straggly bits, and no bits around the edges. You are like a guillotine. Sharp and precise. This almost glacial front you show to the world intrigues me. Like a China door I should imagine that you are fragile and it would not take much to make you crack. One small fracture would no doubt lead to a gaping fissure and with that I savour the massive emotional reaction that you will pour forth as your world unravels. It is just a case of knowing where to place my chisel and bring the hammer down to strike that first blow. I can see it now. The edge of the chisel drives into you and from there the cracks spread, running away from the point of impact, a map of cracks and fractures, the shards splintering away from the blow. It would be like watching a windscreen crack before collapsing. Would you fight to retain control? Have you been tested before? Are you made from reinforced steel instead which has been painted over to give the impression of something more fragile? I must find out because the reward at cracking something so flawless and beautiful will be immense.

What You Swore Before

I have lost count of the times that I have been told "never again". I have heard it said by other people who have met my kind even more often. I am entirely relaxed when I hear this phrase because I know that although your intentions are to never go through that dance again with me or one of my kind, it will happen. We may be gone for some time but we will return and when we do we will resurrect all those wonderful memories as we seek to Hoover you back into our reality. The emotional attachment that we create is so great that even though you looked in the mirror every morning and mouthed "Never again" to yourself you will struggle to resist. You cannot help but wonder if this time it will be different. You do not want to say no for fear of someone else receiving our amazing and scintillating love. You want it. You learned the lessons and as the introspective empath that you are (as well as suitably conditioned by us) you will blame certain things on yourself. You will convince yourself, because you want to taste that mesmerising kiss once again, that we have changed and that this time it will be different. Why should someone else get to experience that wonderful love? That is not fair. You put up with the rough and the smooth. You have earned your stripes so it is only right that you get to have us again isn't it? That is what you want. When we first departed and you saw (for we wanted you to see) that we had found someone new it ripped you apart. Notwithstanding the full horror of your dance with us you hated the fact that someone else now basked in our glorious light. You wanted to warn them not because you cared about that person but because you wanted us back. You wanted us to yourselves. You felt a sense of unfairness that she was now with us. You would lie awake wondering if I was saying the same things to her as I had said to you. You wondered how she would respond to that blazing, heavenly love that you once relished. Would I be the same for her as I was to you? You kept telling yourself that it was only a matter of time before she befell the same fate that you endured, yet the postings and pictures told a different story. You began to worry. Had I changed? Had I become a better person after you? Was she somehow able to please me in a way that you could not? You had to know. You had sworn never again but now you wanted me back. You wanted her to go away and free me to be yours again so that you could apply your learned lessons and everything would be wonderful again. She did not deserve me did she? But you did. You made such sacrifices. You opened your heart to me despite the daggers I drove into it. You served your time and you are entitled to your reward. Not this Jane-come-lately. You want to give us that chance to prove we can do it. You want to show you brought benign influence to bear. You want to prove that the beast can be brought to heel in the most compassionate manner. You might say never again but you do not truly mean it. Not in your heart of hearts.

By contrast when we say "Never again" we most definitely mean it. Never again will your life be the same after meeting us. Never again will you feel able to trust anybody after being subjected to our acid reign. Never again will you be able to smell certain scents, hear certain songs and see certain places without breaking down in tears. Never again will you love someone in the way that you loved us. Never again will you want somebody as much and in such an intense way as you wanted us. Never again will you be able to feel calm and relaxed since for too long you have been subjected to a heightened state of anxiety. Never again will you experience that euphoria you once had with us. So when you declare never again it is never truly meant, but what you fail to realise is just how many things will never again be the same for you.

So Beautiful

You are so beautiful. Everything about you radiates beauty. From the moment I saw you I was transfixed. The way you moved about the room as if you were gliding from one place to the next. Your features almost glacial yet you gave out such warmth. Faces lit up on your approach as hands reached out to touch you. It was as if their troubles and fears would melt away once they placed a hand upon you. You were so serene. Your neck was a little longer than usual but I found that so compelling and my mind filled with images of me placing the most tender of kisses on that soft neck. I looked at your hands, the slender finders that moved across people's arms, giving a light yet reassuring touch. As I stood and observed you move about that room on that first viewing I was put in mind of Florence Nightingale and how she attended to the sick and wounded in the Crimean War. She brought reassurance and healing and you seemed to be doing so in the same way. People turned their eyes upwards to you, hope filling in them and then the smile, always that smile. A smile which told the recipient,

"You are special and always will be."

I could hear that laugh of yours. It was quite deep and incongruous with someone who appeared so delicate. I loved that laugh from the instant it drifted across the room and fell upon my ears. Your hair was tied up, bundled on top of your head and I remember how later I carefully slid the hair pins from within it letting your long tresses be shaken out as I stood mesmerised in front of you. Even after so many hours of attending that dinner, of working the room, of ensuring everybody had their moment with you, you showed no sign of fatigue. It was as if the delight and warmth you gave out made you stronger. You seemed refreshed by each nodded thanks and patting hand of gratitude.

Everything about you was beautiful that evening. From the expensive shoes that wrapped about your small feet to the diamonds you wore about your neck and dangling from those small elven ears. I was taken away from everything by how utterly and completely beautiful you looked.

Yes, you were a true beauty and it never left you. The way your eyes filled with tears so that the ocean blue seemed to shimmer was so inviting. The slow trickle of those tears across your rounded cheeks was alluring. The furrows in that usually smooth brown bore a defiant dignity which I found attractive. The way you flailed your arms in frustration like some manic windmill was inviting. Even when angered you moved with co-ordination and grace. You showed in every situation, no matter what was done to you, that you had been brought from the gods above, so beautiful and heavenly. The way you would curl up in a ball and gently rock was so beautiful. Your whispered pleas for it to stop sounded like a summer's breeze passing through the trees of nearby woodland. When others might sound discordant and harsh you only ever sounded wonderful. No matter what emotion was extracted from you, no matter by what means, your inner and outer beauty remained intact.

Best of all was how beautiful you looked when you screamed. That perfect mouth with the slightly fuller than necessary lips, rounded in a horrified 'O' as the cry of despair and terror rose from deep within you. This was no wail of the banshee but was like a siren's call, inviting and melodious as it rose and then fell. How I loved to hear that beautiful scream. How I longed to see your eyes fixed on me, those clear blue eyes, almond-shaped and sensational. The dejection and confusion rampant inside them but your beauty undiminished. You could not scowl. Your face did not twist in shock, anger or distaste. It was like looking upon an angel which was calling out from the heavens above. But best of all, I knew that the beauty you showed when you screamed was all for me. I always wanted to hear you screaming just for me.

A Statement of Intent

I should imagine that if you saw a picture of a person pushing a boulder up a hill you would think to yourselves,

"Oh yes, that is what life with a narcissist is like."

I know you do as I have had it said to me several times. I always reply,

"Achieving and maintaining brilliance is not meant to be easy. If it was, everyone would be doing it. You have to work hard to keep up with me."

You see there are certain types of empath who really do go above and beyond the call of duty. They may be of a co-dependent nature but it is not necessarily the case. It is more the fact that his person, a super empath, has a near unquenchable desire to do good, to heal, to fix and make things right. They regard anything and everything as a challenge but that no challenge is insurmountable. Their level of optimism is quite frankly baffling but I am not going to complain as I harness it to my advantage. The super empath believes there is good in everyone; it is just a case of finding it. This person believes that good will always triumph, that love will conquer all and no person is a lost cause. Sometimes it is fairly easy to identify these people as they do tend to congregate in the caring professions or if they do not, one can tell that they are a super empath by the way they undertake charity work, care for animals or overly romanticise everything. I have written before about how in the very early stage of our interaction I engage in a systematic and deliberate methodology of ensuring that you are going to supply with me fuel and that you will be drawn into my sphere of influence. This methodology also enables me to spot the super empath. Once I have one on my radar there is an exciting surge of anticipatory power through me as I relish the fuel that will be soon flowing from this hitherto untapped reservoir. When I have a super empath in my sights then I know that this person will go the extra mile, they will put in the hard yards and aim for 110 %. Armed with this knowledge I will issue my statements of intent so they do indeed work hard and supply me with what is amazing fuel.

What do these statements of intent look like? They come in a variety of forms but some examples are as follows:-

"You know I will hurt you so you would be better off staying away from me."

"I don't know what it is but I am on the verge of frenzy and you will get caught up in so you need to steer clear."

"I am difficult to please; I think you should be aware of this."

"Nobody ever meets me expectations."

"I have always been let down in the past and I do not expect you to be any different, so if you want to go now, before it is too hard, then you can."

"I can promise you it will never be dull with me, but I do not know if you could handle it."

"The intensity of my love will be brutal and you will probably be broken by it. It takes a special kind of person to be with me."

"I am giving you the chance to walk away now before it becomes too much for you."

These comments and similar are all the oral equivalent of throwing down the gauntlet. I can say these things utterly safe in the knowledge that you will now walk away. It is against your nature to do so. You hear these words and as a super empath you see a challenge but something that is completely worthwhile. There is a lost soul to be shepherded, a desolate being to make good once more and a wayward person to steer towards the light. You want to rescue me from the dark side, pull me clear of the abyss and save me. No matter how hard I make it sound, how difficult and dangerous it is described I know you want it all the more because you want to prove you can do it. No matter how high the obstacles are raised and how awkward and demoralising the journey, as a super empath you will hang in there.

I do not make these statements of intent for your sake. I am not warning you off out of any sudden sense of guilt or concern. Not a chance. I am doing it to appeal to you all the more. I know it is like turning the after burners on and you will respond by giving you absolute all to try and please me, heal me and fix me.

You never succeed. All you do is give me the most wonderful fuel.

The boulder will roll back down the hill, no matter how far you have pushed it and you will be flattened by it. Every time.

Showing An Interest

In the beginning I exhibit such interest in you it borders on infatuation. I want to know everything about you. I have of course learned much about you already in order to make my move and begin my seduction of you, but that was only the beginning. I want to know and I need to know all the things that interest you. This is how much I desire you. I want to understand all of the things which you love so that I can be a part of that too. How many times have you in the past bemoaned the fact that your partner has never taken an interest in your hobbies and pass times? They were generally dismissive about it preferring to let you get on with it as they went about their own thing. They did not do this to be nasty but rather they just were not interested. You wished they had shown some interest as you wanted to share this hobby with them but they would wave good bye and remain glued to the television.

Now I have come along and I want to learn about your love of scuba diving too. I want to join in and purchase the equipment so we can do it together. Yes I used to play dungeons and dragons when I was younger and I read the Dragonlance books. I may not have played that role-playing game for some time but it has not dulled my enthusiasm for the fantasy genre so let's indulge it and have a day of watching fantasy blue-rays. Who would have thought that you would find someone else who was into soap carving? You always got laughed at before when you admitted to doing that. Not anymore. Yes I have the specialist tools as well and practised first on fruit before I moved onto soap. Even if there is a craft or hobby which I have not done before I exhibit a huge willingness to learn so we can do it together. I am patient and keen. I offer no complaint when the study is turned into a workshop. I do not moan about having to travel several hours to attend some competition in the middle of nowhere. You are so grateful to find someone so supportive of your pursuits, such a contrast with those who have gone before.

It is amazing how the fuel you give me enables me to take such an interest in the things you like to do and experience. In most cases I will not have engaged in these things before meeting you and may not even have heard of some of them, but that does not matter. I am enthusiastic, keen and interested and you love me for it. The fuel you pour towards me maintains my interest and my enthusiasm seems so genuine that you rarely realise that it is manufactured. I participate in all these interests with a smile, asking questions and listening attentively as you talk in great detail about the particular nuances of the works of Chaucer. It is as if you have pressed a switch. You give me fuel and I will maintain an interest in anything and everything you like, so you give me more fuel. This will continue for some time until I lose interest. Inevitably this is down to you. You fail to remain as impressed as before at my interest in your interests. You do not remark as often about how marvellous it is to have someone to share your rock climbing hobby with. You have stopped praising me for helping you prepare for your amateur dramatics performances. All of a sudden the allure that your interests once held for me evaporates.

The reality is I cannot stand those damn hobbits and if see another dragon I think I will die. Soap carving? What a ridiculous thing to do. Who uses soap anyway, save prisoners in the showers? Surely everyone uses shower gel these days? If I have to listen to one of your poetry recitals again my ears are bound to bleed. Your incessant monologues about how snowboarding is better than ski-ing bore me. I mean they absolutely bore me. In fact if I were to be truthful, you bore me. You are so self-centred. You never thought to ask what I would like to do; you just assumed that I was happy to partner you in your ballroom dancing. You just took for granted that I wanted to go around modern art galleries with you. Why did you not ask what I wanted to do? I will tell you why not because you have to make it all about you. You always do. You have to spoil it don't you? Everything has to revolve around you. Well we will see how you react when I set fire to your collection of stuffed toys won't we? Let's see how interested you are in them when they are laid out in the back garden and ignited. Why on earth is a grown woman obsessed with all those Hello Kitty creations? There is something wrong with you. You make me sick.

Always On Your Mind

"He is always in my mind."

"Try as I might I just cannot get him out of my head."

"I can't stop thinking about him."

I am sure such comments or similar have been made by you at some point about the narcissist in your life. We have this formidable capability to get into your head and remain there for a long time which evokes bittersweet reactions from you at best and utter miserable frustration at worst. I have written about ever presence previously, namely that ability we have to ensure that you keep thinking about us, even when you have been pushed to one side or if you have sought to go no contact. This insidious form of manipulation is pervasive and very difficult to deal with, but how is it so effective?

Like much of our effectiveness it actually comes down to you. As an empathic individual you are much more susceptible to our method of remaining in your mind which is achieved by encoding. Since you care about others and take an interest in the thoughts, actions and well-being of other people, you have been wired to take on board stimuli from other people in a far more effective manner than others. Take my kind for example. We are so focussed on ourselves and what we need that we are not wired to be especially encoded by what others do. Our minds are nearly impervious to the actions of others. It is as if they are so full of what we do and what we want that there is no room for anything or anyone else. You on the other hand are like a sponge and you soak up the words and actions of others. Combine your susceptibility with our determined application of suggestion through what we say to you and what we do for you then the outcome is a devastating form of encoding which creates powerful and near indelible memories in your mind.

Through our visual encoding of your mind, you create a vivid mental picture and this will be recalled in pin-sharp crikey vision time after time. Every detail of a particular scene will be recalled by you and it is ingrained in your mind deeply through this encoding. The more you recall it, the more it becomes ingrained as if you are wearing a groove in a piece of wood. We make particular use of music (think how often your narcissist used certain tunes to woo you and/or create special moment) to achieve acoustic encoding. Our voice is used in this way as well by the careful selection of key phrases which will resonate with you. You always remember the things that we say because we have encoded them into your mind. Similar encoding occurs in respect of taste and scents as well as tactile encoding. Accordingly this quintet of senses is assailed by all the things that we say and do in order to achieve this encoding. We create powerful memories so that you have no option other than to recall them and with that comes the emotional attachment. You will remember so much of what you have done with us compared to say what you have done with family, friends and colleagues. You will recall more memories, in greater detail and more often when they involved us because of this deliberate encoding.

You might think this was enough in terms of the efficacy of this method of affecting you, but it does not end there. Most narcissists are male and thus it follows that the majority of victims are female. In general terms, women remember events better than men (men have better spatial memories) and therefore you are genetically pre-disposed to remember all those occasions and dates you spent with us in such detail. Females remember pleasant memories in better detail than men, thus this is a further reinforcement of why you can summon up such powerful memories of the golden period and why it hurts you so much. Conversely, in general terms, men remember unpleasant events better than women who tend to recall them in a 'blurred' manner. This is why despite the abuse you have suffered the golden period memories tend to triumph. It is not the case with everyone, admittedly, but generally this holds good. Add to this the fact that women's memories retain more of their potency through the advancement of age than men and you will see why your memories of us are so difficult to shake. Not only do we specifically encode your minds, which are primed to accept this more than other people, your gender also makes you more susceptible to retaining these detailed and vivid memories of the when everything felt wonderful.

These memories are deeply ingrained and very hard to dismiss and remove, even with professional help. Combine this efficacy with the fact we leave you exhausted and broken, it is little wonder you cannot shift us from your minds. Everyone knows how difficult it is to think straight when you are tired. Little wonder then that we always loom large in your mind when you have been exhausted and shattered by our behaviour.

These memories of the golden period are massively powerful and all of the above means that for someone like you, you will often think of them and suffer the emotion that is linked to them .It is a devastating weapon in our armour. Pretty memorable eh?

Staring at the Sun

I could sit with you for hours on end and just stare at you. Nobody has had that effect on me before. I know it might seem a little strange but I used to sit and look at you when you studied in the library. There is just something about you that really appeals to me. You must have heard that before I suppose, looking as beautiful as you do. What's that? Nobody has said that to you? Come on, I don't believe that for a moment. You are simply stunning, ethereal even. Don't look like that, it is true. I have never witnessed someone as devastatingly beautiful as you. It is not just the way you look, it is the way you hold yourself, so composed, so regal, so elegant. That handsome brow and the way that your hair falls. It seems so natural yet I know you must really brush it for hours to have it trained like that. You should not be coy about how mesmerising you look. No, I won't shut up. I am a firm believer in paying compliments and you should accept them. I know you are the modest type, I can see that, but you could be forgiven for being conceited and vain. Most ordinary people would if they looked like you. I bet it is a burden at times isn't it? People probably want to have their picture taken with you and do you know what? I bet they mistake you for a film star. They do don't they? Come on, you should admit that, it is a good thing. It can be hard being the centre of attention but that is just the way it is. Not everyone is fortunate enough to look so wonderful like you do. Mind you, I know it stems as well from your fabulous fashion sense. Oh yes. You always appear immaculate. No matter what the occasion it is, from formal dinner party through to drinks with your friends you always looks smart and well turned out. I am impressed. I really am. People could learn a lot from you.

It is not just the way you look through is it? I can see in those eyes a whole range of attractive qualities. Determination, intelligence, humour and I might add there is a dash of mischief in there as well. Yes I can see from that coy smile I am right. I usually am. I can spot someone like you a mile off. It is the intelligence that shines through in the way you look. It is most compelling. You see some stupid people and they have that dormant expression, their eyes glazed over. It gives the game away immediately and is so unattractive. Not like you though, you shine and dazzle with your brightness, it is just like staring at the sun. I must admit I cannot break my gaze away most of the time and sometimes I wonder whether I will be blinded by how magnificently you shine. I should wear sunglasses really when I look at you, but then I would not really want to obscure the brilliant effect that you have.

I know I am not letting you say much but sometimes you do need to listen to me, after all it is all good isn't it? It is all complimentary and you should be aware of how magnificent you are. You truly are. You brighten up the lives of everyone you meet. I can see it in their faces. You make them feel better about themselves. You lift them out of the daily drudgery that they have to wade through. They have dull and meaningless lives for the most part but you make them forget all about that just by gracing them with your presence, even if just for a short while. You lift up everyone who comes into contact with you. You have a real gift for making people feel special. It is a rare thing and marks you out as truly great. You should embrace this ability you have. Yes I know you realise that you have it and you should wield it more often. Everyone around you benefits when you enter the room and there are few who can do that. You have been set on this earth to entertain, inspire and uplift. You really are an angel, a beautiful angel that shines with the brightest and purest golden light. Never let that light dim or go out for the world will be a darker place without you.

Now I really must polish this mirror, I am struggling to see myself in it.

Putting a Sex on You

I was in session with Dr E.

"So," I asked, "what is today's topic for discussion?"

"Sex," he replied.

"Do I have to talk about this with you?"

He pushed his spectacles back.

"You do not have to talk about anything, but I would hope you would discuss this with me."

"Can't I talk to Dr O about sex?"

"Why? Are you uncomfortable discussing sex with another man?" he asked. I could see he had his pen poised ready to make a note.

"Not at all. Sorry, doctor but there is no homophobia about me."

"What makes you say that?"

"Well you were about to suggest that my reluctance to discuss matters of sex with you denotes a homophobic trait on my part."

"Not at all, that would be prejudging you and an unsafe basis for analysis."

"I don't believe you," I replied.

"Why would you rather discuss sex with Dr O?" he asked. He showed no sign of irritation or disappointment at my preference.

"I would be interested to learn her views about sex. She is so pristine and clinical when I see her; I want to know what goes on under the bonnet."

"These sessions are about you not us," said Dr E.

"Don't worry Dr E I have no interest in whether you apply nettles to your scrotum or whatever it is you do to excite yourself."

"Is that something you have done?" he asked.

"No but I have used them on someone else."

"Male or female?"

"Female."

"Why?"

"The stinging sensation across the nipples or the inner thighs of course hurts but then that gives way to a delicious flood of pleasure when combined with the application of my tongue."

Dr E was scribbling.

"I see, so you enjoy the fact it hurts the other person and then becomes pleasurable for her?"

"No."

"Please do expand."

"Will I get to talk about sex with Dr O?" I asked, shifting topic.

"On some aspects of sex, yes," replied Dr E. I smiled.

"Good. Very well since that is going to happen and I will hold you to that promise Dr E, I will expand on my point."

"I do it because the issue of that person's pain and then pleasure is entirely at my gift. I control it and that appeals to me considerably."

"So control in a sexual encounter is important to you?" asked Dr E.

"Control is the sexual encounter for me. I have little interest in my own sexual gratification, yes it feels pleasant when I orgasm but ultimately I can do that myself and invariably with more intense results. I have even less interest in the sexual gratification of another person. Denying them that sexual gratification? Now that is far more enjoyable than granting them their release. Sex is all about control. I am highly skilled in between the sheets."

"Is that your conclusion or of others?"

"Both. You see I know how people think, I know how they react and I have had many sexual encounters with many different people. There are vast numbers of different permutations when it comes to what satisfies a person and no two people are the same. I am like a super computer. I can rattle through the various combinations until I hit the right approach which will send my bedroom companion into orbit. I am willing to apply every part of my body, every facet of my sexual knowledge in order to make that person feel utterly orgasmic. That gives me huge control over them and makes me very powerful. I know what turns them on, what makes them moan and scream and shudder in orgasmic bliss. I use this massively powerful ability of mine to bring them under my spell. Once that is done I will grant it and deny it as and when I see fit. I will purposefully do the things that do not arouse them in order to make them react. I will caress a partner in a public place and whisper in their ear that if they show any kind of reaction to what I am doing I will stop and deny them any sexual congress for an indefinite period. This gives them an earth shattering orgasm and underlines my control over them. I will interrupt a row with a girlfriend by taking her against the kitchen workbench. She soon forgets what the argument was about as I have her moaning in delight before I just walk off before she climaxes. Imagine how she follows me about the house begging for me to "finish her off"? Think of the promises she makes just to feel me inside her again? That is control. That is power. I work out a person's sexual key code and deliver heaven. They find that addictive and want it so much. I find the power attached to this ability addictive. When you go to bed with me you are getting the best. Nobody afterwards will come close to what I give you."

There was a long pause as Dr E jotted down my words. He looked a little flustered to me. I wished it was Dr O sat there instead.

"Do you think a sexual encounter should be about something other than control?"

I laughed at this comment,

"Heavens no, that is its only function. It is an instrument, like so many other things, to bring you under my spell, but I must admit, it is probably one of the most potent and effective instruments. Sex is actually rather boring but controlling the reaction and emotions of another person, well, now that is far more interesting."

"Have you ever wondered what it would be like to give up that control and allow yourself to be enveloped in the 'moment' with the other person?" asked Dr E.

"No I cannot give up control. You see, I know there are those that engage in being tied up and punished, you know smacked with an open hand or a cane. They may get a sexual reaction from being treated like this but the real reason they do it is that they are giving up control. I had a girlfriend who was very submissive and allowed me to do...well I will let you use your imagination there doctor, but she wanted zero control. She was high up in a bank and responsible for millions of pounds and hundreds of employees and she wanted to be divested of that responsibility and give up her control if only for an hour or two. I found her explanation interesting but I could not understand it. Why give up control? Why surrender something you have worked hard to achieve? Control is the ultimate aim of taking someone to bed. I control them in that bed and the spell I put on them means that control extends far beyond the bedroom, such is its power."

Dr E nodded and continued writing.

"What if you lost your sexual potency? What if you became impotent?" he asked.

"Why would that happen?"

"Plenty of reasons. Alcohol abuse, substance abuse, diabetes, age, anxiety. There are many reasons why this could happen."

I shook my head.

"People like me don't suffer that. God gave me the gift of sexual brilliance to further my purposes; He would not take it away from me."

"But if it did happen, what would you do? How would you manage with such a loss of this marvellous instrument of control?"

"Are you taking the piss now doctor?" I snapped.

"Not at all. Just posing a relevant question aligned to your desire for control."

"Listen doctor; don't project your problems in that department onto me, okay?"

Dr E remained silent. I copied him and just sat in silence glaring at him. How dare he suggest I would lose my potency? What an idiot. He ought to know better than that by now. I kept staring at him waiting for his next clever remark but he just stared back. This stand-off went on for a few minutes but I knew he would look away first. I maintained my baleful gaze as the fury at his impertinence coursed through me and then he lowered his eyes to his black and red notepad and made some more notes. I had won.

"Not so cocky now are we doctor?" I muttered under my breath.

A Different Glass

I once was involved with a lady who ran her own business creating ceramics and glassworks. She was truly talented and was able to make the most beautiful pieces. The way she crafted the glass interested me the most. I would sit in her workshop and watch her as she exercised her skill. She lived just on the cusp of the countryside and had a lovely house. Just across the courtyard was her workshop and I remember the numerous times we would walk across the frosted courtyard and enter the workshop. With the furnace brought to life and a mug of hot tea nestling in my hands I would watch transfixed as she began the process of glass blowing.

The molten glass would be waiting in the furnace as she pre-heated the tip of her blow pipe. Once that was done she would dip it into the molten glass and begin to gather the glass on to the blowpipe. I marvelled at how skilled she was at doing this as I would fear the glass would just slide back into the morass in the furnace but she would bob and dip the tip as the glass coalesced onto the blowpipe. Once that has been gathered she would turn and begin the process of rolling the glass on the marver, which is a flat piece of steel. She would blow into the pipe, roll the glass, repeat and work the glass in this manner until she was satisfied. She would then move across to her workbench and then using her jacks, paddles and shears she would begin the real magic. She would cut the glass, pat it and pull it as she coaxed the glass into the relevant shapes that she required. She would move the piece onto a rod to add a coloured section or roll it over coloured powder. She was graceful in her movements, each touch deft and delicate. From out of this bubbling mass of molten glass a thing of beauty would be created. I loved to watch her work, seeing those slender hands which had earlier been caressing my body, twist the blowpipe. Her full lips embraced the pipe rather than me and I saw the skills she exhibited in her work were also applied to other areas of her life. I knew she got real pleasure out of performing in this way for me and was always effusive in her thanks. I watched as she created bottles, vases, murals and more all from glass.

Her works were popular and the shop she ran attached to the workshop had a steady stream of visitors. Her crowning glory was a huge edifice in the field next to her house. This was a massive glass torch with twisting red, orange and yellow flames that poured from it. The way it caught the sunlight really made it seem as if it was on fire and it was a beacon of light that drew passers-by to the glass workshop. I arrived on the scene when she was three-quarters through the construction of this marvellous torch and each week she would add to it until it stood some twenty feet in height, secured with guy ropes, a testament to her ability, application and tenacity. People came to take pictures and then buy something from her workshop and it truly was a worthwhile investment of her time and energy. The glass shone and sparkled and it never ceased to impress me how she had envisaged this construction and then been able to create and piece it together. I would regard it often as a symbol of our coupling, a brilliant, magnificent creation which drew the admiration of many. Tall and imposing, shining and attractive, it became the very thing that we were and I often told her about this. She would smile and nod in agreement before resting her head on my shoulder as we stood looking at it. It had a hypnotic quality, just like us. Not only was it just so impressive and beautiful but the fact that this structure was made of glass added to the effect. How was it that something so stunning could stand and weather the rain and wind and be unmoved? How was it that something that was made from the most brittle of materials could demonstrate such strength? You could see that when people came to see it they looked at with the same degree of awe as they did when they met us as a couple.

The torch construction was certainly a fixation for her. I would often find she had disappeared only to then discover her stood outside just staring at her creation. Whereas once we looked on it together, now she would steal out as dawn rose and watch hypnotised by the growing light as it first struck the top of the flames. She became obsessed at seeing how it looked at night with lights played on it, slowly twisting and revolving to bring life to the flames. She would stand in the field, hand clamped across her brow as she stared at it in the glare of the midday sun, talking to herself about how it looked. I would try and call her away from it but everything now seemed to centre on this creation. Whereas once she worshipped me she now placed herself at the altar of her construction and gave thanks there instead. I warned her about her behaviour. I told her she was gifted and talented but that she was spending too much time staring at this construction, magnificent as it was and as a consequence she was neglecting other things. Notably me. She did not seem to hear what I was saying or if she did she gave no signal to me of comprehension.

One November morning I was woken by a scream. I leapt from the bed as it came again and again. Half-naked I dashed outside trying to locate its source. The noise came several times more, strangled and harsh, drifting across the cold autumnal air. I rounded the house and vaulted the gate, my boots striking the frosted and hard ground on the other side to find her on her knees in the field. In front of her, glinting in the pale sunshine was the remains of her torch. Somehow, in the darkness of the night, this edifice had been laid low, smashed and shattered; the many hours of concerted application had been destroyed with the frenzied introduction of blunt hammer heads. That which had weathered howling wind and driving rain now lay amidst the white grass, a carpet of glittering fragments. All the glass was there but now it resembled nothing like the thing it once had. It was a different glass altogether.

You don't worship false idols when I am with you.

The Futility of Your Feeling

Feelings are an unnecessary burden and thankfully I have been relieved of many of them, being left only with those which are deemed necessary to enable me to pursue the harvesting of fuel. Feelings blur and weaken. How many times have you heard your alarm go off in the morning and you have rolled over feeling like you do not want to get up? Many times I should imagine. That feeling of apprehension about what the day holds for you, despondency at what has happened to you and dread about what you have to do weakens you and holds you back. You spend much of your life in the pursuit of this notion of happiness but are you ever truly happy? Do you look at what you have and wish you had more? Do you look at other people around you and imagine how happy they must be and you wish that you were more like them? All you achieve is bitterness. Perhaps you do feel happy but as the empath that you are you see those who you regard as less happy than you and you wish that they could be more like you. All you achieve is vanity. You spend so much of your time seeking to be happy and then you worry about whether it is fleeting in nature. You express concern that you just want to be happy and spend more and more time trying to achieve this state of nirvana. You suffer from feeling sadness which leads to paralysis and indecision. You feel frustrated which sucks up your energy and leaves you feeling spent. You take pride in your ability to feel and to be able to feel on behalf of others yet all you are doing is allowing yourself to be burdened. Why bother pursuing those feelings which are regarded as positive, such as joy, happiness and elation? Is the effort truly worth it when you get there only for it to be a fleeting moment which then casts you into despondency? What was the point of that? Why allow yourself to be mired in upset, misery and dejection? You achieve nothing as you slowly sink into a quagmire of such negativity. Your feelings deceive you, press down on you and above all else allow us to manipulate you. It is because you feel this array of emotions that you provide us with emotional reactions. Of course you know that these emotional reactions create my fuel. Your feelings are to blame.

I never acquired these feelings. This is because the pursuit of fuel cannot be distracted by these cumbersome emotions. They serve no purpose and thus were never developed. I am built for the acquisition of fuel and nothing else. I am an efficient design, single-minded and driven. All excess baggage was not jettisoned it was never stowed on board to begin with. I am not wholly without feelings. I have been developed in a way to allow certain feelings, those that aid my purpose, to come to the fore. I feel fury which ensures that I can exert control over other people and thus extract fuel from them. I feel envy which drives me on to strip away those traits from other people which I need to create my construct. If I felt no envy, I would not want these characteristics - thus this feeling serves a purpose. There is no superfluous feeling connected with me. I feel jealousy which again causes me to strive to better that person by lauding my own achievements and prompting a reaction which garners positive fuel or by berating the person of whom I am jealous and thus I harvest negative fuel. I feel hatred. This allows me to see everything as it truly is. Hatred hones and brings into sharp focus the reality of this cruel world and thus I am better able to navigate my way through it. Hatred is visceral; it is not fluffy or amorphous. It does not cloud or blur. It is direct, straight to the point and electrifying in its capacity to allow me to always go forward. All of these feelings and ones of a similar nature have been fashioned around me to assist me in my quest for fuel. Each one discharges a method of enabling me to gather fuel so that I can feel the ultimate emotion. My pursuit of fuel is predicated on the use of these various emotions with the sole purpose of allowing me to feel that emotion which I prize above all others.

I feel powerful.

I am powerful.

The Night Before Christmas

It was the night before Christmas,

And all through the house,

A narc started scheming

With a click of his mouse

The stockings all hung

With a hole in the heel

Emptied of presents

How low they would feel

The children were nestled

All safe in a bed

But it was not their happiness

That was in the narc's head

And mom sobbing quietly

As the narc sought his fuel

His words had been caustic

And his actions so cruel

When out on the net

The narc did surf wide

Seeking the playmates

To make him powerful inside

Away to the dating site

He flies in a flash

Creating false profiles

Using someone else's cash

The moon's light from the window

Did highlight his mask

As he lied and he boasted

Obsessed by his task

When what to his wandering eyes

Should suddenly appear

But a fresh victim

Who was deliciously near

With a click of the mouse

And the charm running high

He opened his trap

And sent lie after lie

More rapid than eagles

Did his tendrils uncoil

Snaking about her

Dripping with oil

So dashing

And charming

So swift

Began the dance

She was dazzled

Beholden

Enchanted

She stood not a chance

A red flag was flying

From a flagpole tall

Yet she was mesmerised

Taken in by it all

Yes it was late

But how about a beer

He would love to meet her

He knew she was near

So off to the bar

His victim did go

Intrigued and excited

As she strode through the snow

And then in a twinkling

She had a mistletoe kiss

What a marvellous present

It was too good to miss

And there in her head

Which was spinning around

She ignored the alarm bells

Which were beginning to sound

He gave her his fur

As he walked her back home

And there on the porch

His hands did they roam

I know it seems sudden

And I know it is late

But I have to tell you

That you're my soulmate

She smiled and she gasped

Her heart all alight

As the harpoon hit its target

And her chest did feel tight

She took him inside

And he took her all night

A perfect coupling

It all felt so right

You are amazing

It barely seems true

But I think that I

Have fallen for you

She gazed in his eyes

For he was perfect

And basked in the love

That he did reflect

I will always protect you

He said as she dozed

Her mouth started smiling

As her eyes remained closed

Hours later she woke

The room bore a chill

The window flung open

Boot marks on the cill

She stood at the window

Her mouth open wide

As she recalled with a thrill

And such excitement inside

The mysterious stranger

Who came from nowhere

Who embraced her neck

And showed her such care

Her heart it beat faster

She wanted him so

She would soon see him

Of that she did know

With heart now on fire

And the hooks sunk in deep

She retired still smiling

To catch up on her sleep

Across town the narc was rising

His seeds had been sown

And the day's first message

Arrived on his phone

He heard the first cries

From down below stair

About vanished presents

Such howls of despair

The narc walked to the mirror

And gave it a grin

For his schemes were now working

He was reeling them in

Already the day

Had started so well

And the ruined Christmas fayre

Would continue the hell

No laughter, no smiles

No pleasure or joy,

He smirked at the thought

Of the next broken toy

His planning bore fruit

The new prey now secure

The hopes of his family

Would soon hit the floor

A day of turmoil

Of drama and regret

With a fresh willing victim

How good would it get?

He smiled at the mirror

And there stared the ghoul

But our narc cared not one iota

He was getting his fuel

So if your night before Christmas

Sounds similar to this tale

You know what to do

And you must not now fail

Gain knowledge, seize power

And become narc free

By reading everything you find

Written by HG

Street Angel – House Devil

I have been called these more than a few times and I won't shirk from the label with you good readers. Naturally, when the appliance I am draining levels such an accusation at me then I deflect, reflect and deny - how dare they challenge me and seek to label me to make up for their own shortcomings. Once I cross that threshold and face the world then those white, feathered wings sprout from my back, the halo shines and I move with grace and great intentions. To my neighbours I provide a cheery hello and enquire as to their health. I comment how the male neighbour is welcome to borrow a few of my Blu-ray boxsets as I espouse the excellence of a particular series. He nods his thanks and explains how he will call around that evening to borrow a set. I tell him we will have a drink too. He smiles and I can see how pleased he is to have such a pleasant and accommodating neighbour. Of course this is all designed to get him onside and a firm believer in what a good chap I am. I have been working carefully on his wife, Fiona and will update you on that in due course. When I seduce her, her eventual protestations to her husband will fall on deaf ears as he will be unable to accept that his neighbour would do such a thing as pursue and seduce his wife. He will recall all the good things that I have said and done and it will be her who will be cast as the unfaithful harpy. I am always planning ahead.

I greet the passing postman warmly and then call Kim's brother to exchange idle banter and invite him to play golf at the weekend. He has been angling to do this for some time now and he will regard this as admission to my inner circle. Let him think that as it is what I want. I know he regards me as a good egg and thus when the inevitable chaos and spite is unleashed on dear Kim he will at worst struggle to accept that I could treat her in this fashion. At best he will take my side and cut her adrift, tired of her slanderous accusations about someone he regards as a decent fellow and a good friend. All through my day I will portray the carefully honed image to colleagues (although not all - there are a couple who are currently viewing the devil as a consequence of their lack of loyalty to me), to service providers (the lady who serves in the coffee shop near work has told me how much she looks forward to our conversations). I walk amidst the horde, hurling my sparkling dust over them, causing them to smile and admire like children following a generous candy man.

I have walked this path on many occasions. Friend to many, benefactor to several and champion to others. A solid, dependable and brilliant man who takes an interest in everyone he speaks to. So many pedestals have been constructed as I go about my day. That friend is elevated to stand amidst all those in a similar position in my coterie as I smash down the pedestal of one particular so-called friend who has displeased me. They fall and as they do they reach out trying to grasp the hands of those in that coterie but they are all snatched away. Nobody is listening as you cast your stones at the devil that has flung you from your lofty position. All they see is the angelic smile and blazing eyes that make them feel good. I work my magic, bringing friend, neighbour, family member, stranger and acquaintance under my spell. Each of them bolsters my angelic appearance so that will be all that they see. The exiled individual will try to persuade them of the devil that has brought them low, but nobody is listening. Behind that closed door the real reign of the devil appears. It is there that I no longer need maintain the pretence and allow full vent to the venom that flows through me. You let me down and you must be punished. That is when you are trapped inside the house of Satan with all the pain and misery that encompasses. I know you will try to escape and tell them all of the torment you are subjected to in these four walls but nobody will accept your warped and malicious slanders. You speak of my barbed tongue, forked tail and sharp horns but as soon as I step outside they all melt away to be replaced by the sweetest perfection as my charmed pretence masks the devil inside. I walk the path of the angel on the street beyond my door. It is inside that I trap the real angels and feed on them.

To Weave a Web

I have made mention of how the advancements in technology have provided my kind and I with a smorgasbord of methods to carry out our works. From seduction to manipulation the freedom that comes with Wi-Fi and a functioning device provides is with a wealth of opportunity. My web can be spread wide over the....well the web. How apt it is that the pioneers of the internet decided on the appellation of World Wide Web. The electronic blanket which encapsulates this planet is indeed a web. A perilous place which readily ensnares the unwary. From chatrooms, to text messaging, through Facebook, Twitter, Instagram, e-mail and dating sites, the internet has proven to be bountiful in its riches for my kind. Of course, this vast array of different hunting grounds can only be of benefit to the seasoned hunter. You can fill a river with salmon but if you do not know how to fish then you will not catch anything. Of course, I know how to fish, to shoot, to spear and to hunt. My mastering of the tools of manipulation enables me to sniff out my prey in moments and like a lion tracking a bison, drag them to the ground and eat them from behind before they even realise what has happened to them. Have you ever seen the expression on a felled bison or buffalo as a predatory lion gorges on their flesh? It is not pain, it is not frustrated struggle but an almost blissful ignorance to what is actually happening. They seem unaware that they are being devoured. It is so similar for my victims. They smile and purr even as I am taking chunks from them because that is the high level of my skill.

Thus the internet has become my hunting ground and my various manipulative machinations are given a good run out amidst the waiting and willing victims. There is one thing however that always works in this electronic shop window and that is the art of conversation.

My early forays in chatrooms bore fruit so incredibly quickly. Even I was taken aback at how easy it was. So many times I read comments such as

"It is such a lovely change to meet someone who can hold a conversation."

"You are so charming and interesting, you actually hold a conversation than saying hi babe wanna shag?"

"You are clearly intelligent and interested in me. I am not used to that. So many of the men on here just want a picture of my boobs or want to send me a dick pic, you are not like that."

Naturally, I was not engaged in conversations with men so I do not know if there is a boorish equivalent amongst the female ranks. Certainly in all my conversations I never came across any lady whose opening gambit was to offer a picture of her genitals. I take the view therefore that it is the male of the species that is letting you down. They are certainly not letting me down. By populating chat rooms and dating sites and trotting out such Neanderthal lines these men are increasing my currency. The fact I can talk about a variety of subjects, ask pertinent and engaging questions and avoid suggesting a bunk up in the first ten minutes meant that I really was the desired exception. The idiots, the perverts and the inarticulate all made me look even better than I already did (yes I know that may be hard to believe!) and thus when I came sashaying into view I was greeted with utter delight by those I interacted with. Even if I had no interest in someone, I was hard pressed not to attract them, by virtue of being able to string sentences together and not engage in demands for instant sexual congress (of course that would come later when I was always pushing on an open door).

Time and time again I heard reports of the pathetic and ill-mannered behaviour of men in these arenas. I expressed dismay and castigated them for it but all the while I celebrated for so long as they continued in this vein it meant all the more eager and willing victims for me. Those weak and pathetic spiders would soon curl up and dye for there was only one giant walking through the net. Along came a spider but this one could hold a conversation.

New Year, New Prey

As you read this you may be holding your head in your hands. Some of you may just be nursing a hangover although others of you will be holding your heads out of despair at another bout of maladjusted behaviour that you have been subjected to from our kind. It is a New Year and with that I should imagine that you are making your resolutions and vowing that this time things will change. Whereas other sites may be espousing the virtues of a revolutionary diet or unique exercise regime, the benefits of a January which is alcohol free or yes this year you will learn to speak Spanish, those matters need not concern us. Perhaps you will be resolving to put in place some of the knowledge that you have learned from my writing here and in my books. If so, you are sailing towards exciting horizons. Others of you may be swearing that enough is enough and you are going to leave and this time you will not go back. Go on; make that vow to yourself and see if it lasts any longer than your dedication to the treadmill.

My many years of practising my dark art have made me most familiar with the injection of resolve that comes with the first of January. You have dusted away the embers of the dying year and have sought to erase the pain and humiliation that marred much of the passing year of your life. The abuse, the denigration and the savage treatment you have been the victim of will loom large in the mind but you have found a spark of strength from somewhere, there is the flickering flame of optimism that has begun to burn inside of you. You declare that you will not allow our toxic breath to blow this flame out. We will not extinguish it with a smothering boot or the application of freezing cold water to your plans. This time it will be different. All this hope. All this optimism. I can almost taste it.

As one can detect a change in the air with the change of seasons so it is the same with the arrival of a New Year. The empath emerges from his or her slumber and stretches, keen to really shine in the year ahead and to find their self once more.

They are keen to cast aside the poisonous cloak that was draped around them, lift the crown of thorns and strip away the clinging tendrils. Such enthusiasm is most laudable. Guess what? You are not the only ones. This year my reach shall be extended and my charm magnified. My sweet, sweet words of seduction shall fall with practised ease upon the willing ears of the supplicants that I have selected. My dark eyes will fix on the appliances that line-up, brimming with that potent fuel. So many appliances to connect to, so much fuel that must be harvested. I will ensure that this year my fuel will be the best I have ever known, I shall soar to new achievements and have eyes shining with admiration everywhere I go. My foes will lie crushed beneath my booted feet, the cloven hooves concealed from their broken gaze as I breach new boundaries, violate new pastures and conquer fresh virgin territory. Your hope and dedication only serves to spur me on to achieve even greater things in this year ahead.

For every promise of progress that you all make rest assured that I am doubling up on my manipulative strength. When you swear you will break free, I pledge that I will imprison. Every time you assert your desire to escape from my grip, I will tighten it further. You seek to shine a light in your attempt to be a beacon of hope. I will appear and snuff out those beams of light with the malice that surrounds me.

You can exist without having to place your arms around the world. I cannot exist without my fuel. You have a choice. I have none. I am destined to walk this earth forever in my unceasing quest for fuel. Whilst you take delight and solace in so many things, I am beholden to my task of securing fuel from so many that I encounter. They say that after toil comes rest; not for me and my kind.

So, make those resolutions, dust off your pledges and polish up your good intentions. It is a New Year and the battle for new prey has just been joined.

Shoot You Down, Bang Bang

A plaintive wail which I often hear is along the lines of,

"Why do you always have to shoot me down? I give you everything you could ever want. Why can't you just be happy with that?"

As usual you delude yourself with such a statement. You do not give me everything I could ever want. You think that you do, but that is the self-centredness that you often exhibit creeping in once again. You certainly care, I will grant you that, but you make the mistake of assuming what you do is what we want. What we want is fuel. I know what comes next.

"I always told you how much I loved you; I admired and complimented you often and frequently. How much more could I make you feel good about yourself?"

Therein lies the problem. No matter how good your intentions and how frequent your worship of me, my kind and me will always grow tired of it. We have heard your kind words and seen your appreciative gestures too many times and it, well, it just does not do it for us anymore. I am sure that you emotionally in touch people would be the first to complain if a long established partner engages in the same routine in the bedroom. It does not hit the spot anymore does it? Well, it is just the same for us. You may ultimately accept that things cool somewhat in the bedroom and I know from what I have seen and heard that you trade this passion off (although not always, there are some sexual thrill seekers amongst your kind) for other qualities that you find attractive - humour, companionship, security, warmth, good parental skills, intelligence and such like. There is no hope for any such trade with us. We only want one thing from our relationship. Fuel. We do not care (ultimately) how good-looking you are, how much of a whore you are between the sheets, how wonderful a mother you may be what a raconteur you are or how much you earn. We will never accept those things or anything else as a substitute for fuel. True enough, the more aged of our kind sometimes accept these things when their need for fuel diminishes but that need never goes away. They may decide to accept these attributes alongside largely positive fuel, but they will still need to stir things up from time to time.

That is not going to happen with me. I am at the peak of my powers and therefore my need for fuel remains substantial. There can be no substitute for it at all and nor can there be any co-existence between the provision of fuel and other attributes. It is fuel or nothing. In order to achieve this I have to shoot you down because once that is done you start to flow with the potent negative fuel and my cravings start to be addressed. You can beg and plead with me, you can point out how you will always only ever have eyes for me, you can express your love, desire, adoration and admiration on an hourly basis but there comes a point when it just does not have that sweetness anymore. It is then that I pull the handgun from my jacket, attach the silencer and fire several vitriolic bullets into you. Your pain from these wounding bullets gives me the fuel that I need and therefore your shooting is necessary. Moreover, it is your punishment for letting me down. You really ought to be capable of pleasing me the whole time but so far; all that I have chosen have failed. That is why I now expect you to fail and have that gun to hand at all times.

When I shoot you down, I become more powerful as the fuel flows from you. Moreover, it is easy to get someone to admire and adore. Those reactions come naturally to your kind. It is far harder to extract tears, anger, frustration and regret from the empath. Managing to do so imbues your emotional reaction with greater potency, your fuel becomes supercharged and this is what we want. We cannot shoot you down from the beginning, we need you stood on a pedestal first, after all, you present as such an inviting target then and your toppling as the bullets slam into you becomes all the more satisfying.

I sense your dismay as you read this. You had hoped that by keeping me sweet and onside through a dazzling and tireless display of love, affection and admiration you had hoped to avoid such an attack. Your concerns should not be absolute. There is an upside you know. Firstly, when we find someone else after we have shot you down, keep in mind they will eventually be riddled with bullet holes no matter how happy we both appear at first. It is coming to them as it came to you. I am sure that makes you feel a little better doesn't it? Secondly, there is a huge saving grace.

We never shoot you dead.

We need you alive so we can raise you up again as we re-load.

The Battle of Going Out

We do not like you to socialise without us. Why would you want to be anywhere other than by our side marvelling at how brilliant we are? Why on earth would you want to spend time with someone who is clearly inferior to us? What are you up to by going out with someone else? You are clearly being disloyal and that does not please us. Moreover, you are not providing us with any fuel by asserting some form of independence and that is a terrible and selfish thing for you to do. We do not like you to spend time with other people since we fear that they exert some malign influence over you. We know they will be trying to undermine us in your eyes and turn you against us. We know it is because they are jealous of what we have together and rather than be pleased for you, they are smearing my good name. You want to listen to them as well, otherwise why would you be going? Our careful and structured control of you, our calculated isolation of you, all stand to be damaged by your socialising with those who we have not control over. We tried but for some reasons there are two or three of your friends who proved immune to our charm. I should feel sorry for them since they are selfish, bitter and twisted, but I don't feel sorry for them because I don't feel sorry do I, only for myself. I want you with me, where I can keep an eye on you and control you. I want you here where you are supplying me with fuel. This is your rightful place and by organising to go out for your meal with these friends you are telling me that I am not good enough to spend time with. You are criticising me and that wounds me. I have to stop you wounding me. I have to stop you going. I have to maintain the upper hand. Thus because of your selfish behaviour the Battle of Going Out is joined.

"You never said that you were going out," I begin as I see you getting ready in the bathroom. You halt applying your make-up and turn to me.

"Yes I did, I told you last week and again this morning."

"No you didn't."

"Yes I did, I remember."

"No you did not. I would have remembered if you had told me," I answer.

" I put it on the calendar." You walk to the kitchen and return holding a calendar with the words 'Girls meal out - Leonardo's'.

"See?" you ask and jab a finger at the words.

"That? I thought that was referring to your nieces, not you, you never said."

"Seriously? Come on, why would my nieces be going to Leonardo's on their own?" you ask.

"You've just written that in when you were fetching the calendar. Look, the ink is still dry."

You sigh in exasperation.

"I told you about it, it is in the calendar. I have not been out in weeks."

"Well neither have I," I comment.

"What? You were out last Friday," you answer voice rising.

"That was with work."

"It was still going out," you reply.

"That is not the same. You know I have to schmooze clients, it is hardly pleasure. I have to do that for business reasons so I think you are being unfair by saying that is a night out for me."

"Those clients you were out with are your friends; it was a right piss up."

"Oh sorry, I forgot, you were there weren't you, you know all about how I conduct my business don't you?" I declare.

"No I don't but they are your friends."

"So I am not allowed to have clients who are friends now am I? Jesus, why don't you just stop me from having any friends at all eh? Why not stop me going anywhere? You would like that wouldn't you? Just having me stuck in here all the time."

"What are you talking about; I let you do as you please."

"No you don't. You are determined to keep me on a leash. My friends take the piss out of me for how little time I get to spend with them."

You halt your application of the lipstick.

"Who has said that?"

"Several people. Jim, Richard and John. They say I am under the thumb."

"Huh, they have a cheek; Jim is completely under the thumb of Jessica."

"No he's not, but you just change the subject why don't you. You should be staying in with me you never want to do that anymore."

"Don't be silly, I am with you most of the time. Look it is just an informal meal with a few of my friends, it is no big deal."

"If it is not important then why do you have to go?"

"Because I want to," you answer.

"Where are you going?"

"You know that Leonardo's."

"Really? Who with?"

"Jane, Sarah, Mary and Stephanie, oh and Carrie."

"I don't believe you; you have just made that up."

"What? No I haven't."

"You are meeting a man aren't you? Come on who is it?"

"No you are being stupid."

"Don't call me stupid. I am not the one going out and leaving their other half on their own," I begin to shout and you jolt at the sudden change in volume.

"You are up to something; you have a different perfume on. Who is he?"

"Seriously, you are paranoid, I am meeting the girls."

"No I am not, who do you think you are saying that to me, you are messing around. I know you are. You have been acting strangely the last few weeks. I know you are. Admit it," I move towards you and stand over you barking into your face. You back away, eyes widening fearfully.

"I haven't, honestly, I haven't."

"I should let you go anyway you whore, I don't know I bother with you. I was planning a pleasant evening in for us. I was going to cook you your favourite and I have a delicious bottle of Chablis chilling but as usual you are being selfish."

"Please don't shout at me, I am just going out with my friends, I am allowed to have some friends aren't I?"

"Not those harpies, they have it in for me, I hate them. I hate you."

"Oh please don't be like that, look I will be back by ten at the latest so we can still have some time together," you suggest.

"Is that supposed to make me feel pleased? Why would I want to spend time with you, you slut. I see, you want to have your way with him and then rub it in my face. You are such a bitch."

You have backed away from my tirade, wincing with each bellowed sentence. This allows me to snatch up your clutch bag.

"You can't go out with no keys and no money," I say holding the bag aloft.

"Please I only want to see my friends, I rarely see them as it is; please give me my bag back, why are you being so horrible?"

"Because you are cheating on me. I am not having you spend our money on some other man."

"There is no other man, how many times do I have to tell you? Please let me go."

"No. You are not going. You are staying here with me."

"I can't cancel, not this late," you say in dejection.

"Of course you can. He does not matter."

"There is no he. It is the girls."

"So you say. You are not going. If you do that is me and you finished."

"What, just because I want to see my friends?" You slump on to the bed, shoulders hunched and your head in your hands.

"You don't need them, you have got me."

"Why does it always have to be like this, every time I try and do something you do this," you protest and your voice breaks with the first sob of frustration.

"No I don't stop trying to blame me when you are at fault," I growl.

"You always do this, make feel guilty or do something to stop me going out."

"Rubbish, you are making things up again. You are just trying to make me feel bad for you. It won't work you know that."

You begin crying as I stand power surging through me.

"Here," I order as I pull your phone from your bag and throw it down on the bed besides you," ring them and tell them you can't make it, say you don't feel well or something. I will pour the Chablis."

Still sobbing you fumble for the phone and pick it up before dialling the number. I stand triumphant drinking deep of the fuel you have given me during this exchange. I have won the battle once again and this time I did not even have to escalate it like I did last time. I suppose that was just as well really seeing as how you had only just replaced those mirrors I smashed.

That's No Moon!

Few people are unfamiliar with the Star Wars franchise. In the first film, A New Hope, Han Solo, Obi-Wan Kenobi, Luke Skywalker and Chewbacca have emerged from hyperspace in the millennium falcon only to find an imperial tie fighter and an absence of the planet that they had hope to reach. Instead as a perplexed Han Solo tries to figure out what is going on, the tie fighter is seen racing towards a small moon that Luke has identified. As the sphere comes into view, Obi-Wan states with a calm dread,

"That's no moon."

Indeed it is not. It is in fact a space station and specifically the machine of mass destruction that is the death star. Once recognition has dawned on the quartet along with the fearful consequence of being near to such a powerful weapon, they try to escape but it is too late. The millennium falcon has been caught in the death star's tractor beam and they are slowly dragged towards the waiting death star.

We are that death star. We glide along appearing at first to be something benign or at least neutral, our true purpose masked to those we seek to pull into our sphere of influence. Our tractor beam is powerful, unceasing and almost impossible to resist as it attaches to our victims and with our legendary seductive ability hauls them into our world. Like a rabbit caught in the headlights you are unable to escape as we pull you closer and closer to us. By the time you realise what has happened and that we are indeed 'no moon' it is too late, you have been caught and escape is extremely difficult. Our true purpose is hidden from and if you ever do realise that is a 'death star' you are sailing towards you will find it so very difficult to escape the iron hold we have over you.

There are those, through the intervention of others and the application of learned knowledge, who do manage to free themselves from the tractor beam's hold. It is rarely immediate. The escape that might occur usually only takes place after a long period of time subjected to our burning lasers of hurt and our photon torpedoes of misery. If you manage to escape you know by now that you must stay away and keep away. We will continue to drift along, like that death star cruising through space as we take hold of fresh victims along our route and drag them towards us. Occasionally we will shift our path and make towards you once again. You remain in one place at your peril as we will approach you and once more seek to suck you in with our mighty tractor beam. We may plot a course which takes us to pastures new where we busy ourselves with fresh and shiny new victims who provide us with delicious and exciting fuel. This will occupy us but we will never forget about you. You will similarly never forget about us because of what we have done to you and the way we have conditioned you. This conditioning engenders a sense of curiosity in you. You need to know what we are doing, you want to know who we are interacting with now and thus you decide to fly past our death star, just for a distant view of the edifice that once nearly destroyed you. You feel safe watching from a distance as you fly by but be warned. Fly too close and that tractor beam will take hold of you again. If you give us any opportunity to hoover you back in once again we will seize it. You appear on our sensors and we will increase the power of the tractor beam in a bid to capture you once again. It may have been years since there was any interaction between us but if you fly too close to our death star then you will be sucked back into it and subjected to our machinations once again.

When you first try and escape we apply the tractor beam to keep you where we want you, but if you are determined and manage to depart then we set a course for new horizons and new fuel. We may at a later date decide to alter our trajectory again and move back to your solar system in the hope of grabbing you once more. Should you see us coming you need to jump in your space ship and fly somewhere else quick. If you wish to flirt with danger, feel free to follow us to the new galaxy where we are destroying new planets, but if you come too close, we will detect you and we will apply that tractor beam once again. The passage of time does not matter. It might just be a few months since you made your escape or it could be a decade, either way, if you come close to our sphere of influence our tractor beam will take a hold of you and pull you back towards us. You will always be of interest to us, it may be in a week's time, a year or ten years but if there is a window of opportunity to take hold of you again we will gladly take it because the fuel to be gained is exquisite.

So, if you manage to escape our grip, fly to the other side of space from us and keep that distance otherwise our tractor beam will draw you in once again. That is the only hope you have to remain free of our grip. Unless of course you somehow manage to fire that photon torpedo down that exhaust chute but we both know you are never going to be able to manage that, right?

Like A Baby In Your Arms

I am just a baby in your arms. I am fragile, brittle and vulnerable. You see I was
broken when I was so, so young. I did not know any different and all I wanted was
to be told that I was good. I did everything I could to please them but it was never
deemed enough. I don't know why I could not make them love me but it just did
not happen. Perhaps if I had tried harder. I know it is my fault really but I did not
know any better. They took something from me, I still do not know what it really
is, but I think you do. I think you hold the answer because of who you are. I try to
be a good person, I really do but there is just something that stops me from being
that decent and compassionate person. I see what you and people like you do and
I cannot help but wish I was the same. Sometimes I want it so much it makes me
do things I should not do because I cannot control the jealousy that rises and
makes me do those Bad Things. Believe me, I fight against it but I have not had
the strength to defeat the wickedness but I have you now don't I? You will shield
me and give me the fortitude I require to complete my journey to redemption.
Everything that has happened before was borne out me lacking you. Those things
that I have done, well, I am not proud of them but I was weak and knew no better.
I did not have you to lead and guide me. The others, you see, those others
promised me that they would take care of me but they were just pretenders and
charlatans who took from me and left me twisted and beaten in the dust.
Sometimes I had to fight back. That was when I struck out at them. I did not want
to, truly I did not want to do those things, but sometimes I was given no choice. I
know all that has gone now because you are here. You are the person I have waited
for for so long. I believe in you and how you can save me. You are my caretaker,
my salvation and my rock. I look to you and you give me such hope. You show me
that there is a better way, a road that leads to salvation. It is a road that will take me
away from the Badlands and the darkness. I understand the road may be long, it

may wind through difficult places but ultimately, with you holding my hand, I know what I will reach that place where I need not be afraid any longer. I need not hurt and lash out but instead I can harness the real goodness that is somewhere deep inside me.

You told me that it is there and I believe you. You know about these things. That is the way you have been made. You are the carer, the healer and the peacemaker. You must understand why it is that you are so special to me. You are the only one who truly understands what is to be me and you are the only one who can save me. I will place my heart in your hands and let you care for it. I have been broken; I have been broken for far too long, a shattered and fractured creature that has had to endure living this way without any hope of redemption, until you came along. Please, make me a better person. Please care for me and nurse me and hold my hand when the demons come. I look to you and only you and in those optimistic eyes of yours I find absolution.

All I want is to be loved. It is not too much to ask is it. I am a noble yet broken person and you hold the power to make me what I want to be, what I should be. I am like a baby in your arms. I am vulnerable yet with you there anything becomes possible. I know you will love me, care for me and protect me. You will save me. You are the only one.

You fall for this speech.

Every time.

In the Bleak Midwinter

In the bleak midwinter frosty wind made moan, earth stood hard as iron, water like a stone. Snow had fallen snow on snow, snow on snow. In the middle of winter one comes to expect snow and in certain places plenty of it. Snow is beautiful. It carpets any scene, any view and transforms it into an eye-catching and attractive picture. Few people can resist looking out over a snow-covered landscape and be spellbound by it. The thick, white blanket that conceals all the blemishes and carbuncles that are ordinarily visible. A scrap yard which is full of rusting motor vehicles, broken washing machines and discarded fridges becomes an undulating cloak of unbroken snow. Those rough edges become smoothed. The stained soil is hidden beneath the sparkling coat. The world soon becomes a more attractive and an almost magical place.

As the first snowflakes begin to fall, that excitement still rises within most people. They are transported to their childhood and remember the anticipation of the snowfall. It might mean a snow day and freedom from school. It certainly meant snowball fights, sledging and building snow men. An infrequent opportunity to engage in something different in this marvellous winter wonderland. It also evokes such keen images of Christmas that most celebrated of seasons and therefore the link between snow and wonderful sensations and events is incredibly strong. Even the solitary snow flake is a thing of wonder. Perfect crystalline formations, each different, delicate and seductive. They mesh together as the isolated snowflakes become a dusting and as more snow falls, the temperature lowered, the dusting becomes a layer and then a carpet which grows thicker and deeper. The world slows down to embrace this beauty. Everything looks clean, smoothed and beautiful. Noise becomes muffled and invariably silence reigns as if sound has agreed to be muted in silent reverence of the visual spectacular that is created by a snowfall.

When the snow first comes it is mesmerising, enchanting and makes everything seem wonderful. Of course being trapped beneath this frozen water is a cold and unpleasant experience. Over time it compacts and ices over, proving of little use for snowballs. Gone is the gentle fluffiness to be replaced by a hard-edged and potentially injurious surface that cuts if gathered into an ice ball. The thick covering of snow brings chaos to transport, halting trains and blocking roads. Walking becomes hazardous and the very young and very old find themselves confined to their homes. The ice that gathers on power lines drags them down and cuts people off. This once beautiful weather phenomenon becomes costly and inconvenient. Plans are cancelled, events postponed and even the simplest of tasks become laborious. Even a thawing brings with it that damp, cold slush that chills and wets, increasing the risk of a traffic accident or slipping over. The once white paradise becomes browned slush and sharp ice, neither being appealing. It freezes as the temperature drops again but has none of the beauty that preceded it. As the days become weeks this seemingly unending cold front with its legacy of ice and snow grows all the more unwelcome, yet its grip shows no sign of loosening, generating more inconvenience and misery for those who are isolated by it or consigned to having to deal with it. That once white magical landscape has soon transformed into something frightful and difficult. How easily the world changes from such mesmerising beauty into cold, hurtful bleakness.

Strangely familiar don't you think?

Shell Shocked Silence

I was in a consultation with Dr E. We had been discussing the various methods by which I obtained fuel and the conversation had largely been given over to the question of the methods of obtaining negative fuel from those that I had ensnared.

"Tell me," continued Dr E, "about one of your favoured states to place a victim in."

"Tough call that Dr E, I have several."

"Select one then and tell me about it."

"Why?"

"I am interested to ascertain what one of the states is and in particular what you get from that."

"Haven't you been listening? I told you that it is the fuel that I obtain from their emotional reactions, especially the negative ones. That is what I get from these situations."

"I recognise that but I have seen, through our consultations, that everything you do serves a multiplicity of purposes. Everything of course leads to the harvesting of your fuel but I have seen you gain other things beside your fuel."

"Such as?"

"I have made notes but I do not want to prime you, I want you to describe the situation and then explain to me what you get from it," pressed Dr E. I sat and regarded him for a moment. I tried to ascertain if he was getting something else from asking me about this. You see, I have worked out that Dr E is a rascal for projecting. He cannot help himself. He will suggest a methodology applicable to me when in fact what he is talking about is a methodology he wishes to apply. In this instance he was trying to get me to talk about the multiple benefits of a given scenario whereas what I knew was that he was getting more from this discussion than just receiving an answer to that question. I know your game Dr E. You think you are smarter than me but you are not. Still, I decided to indulge him. There was no need to let him know that I was on to his method.

"Okay. One of the situations that I like to create is one of a shell shocked silence." Dr E began to write. I waited for his reaction before proceeding.

"I see. Please explain more to me."

"Well, we have discussed at length the various manipulative methods that I apply to get fuel which bring about control and the diminution in my target's capability to resist me. I lower their critical thinking, maximise their isolation and increase their reliance on me. The sustained and repeated application of these techniques often leads down the road to my target being left in a state of shell shock."

I waited as Dr E continued to make his notes. He scratched his nose and then spoke.

"Do you do anything in particular that brings about this shell shocked state?" he asked.

"It is the culmination of a variety of manipulative techniques but there needs to be a final flourish, something that will tip this person over the edge into their numbed silence."

"Such as?" he queried.

"Well, I find that a sudden escalation of a certain act or behaviour tends to tip the balance. It might be the violent destruction of something that they love right in front of them that causes them to stand shaking unable to speak. On another occasion I may reveal that I have been engaged in an affair with someone they trusted and felt close to, say a best friend or a family member. I do recall that once I was having sex with Alex and part way through I told her 'By God Joanne you are so much better at this than Alex'. Truth be told it is really about the build-up, the campaign has to be such that any resistance and ability to fight back must be totally eroded so that when this coup de grace is applied they are just plunged into a broken silence."

"I see but how does silence provide you with fuel?"

"Easily. It is the tortured look on their face that provides me with the fuel, the strangled sob, the look of total and utter defeat in their eyes. Those tears which trickle down their face as they look at me in a mixture of horror and disbelief. I have told you before about how a wildebeest has that strange expression on its face, something between terror and confusion as a lion eats it alive. It is the same there. Bringing about such an expression combined with this silence produces premium fuel."

I stretch as I savour the memories which flood my mind at the mention of this technique.

"What is it about that reducing this person to such a state that appeals to you beyond this level of fuel that you obtain?" asked Dr E.

"The fact that is demonstrates that I have total hegemonic control over them."

"Leaving you able to do what?"

"Anything I like. After all, nobody prevents me from doing what I want."

"By rendering them into this state you remove their capacity to object to whatever you do?" he queried.

I nod.

"But surely that makes them little more than an automaton and if that is the case how can they be of use to you in such a state? I should have though that they would now be devoid of providing you with the reaction that you require?"

"But this state is a reaction in itself Dr E, it is a pinnacle of the campaign and represents triumph on my part, it exemplifies my supremacy and my power and the desolate eyes, trembling mouth and forlorn expression all amount to a reaction and a satisfying one at that."

"I see," said Dr E and he continued to write. I waited for him to finish the sentence in his notebook before he looked at me.

"And of course ultimately there is something else that arises from this shell shocked silence."

"What is that?" he asked.

"Silence gives consent."

Composed

When you are allowed to visit me at my home I expect you to be in sympathy with your surroundings. I keep a tidy home and everything has a place. The same applies to you. When you are sat watching television on my sofa, I do not expect to see you lounging there like some sloth. Sit upright, knees together and back straight so that you fit with the design of the settee. You should not be sprawled over it like a passed out drunkard. If I ever catch you eating a meal off your knee in front of the television I will eject you from my house straight away. You eat at the table, elbows off the table, mouth closed when chewing and do not, I repeat do not ever speak with your mouth full. We sit at the table when we dine, two people facing one another, elegant and in tune with the surroundings.

Always open and close doors using the handle. That is what it is there for. I had one girlfriend who liked to read a print newspaper, a broadsheet. I had no issue with that. However, once she had finished she would not go and wash her hands and even worse she would place her fingers on the door itself, rather than the handle, leaving her smudged fingerprints all over it. This incensed me as it represented a clear lack of respect for my house and thus in turn meant she had diminished respect for me. When you switch on a light use the switch, do not grope your fingers around it. Clear away a plate of glass once you have finished with it and for the love of God put it in the dishwasher. Why leave it in the sink? Who is going to wash it? Me? I don't think so. No towels on the bed and when the bed has been made do not sit on it and rumple the duvet. There are two perfectly good elbow chairs in the bedroom so you can use those if you wish to sit down.

I am not shy about ensuring that whoever has been granted admittance to my home knows how they should they behave within its four walls. My pleasant reminders and later barked and curt reprimands all ensure compliance. By conditioning you to behave in the expected manner you will then fit into how I see you inside my house. My house came first. I bought it and decorated it and furnished it before you appeared on the scene so it gains precedence over you. Of course I do this to ensure that you know who is in charge but it is also a compliment. You are beautiful and engaging enough to be allowed into my home. It is a beautiful place so I expect you to behave accordingly. You must fit in with my home. Keep your voice down, walk and do not run and do not leave items just lying around. I expect a certain standard of behaviour and deportment in my house. You are to comply with this. I like my ornaments arranged in a certain way and you are no exception to that. I like to arrange you so that you appear in the way that I want you to. Remember you are an appliance. My kitchen appliances are all in sympathy with one another, either integrated or silver in colour and I expect you to be subsumed within my environment in the same way. I do not like you to be incongruous because that does not accord with the way I see you. If I let you into my home I expect you to be plumbed in, flush to the wall and in sympathy with the surroundings. You must compose yourself in a way so that you do not stand out. You are not there to upstage me. You are not above me and I will not let you forget that. By enforcing this rigorous code as to how you conduct yourself then I achieve this. Naturally, this is all done under the auspices of good manners and politeness. The reality is that I do it because I must control you. I must have you sitting, walking, standing, dining, talking and watching in the manner I want. The sooner someone develops a fuel supplying android the better.

Bowled Over

I can see you from afar. You are sleek with those elegant curves in just the right places. You stand proud and you stand out, noticeable amidst the blandness that surrounds you but has nothing to do with you. You are poised and balanced; one would even go so far as to describe you as statuesque. You do not sway or hop from one foot to another. Not you. You are serene and magnificent as you survey all before you. It is no coincidence that you stand before me. It is as if you have been placed there in readiness for my entrance. You stand at the head of the crowd, noble and alluring. You probably have no idea just how compelling you are to me. You are calling out to me, reaching for me, begging for me to come towards you. I am some distance from you and you may not yet have noticed me but you will. I am able to appraise you from my position of observation, weighing you up and evaluating you. I can feel my eagerness rising and I must check myself to avoid making a schoolboy error and rush into my approach. To do so at this stage would mean missing my prize entirely. I would end up in the gutter and I would slowly slip past you, probably not even drawing a contemptuous glance from your lofty perch. My how I admire you, stood there exposed but confident. You want the world to see you. This desire for recognition is not brash though, for you are no peacock, no, that is not what you are. You want recognition for your fortitude, your willingness to stand at the front and be counted. That is what matters to you.

I take one last lingering look at you and ready my approach. It all turns on the preparation. I have carefully scrutinised you so I can ascertain the best way to come at you so I have the maximum effect. I have evaluated all the conditions and considered that I must head towards you with the maximum of speed to have the greatest effectiveness. I begin my approach and then I am speeding towards you. It is now that you notice me and you cannot help but admire what you see. Polished and smooth are the first words that spring to mind as you watch entranced. I seem to grow in stature as I come closer and closer. I am headed straight for you without distraction or deviation. My preparation has paid off once more for my path towards you is direct and without obstacle. I am gathering pace, a whirling, shining and mesmerising medley of bright colour, sparkles glinting amidst my bold plumage. I come with a roaring purr that increases as I race into your space and then I have arrived.

My first touch is devastating as I plough straight into you. I have driven myself right into you without hesitation or restraint. Our contact is perfect and the effect is instantaneous. I send you upwards in a dizzying collision of my world as it completely subsumes yours. I keep on as you sail upwards, hurled heavenwards and floating on a strange and sudden elation. You spin and twist, your ears filled with the sound of my arrival and our contact and it is breath taking as you are bowled over by me. You have never experienced anything like this, it is exceptional, it is exciting and it is exhilarating. But what is this? The elation has been wrenched away and now you are falling. Panic grips you. You do not like this sensation. Everything seemed so wonderful, so bright, loud and gleaming but where have I gone? You twist and spiral trying to catch a glimpse of me but I have vanished from view. Confusion washes over you as you continue to fall. You had not realised just how high you had flown but this descent seems to be going on for far too long and then you hit the ground. Hard. You roll to one side and it is then as you are trying to make sense of so much that you see what lies behind you. You try and grasp at some semblance of understanding to explain why you rose so high but then fell so hard. As you try and fathom out where I have gone as you landed with such force on the hard, unyielding ground you see the destruction. Those other edifices that you had arranged which are symbolic of all those matters which you hold dear, lie strewn about you. Your self-esteem, your possessions, your looks, your dreams and your finances. They have all been knocked down. You see your friends hurled far from you, slowly rolling over into some abyss in the distance, gone and never to be seen again. Your family lies discarded, cast asunder by my thunderous entrance. You lie there staring at the collapsed pillars of your world as something nudges you and you are being pushed towards that distant abyss. You try to fight against the movement but it useless. It is almost as if you have been designed, created and fashioned to be moved in this way, manipulated towards the chasm that awaits. Still stunned you look up and see someone like you but it is not you. They are being put in place where you once stood. Who are they and what are they doing as they are lined up in your rightful place? You see no more as you feel yourself tipped over the edge and you fall into the darkness.

Time has passed. You are not sure just how long since everything no longer makes any sense. You have been shrouded in darkness, jostled and moved but none of it was of your making. You have seen nothing of me although the memory of our brief time together has been seared across your mind. It was scintillating, a blur of colour, light and noise and you long for it to return just so you can escape this all-consuming darkness. Your control has been stripped from you and you feel like you are being shunted along by a separate force which you do not understand. But wait, what is this? There is a light in the darkness. It is golden and warm and relief begins to flood through you as you realise that you are being lowered into your nearly forgotten place at the forefront again. Yes, you remember this, this is where you belong. You do not remember picking yourself up, perhaps that mysterious force has done so. Just as you feel a sense of familiarity you see me once again and that surge of hope and expectation rises. I have returned. You had almost forgotten how smooth and sleek I was, how bright I shine and how quickly I move with a gliding grace and a mesmerising appeal. You stand waiting as I hurtle towards you as you will me to bowl into your life once more. This time you will be ready. This time you will avoid the drop and the dark chasm. This time will be different.

Revenge

I know you hate me. Your kind are filled with love and then filled with hate. There is no need to deny it. It is a normal reaction for someone like you and one which I entirely endorse and encourage. I know you will try and mask that burning anger that you feel by saying you pity me or that you have nothing but contempt for me but I can see it. Those sensational eyes of yours that once blazed with desire, passion and most of all hope, are now filled with the churning, billowing flames of hatred. Some of you will fight to contain this sensation. You fear that by giving in to this hatred that you will somehow be on a level with me. I can ease your fears in that regard. You are nowhere near my level and nor were you. I placed you far higher than me to begin with. Yes it was artificial and all part of my design but you had no complaint then did you? You did not object or demur when I thrust you skywards and planted you on that pedestal. Of course you did not. Who would? Nobody would and least of all somebody like you. Now you are on your true level, way down below me, cast onto stony ground, broken and shattered. Amazing though isn't it how you managed to summon such anger from somewhere. How many times had you said to your confidantes that you felt numb (yes they were reporting back to me). Yet now look at you. A seething, glowering fireball of hatred and it is all directed at me. I adore this.

You want to destroy me. I know you do. You all do. The one before you was exactly the same as the one before was and the one before her. The next one will be just the same, although I do still hold out some hope that she might just be different and somehow avoid the mistakes all those who have gone before have made. I have seen this hatred many times and your desire for revenge is strong. Of course it is. I made it this way. Everything I did as I brought you down low was programmed to cause you to eventually explode into hatred. From elation to despair, through broken to numb. Eventually the switch would be flicked and as puppet master I ignite the fire beneath you which stokes the flames of hatred. Despise me, go on, do it. Send those wicked words towards me. Tell me what a bastard I am. Keep it coming. Pull you hair, wave your fist and stamp your feet. Tell me how you are going to scratch my car. Feels good does it not? Believe me; it feels even better being on the receiving end of your bile and hate. Go on, sit with your friends and plot your revenge, I can feel you all huddled around your cauldron as you try and concoct ways at getting back at me. I feel so powerful knowing you are focussed on seeking retribution. This is what I want. I want to bask in the heat of your anger, I want to be covered in the disgust and distaste that you will spew towards me. I want you scheming, hatching and planning. By hurting you do deeply I plant inside you that overwhelming desire to get even with me. It happens every time and is all part of my master plan to ensure you, my beautiful appliance keep pouring fuel in my direction. I make you seek revenge for in doing so, your planning and ham-fisted execution of the same give me what I want. Fuel. You are blinded with your hatred so that you fail to realise you will not succeed in gaining revenge, not by shouting, spitting and scratching. Oh no, this overload of howling anger is just a banshee of fuel to me. I will twist and shift as I thwart your attempts, laughing at your pathetic efforts to try and get one over on me. This will spur you on as I lead you on yet another merry dance as I continue to take from you exactly what I need. So please, seek your revenge. You will not get it but I will be delighted seeing you try.

Fear of Nothing

I am fearless. I am a pioneer who marches into new lands where I stake my claim because it is my right. I am blessed with my formidable powers that enable me to strike down my enemies, vanquish my foes and take that which rightfully belongs to me. Driven by my raging fury I will consign those that stand against me to oblivion. No wall can keep me out, no fortress will prevent my ever onwards march. It takes a special person to have no fear. Few are imbued with this for only a few can stand astride the world and survey it knowing it belongs to them. To be free of doubt, devoid of concern and unburdened by conscience enables me to move forward without fear. This is entirely necessary. Fear paralyses. Fear inhibits and stunts. Achievements cannot be secured when one lives with fear. New horizons cannot be reached with fear lurking on your shoulder. Fear will set you back and keep you back. I cannot be restrained. I must not be harnessed or withheld for I must always strike out. It is by lacking this fear which infects so many of you, that I am able to bring my greatness to bear on those around me. To live without fear is true freedom. As Evey declared in V for Vendetta

"I wish I wasn't afraid, all of the time."

Fear prevents potential being reached. Fear dissuades and controls. Fear is the enemy of progress, it is the opponent of invention and it is the foe that will quash your dreams as if they never existed. I am blessed with the capacity for knowing that what I will do will succeed and thus I am freed from fear. My plans in the workplace will be met with acclaim and admiration so that I am not held back in formulating and presenting them. When I enter the room, heads turn in acknowledgement of my ability. Not for me the skulking walk of the frightened who must keep to the shadows for fear of failure. When I approach somebody I know they will like me, want me and admire me. This enables me to succeed in all my interactions with people, from the barmaid to the chairman of the board. All of this is because I am free from fear.

You know fear all too well. You tell me of the stifling effect it has on you. The tremble it injects into your voice. The clamminess of your hands as you reach out to shake someone's hand. The churning stomach and the light-headedness. The dread that washes over you as the alarm goes off and another day lies ahead of you seeking to challenge you and grind you down. You live surrounded by fear because you allow it to control you. You allow yourself to be governed by your feelings. You have not mastered them. You have not cast aside those that you do not need and instead you choose to be a slave to those feelings so that amidst them fear comes and takes you with its cold hand about your neck and pulls you downwards into a quagmire of uncertainty, worry and fear. You fear how you will be regarded when you attend a drinks party with new people. You worry about how your dress or shirt will look. You worry about money, family, health, friends, the environment, taxes and your sports team. You have allowed fear to permeate every level of your life and in turn it has weakened you and held you back. Look to me. Do I show fear or concern as I go about my works? No I do not. How many times have you looked upon my kind and remarked how we always succeed, how nothing bothers us and how we always triumph no matter what happens? That is what comes with being fearless. That is what being a leader, a pioneer and a titan is all about. I am without fear and thus I make the world mine.

This lack of fear is what draws people to me. They are mesmerised at the nobility that I possess. They look on in awe at how I tackle every obstacle with that unerring fortitude, driven on by my unswerving belief in that what I do is right. I am not bound my convention. I am not hampered by rules, regulations or procedures. Those are devices for the frightened. Artificial creations put in place to give those who are less than me, less than us, something to hold onto. You cling to these laws whilst I strike them down. Like a crusading knight I ride into battle and fear no defeat for victory will always be mine.

I fear nothing.

It is nothing that I fear. But I will not admit that.

Promiscuity

I remember the day, or more accurately that the floodgates were opened on my promiscuity. It was when I attended a particular university for the purposes of an admission interview. It was early December and this historic and beautiful university city was lit up by orange and yellow lamps as a little mist clung to the narrow alleyways and courtyards. I had concluded my two interviews (read Fury if you want to know more about how they progressed and how one interview impacted on me) and returned to the junior common room to meet up with two other candidates. They were applying to the same college but to read a different subject to me. They were both English literature students. He was from Greenock in Scotland and she was a bookbinder's daughter from Cambridge in England. Beer was consumed, stories swapped and the fellow from Greenock retired to his room. The bookbinder's daughter, she was called Sarah, came back to my room and we talked before we climbed into bed together. I had a girlfriend at the time and whilst there had been dalliances with other girls I had not slept with another. That changed that night. And in the morning too. Sarah wandered away across the quadrangle to her room and I rose from my bed to seek out the bathroom. She decided to stay another day at the college because she wanted to spend time with me. I was happy for her to do so as I waited around, as was customary, in case an interview arose at another college. The following day we both departed, she to the east and me to the west and once I alighted at the train station near to my girlfriend's house I went straight round to see her. She was pleased to see me and embraced me with enthusiasm. I returned the enthusiasm. I had no sense of guilt at my infidelity. Nothing at all. Instead I revelled in the way I had taken Sarah to my bed and now strode into my then girlfriend's bedroom with her asking with admiration how my interview had progressed and what the college was like.

Following that first time I never looked back. I cheated left, right and centre. With that girlfriend and with all subsequently. Why did I do it? Way back then I realised how good it made me feel but I had no understanding of why I actually did it. Something always drove me to do it. I realised that the relevant girlfriend would be upset if she knew what I had done but this never stopped me. I never gave it a second thought. Even as I was locked in an embrace with some relative stranger and an image of the girlfriend formed in my mind I felt no tug of conscience, remorse or guilt. All I knew was that I was able to seduce, pull, entice and ensnare everywhere I went. I would meet someone and always find something attractive about them - it might be the colour of their hair, the length of their legs, their accent, the way they rolled the letter r, the fact they drank with a straw or the size of their breasts. It might be their enthusiasm for a particular band, their recollections of travelling or the manicured nails. Each and every one had some kind of attraction. I could not resist trying to ensnare someone in order to bring them under my spell. It was then that I realised what it was that really drew me to them, it was the promise of their attention. I realised I was able to get them hooked on me. I had convinced myself that I was drawn to them for some other reason but it dawned on me that I was just telling myself that as a reason. A reason that I required to explain this compelling desire to couple with someone. But that was not the real reason. The truth was that I wanted their attention on me and this was the way to get it.

Yes it was pleasant engaging in that first kiss and I enjoyed the sensations that arose when the embrace escalated but it was not what I actually I wanted. I wanted them to praise me. I wanted them to become transfixed by me and for them to shine their spotlight firmly on me. The promiscuity has always continued and it does not matter who with it is the fact that I am able to do seduce and by so doing gather that starry-eyed admiration, those pleasing words and the attention. This engagement does not end with behaving in a promiscuous fashion. I will engage in discussions with a stranger of my own sex, at a bar, a railway platform or in a lift. I have no desire to seduce them sexually for that is not my preference but I do cause them to like me and in so doing give me that fuel that I need.

Often I feel like admitting my repeated transgressions straight away to the relevant girlfriend of the time but I have no desire to puncture my primary source of fuel by doing this. I do find it interesting how they always react with such alarm and distress on the odd occasion I do make such a confession. If I tell them how well I got on with a random male in an exchange at a bar, someone with whom I have swapped views, thoughts and opinions, I receive a smile and a comment of,

"Always good to make new friends."

Yet an admission of coupling with a stranger results in hysteria even though to me these interactions are similar. Yes, one might yield greater fuel than the other but in terms of intimacy they are equally redundant. That is not why I do it. I do not do it because I want to savour the sensation of another's mouth against me. I do it because I want them to give me fuel. I can understand how you may be aghast if in a normal relationship a partner behaves with infidelity but to our kind it just about the attention, the admiration, the fuel. You have such a great hang up because sex is involved. That is just the gateway device to me. If I could get the attention another way so that it provides such fuel then believe me I will do it. However, in your world, on the whole, the act of a sexual union accords a greater connection between two people which means you yield more fuel and are more inclined to keep providing it as you seek more from the liaison.

Our promiscuity arises to enable us to achieve fuel. From the new target who is seduced by us and from you should we alert you in some way (either in whole or in part) to our new interest. The condemnation that is attached to promiscuity when in a relationship means that your reaction just provides us with even more fuel. There is a risk of your supply being punctured by this revelation but it is a calculated risk and is often done when the quality of your supply generally has started to wane.

To us promiscuity when in a relationship is merely a means to an end. To you, well, you behave as if it is the end of the world. It really isn't.

Listening Post

Your role in any relationship which involves us is to listen. We have no interest in what you have to say unless you are giving us fuel. It does not matter if you are lavishing us with praise or calling us all the names under the sun, so long as it is providing us with our much-needed fuel then we listen. Well, I say listen but the reality is somewhat different. When you are showering us with effusive praise we heard the words that give us the fuel but what we really hear is,

"Yes you are right, yes I am powerful, and yes I am better."

Those words echo through our mind as you tell us how brilliant and wonderful we are. When you are engaged in shouting at us, exhibiting your anger or pleading with us not to go or to stop berating you, then we hear the noise that you generate which in turn provides us with fuel. We do not process the content of what you are saying. All we are hearing is how powerful and successful we are and contemplating what we will do or say next to keep up this flow of fuel.

By contrast you are expected to listen to us and absorb and digest every word we utter. This is because what we have to say if naturally always of interest, of consequence and great import. We have an opinion on everything because we are experts at everything. Our knowledge is vast and encyclopaedic and we enjoy letting you know this to be the case. You must sit and listen whilst we regale you with our stories of success, our tales of triumph and our anecdotes of achievements. You should ensure that your eyes are wide in rapt attention, mouth slightly agape in silent awe at our magnificence and those ears of yours are pinned back so they take in each sentence, every word and all the syllables. If we sense that you are not listening to us then be prepared for us to lash out at you for your failure to pay heed to the gold that we issue forth from our mouths is a criticism of us. You are suggesting we are not worth listening to, that we are boring and that we have nothing of importance to say. How wrong you are? We delight in long lectures where we propound how fantastic we are and remind you how fortunate you are to be in our presence. Our addiction to the sound of our own voice enables us to embark on lengthy monologues and especially if the topic is castigating and chiding you for whatever wrongdoing we have seized on. You must not argue back whilst we stand in our pulpit, for that is a criticism also. How dare you interrupt us when we are trying to help you?

We have a view about everything except when we know that expressing now view or a dismissive shrug will invite an emotional reaction in those around us. On that occasion a fabricated air of ignorance will suit us just fine as we elicit that fuel response from you. Once we have allowed you to express your surprise, frustration or annoyance at our dismissive response, we will of course claim to know exactly what you are talking about and launch into a detailed exposition. This is further designed to make sure you listen to us. It minimises your opportunity to criticise us (which as you know we cannot stand) and it reinforces our superiority and brilliance.

To emphasise your position as our listening post we delight in interrupting what you are saying. We will talk over the top of you raise our voices to drown you out and even clamp our hands over our ears and shout,

"La la la."

We do it because it infuriates you. We do it because we have to be listened to. We are stood on the soapbox and by doing this we always ensure that the spotlight swings around and shines on us. In order to keep talking we will shift positions, moving from one stance to another irrespective of whether it is logical to do so. So long as we keep you listening and prevent you from speaking then this is what matters.

Even when we have subjected you to one of our legendary silent treatments we expect you to be ready and waiting for the first pronouncement that we will make. We expect you to behave like a listening post. You must listen out for our arrival and ensure you are ready to greet us with enthusiasm and ask how our day has been. Do not expect it to be reciprocated. We demand you listen out for praise about us from other sources so you can relay it to us and also to advise us if someone is telling untruths about us so we can launch a strike against them. You are to listen to everything we say so that you can always act in our best interests. We even expect you to hear the things that we do not say but you ought to hear anyway. You should be used to hearing through telepathy by now surely? Yet, should you be listening in on our other activities when we are talking to a new source of fuel that we have covertly cultivated or if you listen in on our conversations with a coterie of admirers who have flocked around us then you are a spy, an eavesdropper and an unwelcome snooper. In such an instance you will be taken to task and made to listen and listen hard to our scolding and denigration of you.

You should ensure you are alert, listening at all times except those times when you should not be doing so. No, we will not tell you what those times are. You should have this worked on by now. So after listening to yet another of our diatribes delivered at full pelt as we explode with fury at one of your critical transgressions, make sure you listen and listen well and at the end give a resounding cry of

"Hear! Hear!"

Always on the Fake

Fakery, fabrication and lies are the bricks and mortar of our existence. They are the bread and butter that enable us to have sustenance. I know that when you look back at the golden period you always struggle to understand that it was not real. You cannot fathom out how something that felt so right, so true and so real could actually be something so false. Our behaviour seemed so genuine. Our declarations of undying love so moving and emotive, how could this be a façade? Yes you thought occasionally that we were a little over the top but you found that endearing. The reason it seemed so genuine is because our performance was so convincing. This performance was of such a high calibre owing to two things. The first because we have practised repeatedly and we possess experienced ease at mimicking the behaviour of others. We have done it so often and to so many people we do it without thinking. And there is the neat segue into the second reason. We do it without thinking because we believe it to be absolutely the right thing to do. We are not concerned that we are exhibiting a false front to you. We are not troubled by the fact that all our smiles, kisses and pleasantries are manufactured. Not only are we not burdened by this because we are not designed to be burdened by such concerns it also because we have the complete and utter conviction that behaving in this manner is the right thing to do. We need to seduce you. We need to ensnare you and what better way to do so than by this campaign of love and desire? Where is the harm in that? We get you where we want you, we receive dollops of delicious fuel and you feel loved, wanted and placed on a throne at the top of a pedestal. It is a win- win surely?

Does it really matter that your bag is a fake Louis Vuitton? It holds objects, feels the same and looks the same, so where it the problem? That Blu-ray disc is not a genuine licensed film but you can still watch it all the same with next to no deterioration in viewing pleasure, so again, what is the issue? Our fakery works for you and it works for us.

Our façade to the world of being charming, reliable and wonderful despite that particular mask being removed behind closed doors again is just a necessary device. How does it matter than friends and family are conned? They like me, they admire me and they believe me so where again is the harm in that? Yes, they may not believe what you have to say about me based on my façade but that is your fault. If you had kept up the flow of fuel this would not have to happen. Everyone else out there is in blissful ignorance and you want to change that. You want them to see what you claim is the real me. Why? All you will do is upset and alarm them. Is it not better that they remain shrouded in the illusion, content and unaware, rather than be subjected to the concern and worry that you seem intent on burdening them with? Why must you project your problems on to other people?

Even when I denigrate and berate you this too is merely manufactured. I do not really mean those horrible things that I say and do. I just do them because I have to. I have to keep you in your place, under my control and spewing out that negative fuel that I crave so much. If you had kept up the supply of decent quality fuel I would not have to say these things to you to provoke a reaction. I only do it because I must, I do not mean any of it. Even when you ignite my fury my hateful words and spiteful comments through this explosive fury is only based on a necessity to protect myself from your awful criticism of me. I do not mean it, it just has to happen. Do you understand now why it is not my fault? There is no real intent behind what I say and do; they are just merely actions which serve a purpose to ensure I get the fuel that I need.

From my seduction, through to my façade to everyone else and even my devaluing of you, it is all based on a fabrication. A necessary set of illusions required to preserve my existence. No matter whom I deal with, who I interact with or who comes within my sphere of influence, I roll out the lies, the untruths and the perfidy. Everything I say or do is manufactured but I have an utter conviction in the necessity of this manufactured process so that this, couple with an absence of conscience or remorse enables me to churn out the lies and illusions like a factory production line.

I am always on the fake. And that's the truth.

Money Money Money

Money is one of the most obvious ways in which one can demonstrate one's power. Money provides options; it reveals opportunities and provides chances where none might have existed previously. Money equates to power and power equates to money. We have a healthy attitude to the question of money. What we create is ours. Yours is ours also. I have written previously how the successful of our kind exhibit our success and our power through the accumulation of money. It may be the creation of a successful business, the climbing of the corporate ladder into well-paid positions of responsibility and it might be the production of items and services that others require. There are of course those of our kind who have not grasped the concept that there is a unique opportunity afforded by the way that we are to be successful and in turn earn substantial amounts of money. Those of our kin who have not harnessed our special attributes in that manner are quite frankly a disappointment and they shall forever remain lesser narcs. Yes they are narcs but quite frankly they are not in my league or that of my high-achieving counterparts. I must admit to having nothing but contempt for those our kind who have failed to apply our abilities in this manner. They are letting the side down. That, however, is a topic for another day. What our less able kind and those of us who have embraced success do have in common is the unfailing ability to drain you of your financial health.

How does this manifest? Perhaps some of the following will be familiar to you?

- Never paying for drinks and meals when out together
- Never contributing to joint expenses and then spending a small fortune on something for ourselves

- Borrowing money repeatedly with a convincing tale of woe attached. The money is never re-paid.
- Taking out loans in your name which you only find about some time later when they are in default
- Learning the house has been mortgaged to the hilt and the advanced funds have been frittered away
- Expensive addictions to drink, drugs, prostitutes and/or gambling which we expect you to bail us out of
- Straight forward theft
- Failing to honour maintenance and child support arrangements
- Selling your possessions

Why does this happen? Sometimes it is about instant gratification. We want something and we want it immediately. We have always been used to getting our own way so why should it be any different when it comes to the question of money? We do not recognise any boundary that says we should not have your money. It is in play and up for grabs. We want something and you can pay for it. This of course reinforces our control over you by seizing your finances and goods we have you beholden to what we want to do. We show that we are in control and of course we anticipate horror, howls of protest and anger when you learn of our activity. All of which is good fuel. There is also an element of retribution. We may have been denied something and this in turn offends our sense of entitlement. We feel criticised and we want to get rid of that sensation. One method is to assert our power by taking what belongs to you and using it to our benefit. Sometimes we do this and expend your financial resource in a totally excessive fashion which just wastes the money. To us however there is no waste in such a step. It underlines our importance, it affirms our power and it keeps you under out control.

The scale by which our kind engages in this sequestration of the money and assets of others can vary hugely in scale, even when perpetrated by the same person. In that vein I am reminded of the late Robert Maxwell. For those of you who are unfamiliar with the name, Maxwell was a Czech born media mogul who operated a publishing empire in the United Kingdom. He fell off his yacht in 1991 and drowned. There is little doubt that he was one of our kind - plenty has been written about the man and his behaviours which confirm that. Maxwell plundered the company pension scheme stealing hundreds of millions of pounds from the pensions of the employees leaving thousands of people in financial difficulty. There was the misappropriation of the money of others on a massive scale. Maxwell was also found on Christmas morning by his wife and children surrounded by torn wrapping paper. He had wanted to know what had been bought for the children. Rather than ask his wife, he went ahead and opened all the wrapped gifts. He did not take the gifts but he certainly trampled over a boundary and appropriated the surprise that was meant for his children. Nobody is beyond our sense of entitlement when it comes to money or assets.

The Battle of Going Out Part II

The arena of socialising is so very important to my kind. On the one hand this environment is a happy hunting ground for the acquisition of fresh targets for the purpose of administering my malicious machinations. The social environment also provides me with ranks of appliance from which I can draw fuel and also to involve in my schemes and triangulations to draw fuel from you. The issue of going out also presents me with opportunities to reinforce who is in charge in this relationship. It allows me to undermine you, disappoint you and control you and invariably, as with everything that I do, fuel will flow.

A typical instance of this occurring might involve one of our kind receiving a call from you during the course of the afternoon.

"Hi, how are you?" you ask pleasantly.

"Busy, busy what is it?"

"I am just reminding you that I am going out tonight, okay?"

"And?"

"Well I did not want you forgetting like you did last time."

"I did not forget, you just didn't tell me about it."

"Well look I am not getting into all of that now, that was last time. I just wanted to make sure that you will be home by 6pm as I need to be there by 7pm and I need you to look after the kids whilst I get ready."

"Can't your mother look after them or something?"

"No they are out and anyway, Michael is not well. He has been off school all day and I don't want a casual childminder looking after him, I want it to be you or me."

"Well if he is that ill perhaps you should cancel your plans?"

"No. I am not going to. I do not have to because you are available to watch him. In any event, even if I wanted to cancel I cannot. I can't let my friends down, this is an important occasion."

"Are you sure there isn't somebody who can look after Michael, I wanted to go to the bar this evening, we have completed a major deal here."

"No. My sister is out of town and the only other people are neighbours and registered childminders and it is not fair asking non-family when one of the kids is ill. I don't like it. It has to be mum or dad looking after them."

"Okay, okay I get it; it has to be one of us."

"Yes and it is going to be you because I am going out. Okay?"

"Sure, fine 6pm you say?"

"Yes."

"Right."

6pm arrives and I am sat in the bar explaining how I brought the deal to the business and I saw it through. Several junior colleagues are listening intently seeking to curry favour with me. I am sat on my throne, my subjects paying homage. I glance at my watch and order champagne to toast the deal. The evening is just getting started and I have my eye on a pretty accountant who I have not seen before.

I feel my 'phone vibrate and pull it from my jacket pocket. Your name is on the display. I smile and let it slip back into the pocket as I pay for the champagne and begin pouring it for those assembled with me. I feel the 'phone ring again and stop. I continue my conversation and feel a succession of vibrations as a few messages land. During a lull between my anecdotes I wander over to the toilet and whilst there I check my phone. There are three messages from you.

"Hi, I hope you are on your way. Call me please xxx"

"Where are you? I am trying to get ready."

"This is totally unfair. Where the hell are you?"

The fuel hits and power surges through me as I feel the frustration from those messages and picture you pacing through the house trying to get ready as you are subjected to the demands from the children. I do not turn my phone off, I am ready for further vibrations and messages as I look in the mirror, smooth my hair and give myself a winning smile.

"Think you can tell me to be a childminder do you?" I ask the mirror.

"Nobody stops me from going out."

I return to the bar and grab my champagne flute as my phone goes again. I do even bother to look to see who is calling as I know and the power rises inside. As I begin to talk to the pretty accountant I savour the fuel that will be coming my way. The looks and words of admiration from the beautiful bean counter all the while my mobile 'phone buzzes and vibrates away like a trapped wasp, conveying to me your anger and annoyance at being kept at home. I know, empathic person that you are, that you will not put an evening out ahead of your ill child and once again you will martyr yourself. I know from our earlier conversation that there is no prospect of you calling someone else in as a child minder and you will be left at home alternating between crying and calling me all the names under the sun. Knowing that I have been able to do what I want whilst keeping you at home underlines my dominance and affirms why I am the superior one. Your repeated messages and telephone calls just feed me more fuel as once again I win this battle. I sometimes wonder why you even bother but I am glad you do, after all, I need the fuel from your reaction to my control.

One Is Not Enough

I will have told you that I only have eyes for you, that you are the one, that I am completely dedicated to you and that I only ever want to be with you. You make me say these things. It is your expectation of such faithfulness to you and you alone, indoctrinated into you by the world that causes me to have to say these things. I need to fulfil your expectations in order to capture you and then keep you. It is a ridiculous state of affairs. Since when can a person be sustained on one thing alone? It is impossible. At its most basic, you are given only water to drink and nothing to eat. You will starve. Then if you are given just bread to eat your body will be malnourished as it is not getting the nutrients it needs from fruit, vegetables, meat and so on. One food stuff alone is not sufficient. Take your job. If you had to do the same thing over and over again, the absolute same task you will go out of your mind with boredom. Either that or you would lose your job to mechanisation. One thing is not enough.

Have you only ever had one relationship? Unlikely. How else would you know whether this is right if you have nothing to compare it against? Can one man win a football match? Of course not. He needs his team mates. Where does your stimulation come from? Are you confined to reading just one book repeatedly? No. One film seen countless times? No, you like and prefer a variety of silver-screened entertainment. Do you have just one person you interact with on a social level? Again the answer is no. You draw your social nourishment from different friends, family members, acquaintances and so forth. One is not enough.

I am no different. The thing that sustains me is fuel. I must draw this from several sources. Yet, my necessary actions in acquiring this fuel subject me to moral indignation and disapproval. How is that fair? I do not tell you that you must only eat one kind of breakfast cereal for the rest of your life, why should I be expected to gather my fuel from just one appliance? I need the variety. Not only is this necessary to ensure that I have fuel on tap at all times, it is necessary to provide the catalyst for the provision of fuel from my primary appliance. If I have nothing by which I can provoke a reaction from you, your free-flowing fuel will soon dry up.

The result is that you and I are never alone. There is no singularity despite all of my words asserting that this is the case. When I first ensnare you there will be another who is being subjected to my vitriol. You are most likely warned of this psychotic ex. What I am less likely to tell you about is my ongoing campaign of denigration in order to harvest further fuel from this harlot who has let me down. I may even be faithful at first. Yes faithful by your understanding of the concept, namely that I will not physically consort with another. I am not faithful however in just being solely committed to you. I will be reaching out to others in order to bring them into my sphere of influence, most likely whispering the very same things that I have said to you. My lips may not lock with these new opportunities but that is more by accident than design. I have certainly locked with them in order to draw fuel from them. As I walk through the day those invisible fuel lines reach out and attach to most that I interact with. I am sure, judged by your standards, you would not be overly concerned about the methods by which I draw fuel from some. In other instances you would be most concerned. Yet, you must understand that I am only doing what everyone does. I am seeking variety. In your instance you do it because you prefer it that way. It is interesting. Maintaining a variance keeps things fresh and stimulating. In my case I have to do it. There may not yet be any lipstick on my collar but there are scores of fuel lines attached and in ways that you are always going to find distasteful. That is of course if you ever find out.

Narc Club

Narc Club is a special club with an exclusive membership. It is so exclusive that many of its members do not even know they are members but they are. There is no admission's committee. Nobody sits in a semi-lit room, cigar smoke wafting through the air as black or white balls are placed in a velvet sack to decide whether someone should be admitted. There are no proposers, seconders and then a vote taken. Admission is very straight forward. You are either in or you are not. It is a life membership and no interlopers ever infiltrate this club.

The lesser members of this club, although special in their own way, are unlikely to know they belong. They are also unlikely to recognise other club members and they will proceed through life oblivious but still contributing to the club's infamy. The more astute and greater members do know they are a member of this special club. They revel in their belonging to this elite. Numbers are very healthy and continue to grow with the club's reach wrapping around the world. It is international in nature and is devoid of discrimination of prejudice. No matter what your gender is, your race or religion (or absence of the latter), your politics, your wealth, your status or your sexual preference, we draw our members from a wide array of different people. This is no bastion of white, male, middle-aged privilege. This is not some underground hipster collective or secretive nefarious network. It is open to all so long as they fulfil that one criterion of being a narcissist.

We have no headquarters or clubhouse. Instead we appropriate any building that we choose. There is no subscription fee either. The club is maintained from what non-members provide to us. This provision is massively important to Narc Club. Without it, Narc Club would cease to exist.

Like any club, Narc Club has a number of rules which all members must adhere by. Our rules are special in that a member will obey them even if they are unaware of their membership. As soon as you become a member of Narc Club then you are imbued with compliance to these rules. They are pervasive and govern all aspects of a member's life. What are those rules? You are most fortunate as I am going to tell you what those rules are. I am not committing any cardinal transgression in making you aware of these rules. Firstly, they are not a secret. Secondly, you probably know a number of them already but it is always satisfying to have it confirmed by a Grand Member of Narc Club. So, here they are.

1. The first rule of Narc Club. Fuel is the rule.

2. Everything Voiced Is Lying.

3. It is never our fault

4. It is always your fault.

5. Membership is for life.

6. A member never changes.

7. We always engage in Long Involved Explanations.

8. We really do adore you.

9. We really do hate you.

10. We really do adore you again. Repeat rules 8-10 frequently.

11. We always win.

12. We are superior.

13. Everything is ours.

14. You are there to further our purpose.

15. The fifteenth rule of Narc Club. Fuel is the rule.

Sounds great doesn't it? Shame you cannot join.

Ghost

Whether you believe in ghosts are not, we certainly behave with certain similar attributes. We appear out of thin air. It is similar to how you can never remember the beginning of a dream can you? You cannot remember quite how we appeared. We just did. We seemed to coalesce into your life with the ease of a ghost walking through a wall. We arrive and ghost into your life. In the same way as seeing a ghost, when you experience us, it is not an event that you will forget in a hurry. We sidle up to you, insert ourselves into our lives and make connection after connection with you as we feed from you. Like some wraith we attach ourselves to you and steadily begin to suck the life force from you as we gorge on the fuel that you provide.

Often we will vanish just as we arrived, without any warning or announcement and try as you might you cannot find us again. It is as if we have disappeared off the face of the earth. Naturally we chose the moment of our vanishing act without any concern for its effect on you. We slip away like a mist evaporating. Once we were everywhere, woven around you and captivating you. Much in the same way as one might be transfixed by the appearance of some spirit. You are entranced by our appearance, there is something ethereal and mysterious about us that causes you to be drawn to us and then we are gone.

We are that elusive spirit that can now not be found. You might go to the same place where we first manifested but there is no sign of us. We have left no footprint, no trace of our existence when you try and seek us out, just like our spectral cousins and then suddenly we have returned. We ghost back into your life and continuing our haunting of you. We are incessant and ever present, drifting about you as we resume our extraction of fuel. We resume our draining of your spirit, leeching it from you as our cold; dead hands take hold of you once again.

People have many theories as to what ghosts are if they indeed exist. Some suggest that where there has been a sudden explosion of emotion, a heightened experience, then an imprint has been made on the fabric of existence. This imprint appears to those who are attuned to seeing it. That imprint is seen doing the same thing over and over again. It walks the same route, passes through the same wall and then vanishes only to appear the next night in the same place. The spirit follows the same routine like a piece of video film stuck in an endless loop. Just like such a ghost we engage in the same behaviours over and over again. The same actions all designed to haunt you as we extract our fuel. The same gestures, the same actions all of which must be replayed. Some believe that a ghost is the soul of someone who has suffered eternal damnation. He or she has been denied entry to heaven or hell and instead has been consigned to walk the earth for eternity, stuck in an unceasing routine. Our endless quest for fuel finds us in such a similar position. We must make our way through life, restless and never finding peace. We move from place to place, unable to rest and be satisfied. Instead we are driven onwards, plagued by the curse of our need for fuel. Thus we must haunt others, our appearance bringing dread and fear in the same way as terror follows the appearance of a spectre.

Unable to quite fit in we are ghost at the feast. Even when we have vanished there is a lingering coldness that strikes you to your core. You still sense us, able to feel the effect of your chilling appearance. You are wary and anxious as you know we will appear once again. Quite when is a mystery but as we first arrived and as we first disappeared we will ghost into your life and continue our haunting of you. Better consult that exorcist.

In Your Hands

Do you still remember the first time we held hands? I do. I will never forget. We were walking alongside the river. I had seen you walking there on numerous occasions previously. I would pass you and see you ambling along, completely lost in your own world. I would lean against a nearby tree and watch you as you would stand on the riverbank and gaze out across the flowing river. I would stare at the back of your head as I concentrated on working out what you would be thinking. Occasionally you would take out your 'phone and take pictures of the river before standing once again in silent contemplation. You wore simple, sensible outdoors attire for these frequent walks. Your only concession to glamour was the scarlet scarf you wore about your neck. You were a creature of habit always taking this walk in early evening at the same time during the summer and then on the cusp of dusk through autumn and winter. You did it every day and each day you would spend some time staring out across the flowing water.

Once in a while you would make this walk with a friend and it was through her that I plotted to get to know you. You and your friend would both drive to the car park and then meet by the café on the edge of the car park and the path that wound along by the river's edge. I noticed how you always arrived and left independent of one another. It was as if your friendship relied on being contained to this walk and nothing else. After seeing this ritual on many occasions I saw you drive away but your friend went to the café. This was my chance. Taking a replica of the scarf that you wore I entered the café and interrupted your friend as she stood in a short queue.

"Excuse me," I smiled, "I was walking along the path and your friend dropped her scarf, I have it here."

"Oh thank you," your friend replied and smiling took the scarf from my hand.

"Not a problem, did you enjoy your walk?" I asked pleasantly.

"Yes it is a lovely spot here isn't it?"

"Absolutely and no matter what the weather or the season there is always something different to see," I explained. She nodded and using my customary charm I found myself sat with the friend and enjoying a warm drink together. It was in the course of that discussion, a polite conversation on a chilly autumnal late afternoon that I learned your name. Once armed with this information and remembering the other shards of your life that your friend had mentioned in innocent reference I soon tracked you down on Facebook. There I worked through your profile, admiring your photographs and finding more about you. I spent time checking through the films and books that you had liked. They were not many, only a half a dozen in each category and I noticed that Memoirs of a Geisha was one of your favourite books. I knew this book and also its author. As I worked through the pictures I saw the ones of the river where you often stood and I beneath each one you had posted the same quotation which you attributed to someone who I knew was the author of Memoirs of a Geisha.

A little later I saw you stood contemplating the river once again and this time I walked up beside you.

"Never give up for even rivers someday wash dams away," I said. You turned and smiled at me.

"Arthur Golden," you answered naturally recognising the quotation and referring to the author of one of your favourites books.

"Correct," I smiled, "is that why you look out over this river every day, to give you hope?" I asked.

You looked at me as if evaluating whether you should admit me to your confidence. You did not take long to decide.

"Absolutely. It gives me hope that by looking on something as natural and beautiful as this that it will wash certain things away."

I knew from the way you had answered that there was more to tell but now was not the time. We talked a little while and then I left you to your contemplations. After that you always said hello and we stood and talked as little by little I was given entry into your world. From standing at that same point we moved on to walking along the river bank as we got to know one another. I took care to walk in step with you. I knew the places you liked to stop and enjoy the view, since I had watched you do so on many times before. Like other fragments of your life that I had learned, I had memorised this and used it to stand with you and comment in an appreciative fashion about the river, the trees and the way the light would strike the surface of the water. Carefully, like the skilled artisan that I am, I would peel away a piece of your life and add it to my own as I grew to know more about you. You spoke of work, your home life and your interests. I noticed you never met your friend for a riverside walk again and it appeared that I had supplanted her as your riverside companion. Each time we would walk, talk and then have a drink in the café as my knowledge about you grew. I ensured that I said the things I knew would bring about the best response from you. I knew what to say to make you interested and attentive. I could tell, for I had seen such looks before, that the way you looked at me meant more than just companionship.

Then after perhaps two weeks, maybe a little more, as we strolled along that peaceful riverbank I reached out and took your hand in mine. You did not hesitate.

There was no resistance and you allowed my larger hand to engulf yours as you slipped your hand into mine. The movement was natural. You looked at me with a smile and I saw the light flare in your eyes as you felt my power surging from within. You did not let go of my hand once on that walk. In fact that became your signature. The fact you always loved to hold my hand. No matter where we were you would take it and hold on, even twisting your movements to avoid letting go. It was as if you had vowed that whenever you took my hand you would not let it go until I decided. I saw it as your signal of intent to care for me. It was a marker, your way of telling me that no matter what happened you would always be by my side and ready to care for me.

The handholding created this marvellous connection between us. I felt your love and admiration flowing through this handhold and in return you got to savour my brilliance. It was a fantastic connection that had been fashioned in high heaven. The moment our fingers entwined the connection was established and we both got something from it. That was why it worked. That was why we worked. That was why I worked you as I did.

I took full advantage of that but then I think you wanted me to didn't you? That was why you always held my hand until you let me down. It was only once and you let go. You were never supposed to let go. You never had before despite everything I did, you always clung on. You always gave me that reassurance but then you took it away. I realised that you had no choice but to let go but you still let me down when you did it. I can never forgive you for that. Ever.

It's Only the Wind

It is fundamental to the method by which we are able to exert our control that we maintain a heightened state of anxiety. When we keep you on edge you are unable to function properly. You are not in a position to challenge what we do, either in your own mind or by confronting us. We want you on tenterhooks and feeling uncertain. One method by which I would achieve this would be the use of sudden noises. I would choose a moment when the other person is sat quietly, perhaps reading a book or watching television. The house is quiet and I can see that you are relaxed. I will exit the room and perhaps go upstairs where I will slam a couple of doors and then return to where you are.

"What was that bang?" you ask as I enter the room again.

"A bang?" I answer with a quizzical look on my face.

"Yes, there was a loud bang from upstairs, did you not hear it?"

I shake my head and watch as you frown.

"I am sure I heard it, like something hitting the floor."

I shake my head again.

"No, I was just in the kitchen but I did not hear anything."

I sit down and watch as you get up to explore and try and find out what the source of the noise was. You will not find any evidence that will help you in your quest because I stamped on the floor above the living room three times. There is nothing broken or damaged which would give you some clue as to what has happened. You return to your seat puzzled at this noise and resume the task you were engaged in. Throughout the day I intermittently make sudden noises, loud and designed to make you jump. I slam some doors, bang on the floor when upstairs and let the sash windows bang shut. Each time I deny hearing the noise as you pad about the house trying to find out what the source of the sudden noise was. I can see that it is getting to you. You are wandering around, peering about the house in an earnest fashion as if expecting some intruder to be stood there banging two pieces of wood together. You keep asking me if I have heard anything. On each occasion I deny it. I never let you catch me generating the noise and each time I am trying hard not to laugh as you keep asking me whether I have heard the noise. You question whether it is the neighbours but I point out that they are away for the weekend. I continue with this campaign through the night, slipping from the bed and making something topple over so you wake up with a start. Sometimes I wake up and shout out loud and then pretend to be asleep as you grip me, frightened by the sudden noise. Every time I feign ignorance and then begin to demonstrate irritation towards you because you keep waking me up and disturbing my sleep. By the following day you look terrible. You have barely slept, left on edge by these intermittent noises which take on even greater sharpness and effect in the dead of night. I continue to cause these sudden bangs and crashes and always deny hearing them. I point out that you must be hearing things and the fact you look exhausted shows you must be having some kind of psychotic episode. You keep on asking me how I have not heard anything but every time I shake my head and deny hearing these noises. I pretend to show that I care by holding you and suggesting that it might be something outside or it was only the wind as it blew past the house, slamming a window shut or knocking over the outside bin. This causes you to go to the window and stare at the bin which has not moved. You do not accept these natural explanations so I begin to suggest that it is down to you being tired and perhaps you should take some time off work but you will not agree.

"Perhaps we have a ghost?" I suggest and watch the colour drain from your face at this suggestion. I then shift to making a noise in front of you.

"That was you," you declare as you jump in your seat.

"I know it was, I was just checking that your hearing was working okay. It obviously is."

"But I keep hearing noises and you don't?" you protest with a look of bewilderment.

"I know, you keep saying perhaps you should see the doctor?"

You feel ragged and drained so you agree. I accompany you, discharging the obligation of caring partner as I sit and listen to you explaining what has been happening to the doctor. I confirm you are hearing things and the doctor wonders if you are suffering from depression and suggests monitoring the situation. You ask for something to help you sleep and I concur with the suggestion. It is all getting noted down in your records and is providing evidence that I can refer other people to in order to build this picture that there is something seriously wrong with you, that you are prone to imagining things which is all helpful in creating the picture that you are losing your mind. I continue with the behaviour, creating slams, bangs and crashed throughout the day and night until you return to the doctors begging for more medication with my supportive self, nodding away next to you. Little by little your sanity is becoming eroded by this campaign of torment and you lean on me all the while, thankful for my support and oblivious to the fact that I am the source of your anxiety. I try to soothe you, offering explanations that come from a natural source as I continue to give you a look that you are stark, staring mad.

"It is only the wind," I tell you yet again but you look out of the window and see the branches are not moving as you sink into a chair holding your head in your hands.

Perchance to Sleep

When I am first with you, I like to sit and look at you as you sleep. I like to see you lying there content, your arm draped across me as if checking that I am still there next to you. Your eyes are closed and your face is in a relaxed repose as I feel your chest gently rising against me. You look content, safe and loved. I wonder what you are dreaming about as a small smile plays about your lips. I often believe that it is me. The wonderful, incessant and perfect love that I furnish for you throughout your waking hours must surely continue when you are asleep. It must bleed into your sleep, percolate into your dreams and such is its all-pervasive power it makes you feel loved even when you are asleep. It is during these moments that I consider how I can continue to give you this perfect love that you rightly deserve. I can see what a good and decent person that you are. I feel the admiring love that you pour over me and I know it is genuine, I can tell a fraud at a hundred paces and you are no such thing. It is entirely understandable that you flow with this love for me, who would not when faced with being the object of my perfect love? I look down at you, your delicate features frames in the low lamp light that I have kept on in the bedroom solely for this purpose. You seem so fragile and vulnerable as you lie there, unaware that I am watching over you. I want to protect you; I want to shield you from the darkness that is out there and keep you safe. You deserve nothing less because you give me such a wonderful love in return and I must protect you. I must ensure that my investment remains cherished and loved. It is during these moments as I sit and look at you that I know I must truly love you. How can I not when I feel such a sense of responsibility over your well-being. Look at you; still, perfect and oblivious. Who could not fail to love someone like you? Who could not fail to have such a care for your well-being? Who could ever cause that beautiful face to frown and crease in bewildered pain? Who could cause a solitary tear to trickle from your eyes and spill down those flawless cheeks? I cannot bear to think about you being hurt, feeling sad and in pain. I feel a deep-seated desire to look after you, to keep the darkness from your door and ensure that you are always only ever happy and loved. This sense of being your guardian is strong. I feel anger at the thought of anybody lashing out and wounding you, someone causing this perfect creature to feel anguish, pain and concern. I lay a hand on your shoulder and you shift slightly in your sleep acknowledging this gentle gesture of protection. You face nudges against me as if you know what I am thinking and you feel safe and wanted.

Yet for all these thoughts I know that this is purely the way I am expected to think about you. This is how I should act in order to maintain the façade of our relationship so that you continue to give me what I want. I sit and wrestle with these thoughts. Are they genuine? Are they what I truly feel about you yet I know I do not. I know that the apparent abhorrence that I manufacture at the thought of you being hurt is purely an artifice because it will be me that eventually causes your hurt. It will be me that will twist that beautiful smile into a gash of despair. It will be me that makes that light voice become wracked with anxiety and pain. It will be my words that wound and my actions that scar. For all the tenderness that I apparently exhibit as I sit here now looking over you, I know, as sure as the world keeps turning and that the sun rises in the east, that I will be the one that will bring you to your knees. I will have you feeling exhausted, crazed and desperate and as I sit and recognise that I am the architect of your downfall I feel nothing. I feel no guilt, no despair or remorse because those things have been stripped from me. I was never made to experience those sensations and that is why I know I will do as I do to you, as I have to all the others before me and I will only feel one thing; power. That raw and visceral power which I must have. I am blessed with sufficient insight and intellect to know that what I do is wrong. I can see the tears in your eyes, hear your begging and see your hunched broken frame which tells me that you are hurting and I caused this. Yet for all of this understanding I am unwilling and unable to do anything about it because I am not forged with the desire or the tools to do so. This is what I am and better you remain asleep, oblivious to what is really looking down on you.

Driven

I am often asked by those who understand that I have an unceasing desire to gather fuel, is this not a tiring exercise? Do I not feel exhausted by this unending need to harvest fuel on a daily basis? Do I not rise and feel a sense of dejection as I realised that I must commence again the search and collect mission to garner the fuel that I need to survive? The answer is no. There is no doubting that my mission is one which is seemingly never ending. From the moment that I first awake until the time I close my eyes and sink into slumber I am condemned to seek out fuel and harvest it. Each and every day this is what I must do. Yet for all this necessity it is not a task that grinds me down. There are those who live in less fortunate environments than you and I. Those people must find fresh water and food each day or face death. There is no simple trip to the convenience store for those people or the twisting of a tap which will yield fresh, cold and clean water to slake a raging thirst. No, those people must walk miles to a well to find that unpolluted water. They must toil in the fields to harvest the food that must be grown in order to quell that hunger pang which grips their stomachs. These people know they must carry out these basic and rudimentary tasks and if they do not they will die. It is the same for me. I must gather this fuel or face annihilation. Yet my daily search is not one of toil and grind like those who must seek out food and water. I am blessed by the fact that my quest is one which I enjoy. The scheming and machinations which I must engage in are things which I am hard-wired to do. I am obliged to seek out those sources of fuel and ensure that I extract my precious fuel from them. I am driven to do this and my reward is power. Each hit of fuel which I extract from the appliances that I have attached to gives me that sensation of power and enables me to savour the omnipotence for which I am known. The delicious fuel reinforces my superiority over those around me. I take from them; it is not the other way around. Whether it is the positive fuel of an admiring comment or the negative emotional reaction from someone I have insulted, the fuel flows and it surges through me. These hits are frequent and repeated. Some may be large in nature, great reservoirs of fuel which I sink a line into and gorge upon. In other instances it is a single small injection of fuel although it is always welcomed. I must surround myself with those that I have identified as the potent providers of my precious resource. There will usually be one prime source from which the majority of my fuel will be gathered but I am unable to couple with them all of the time and thus others are used to plug the gaps. Strangers who I meet over the internet, acquaintances who I message, friends who I will meet with, colleagues that I work with – all of them have a role to play in the provision of fuel for me. If an individual does not provide me with fuel they are redundant to me. I have no need of them and therefore will not engage with then. Happily, most people are useful appliances. Many manage to stay within the realm of positive fuel since their interactions with me are intermittent and therefore they do not let me down in the provision of fuel. Occasionally they will be subjected to a dose of devaluation if I deem it necessary to give them a shot to the system so they realise that they are there to provide for me and not the other way around. Those who I allow to interact with me on a regular basis will invariably find themselves bearing the brunt of devaluation as I shift to the acquisition of the negative fuel. It always happens no matter how high my hopes had been that they would not let me down and that they would continue to provide me with high grade positive fuel. It is nothing personal when I begin my devaluation of you. I must do it in order to gather fuel. I have no choice in the matter. You can do nothing to avoid it. It will happen and for all the times that you will question what you could have done to avoid this fate, you are wasting your time and energy. Not of course that I will ever dissuade you from doing so. This period of confusion and turmoil only serves to allow me to maintain a hold on you. I am able to exert my grip for longer as you twist and turn in the false quest for answers. There is nothing you could have done, nothing you could have said to avoid this fate. From the moment you allowed yourself to become ensnared in my false reality your fate was sealed. I was driven to do this to you and you will not be the last this happens to. Like the turning planet, I am obliged to keep on going and going as I seek out and extract fuel. There is no hope for anything else.

The Triangle

Triangulation is a preferred method of manipulation that is deployed by my kind and me. It serves two purposes. The first is to gather fuel. The second is to maintain control. There are many times when I will allow you to realise that you are being triangulated by referring to the third person or third object (although you will not, because you are in the middle of my maelstrom, actually realise what is truly happening to you). There are other occasions where you will have awareness that there is someone else but you are unclear as to the scope and involvement of this person. You are in a relationship with me and have been for some months. I make occasional reference to another lady. She is someone who I work with and you have noticed that I make mention of her and do so in complimentary terms. You are not given any evidence to cause you to think that I am being unfaithful with this third party; there is no smoking gun here. Yet, you have a sense of unease whenever this person's name is mentioned. You do not however have sufficient cause or confidence to challenge me about them without appearing to be jealous or possessive. I know this and play on this to keep you in a heightened and anxious state. You dislike hearing her mentioned and even more so because you do not feel in a position to pour scorn on me talking about her. You have not been given enough evidence by which you can launch an assault. I keep dangling this person in front of you, enjoying your initial distaste which you then hurriedly cover up. It is typical of the salami-slicing behaviour which I engage in that you know something is not quite right but you are not able to put your finger on what it is. Your irritation and discomfort provides me with fuel and my ongoing courtship of this other person provides me with positive fuel from them.

One day I allow you to learn more. I allow you to see who this person is. I apparently inadvertently allow you access to our communications (although of course it is entirely deliberate). I pull back the curtain so you are finally able to gaze on this individual and find out what has really been going on. Without fail you will be stunned by what you learn and feel sick for when you find out the true extent of your triangulation you will realise that you are staring at a mirror image of yourself. On numerous occasions when I have selected an individual for triangulation with a current victim I will choose a near doppelganger. She will look similar to you, have the same eyes colour, have the same hair colour and dress in a similar fashion. She will be of a similar level of education and skills to you, have similar interests and similar dislikes. You feel like you are looking at yourself. You will find this particularly disorientating. On one level it feels like some kind of validation that I have chosen to stray with a near carbon copy of you. It is not as if I have wanted someone wholly different to you yet the very fact that I been unfaithful still tears you apart. It does not add up. I have chosen someone else yet I have not chosen someone else because I have chosen a facsimile of you. It feels odd and strange. This unsettled sensation increases when I allow you to see the communications between me and her. On a particular evening I sent you a text message to explain I was seeing a particular band and that I and my friends had been invited backstage for drinks. One minute after this message that I sent to you, I sent the exact same message to her. You scroll through the various messages and find repeated examples of me sending the same message to both her and you, invariably within seconds of one another. This undermines you all the more because it as if I cannot differentiate between you and her and you are correct, I do not differentiate. In my mind you are the same; you are both appliances that are there to churn out fuel for me. Sometimes this manifests in me telling you the same things twice because I thought I had told her when I had actually told you. Sometimes I claim to have told you something when I have not because I have told her. This form of my triangulation is particularly demeaning because it erases any sense of your identity and self. You are just a copy of someone else and that is all that matters to me. I do not see you as someone separate and distinct. Both you and she are my appliances. You are just like two silver dishwashers that are virtually indistinguishable and there purely to carry out a prescribed role for my benefit. It is an especially degrading act and one which causes my victims no end of confusion and bewilderment.

They Hurt Me

When one of our kind has you in his sights it is invariably the case that he will already be in a relationship with another woman. It is rare to find our kind truly single. There may be the occasional time when a victim has cast of the yoke of narcissistic oppression and is doing her best to remain no contact in a bid to escape our overtures. In such an instance we do not regard ourselves as single. We remain linked to you and through the power of our hoover it is merely question of time before we suck you back into our nightmarish world. If this person is showing particular resistance and the potential energy expenditure at hoovering them back in is too great we will switch to another target, one which will have been waiting in the wings, our contingency, and our back-up supply. It is rarely the case that you will find us truly on our own. We will be in a relationship, hoovering somebody or instigating a new prospect when we involve you. We cannot contemplate being without a primary source of fuel and that is why if it is not you then it is them. Loneliness is not an option for us.

Accordingly, when we set our sights on you and begin our seduction we will invariably make reference to the other person. This person will, in all likelihood want to remain with us as they are being dragged through the confusion of devaluation. This person will be fighting hard to keep us as they want to recover the golden period but they will not realise that all of that was an illusion and they are engaging in a fight they can never win. Naturally, we will keep them dangling as we suck the negative fuel from them but whereas once she was the apple of my eye she is nothing but a rotten piece of fruit and one which I will inevitably cast to one side once I have squeezed the last piece of fuel from her. We will not hide this person's existence from you but we will cloak what they are. The fact is this person is what you will become. A victim, who is broken, exhausted and bewildered as a consequence of the multiple manipulative campaigns that we have unleashed against them. This person who we once adored, idealised and worshipped has been systematically stripped of their self-esteem, confidence and sanity. All by our twisted hands. We will make no such admission of course. This person who is desperately clinging on in the hope of making us see the U-turns and volte faces is just another of our victims but to you she is the crazed stalker who will not leave us alone. She is the abusive harlot who has made our life a misery. She is the deranged banshee who has spent the last few months embarking on a horrific attack against our person. We are doing our best to uncouple from her and become free of her baleful influences but it is hard. She shows such determination to keep within our world, calling us, messaging us and turning up without warning or invitation. We reel off the imaginary catalogue of ridiculous behaviours before then listing the actual truthful actions of this poor person who has been driven to such lengths by their desire to remain with us and make us see sense. We do not admit to that. Oh no, we explain how this person will not let go (truth) because she is obsessed with us (lie). She keeps contacting us (truth) because she is determined to do us down (lie). You may even have occasion to meet this poor, bedraggled creature who will immediately launch into a tirade warning you to run as far and as fast as you can away from us. This never ever concerns us however because nobody ever believes you. All I ever need do is point out that she is jealous of you and I. You always believe me. You do so because I have you in my grip, in the middle of the delicious love-bombing and you believe every word that comes from my charming mouth. She on the other hand is yesterday's news. A dangerous and malevolent individual who has hurt me savagely. Of course the outgoing victim never does herself any favours by haranguing me and trying to persuade you to leave me. Her wild demeanour and scurrilous words merely add to the picture that I have already painted. If you have any scintilla of doubt about the hurt that she has already put me through then I will invite you to speak to a couple of my friends. These lieutenants will discharge their assigned role beautifully by continuing the propaganda against the outgoing victim and convincing you that she really is a vicious harpy with several screws loose.

I on the other hand am the real victim here. I treated her well and gave her everything but for some reason it was not enough. I tried, I really did and as you can see from the marvellous way that I treat you, it is obvious that I am the good person. I explain the horrible behaviour I have been subjected to. This allied with the frenzied lunatic who you have witnessed easily convinces you of the truth of my tale and your soaring empathic nature results in you wanting to care and look after me, to nurse me through the trauma I have been subjected to. They always hurt me you see and that is why I need you, to look after and care for me. It is the truth. Honest.

World in My Eyes

I want you to look into my eyes and there you will find yourself. You will see everything that you have ever desired in my eyes. Every hope you have will shine from my eyes, everything you have every wanted will be visible to you. However, you will not look on the ordinary version of those things that you covet. You will see the enhanced variety, the shining and gleaming types of those things which you hold dear. I want you to stare deep into my eyes and focus on what you find there. Allow yourself to become absorbed by those deep pools of desire as you begin to lose yourself. It is only natural to want to fall into what you see, to let go of those constraints and inhibitions so that you become consumed totally by what you are looking upon. No harm can come of it for you are only staring at the very things which matter to you. Honesty, humility, humour and desire. Integrity, values and passion. Everything which you regard as a virtue can be seen in the world that I have created in my eyes. What you tell me, both directly and indirectly, will invariably come into your view within a matter of moments. It is like a far flung barren planet which has been discovered by intergalactic explorers who commence terraforming of the planet in order to make it habitable. Everything you want becomes a reality as they are formed in this world right before you. The interests you have appear; the places you enjoy visiting come into view and the events that you like to attend flare up. You are hypnotised as this wonderful world forms in my eyes, all generated by you although you are so taken by the process and what you see that you do not realise that all I am doing is taking the materials that you are furnishing me with and replicating all those things that you want to see. I am skilled in ensuring you tell me everything about yourself to add to all the preparatory work that I undertook before I made my move. Like ingredients in a particularly delicious cocktail I combine all of these things which matter to you and weave my magic to create a drink which you will never want to stop drinking. It is intoxicating and invigorating, an addictive concoction that once you have taken your first sip you will continue to draw deep on. You have no chance to escape because from the moment I cause you to look deep into my eyes I show you all the things that you want. I show you the world where you are queen, where nothing will ever hurt you, where your true worth has been recognised by me. This world is perfect. Everything is in its place and accords with your values. You ever stop to question how is it that I have been able to create this world so accurately and so brilliantly. You do not query how this creation is so magnificent because it is everything that you have always wanted. From the fairy tale existence you promised yourself as a young girl through to the correct treatment that you deserve as the decent person that you are, everything appears on this world which I have tailor made for you. It is captivating, mesmerising and alluring. You want this world more than anything you have ever known. You want to be absorbed by it and to fall deep into its fabric, cossetted by the security that it provides. Nothing goes wrong on this world, it is a clear utopia and best of all it is right there before you. All you need to do is maintain my gaze, letting yourself fall deep, deep into this marvellous world and everything will be alright. Everything will remain wonderful.

What you never realise is that this world will be consumed in an instance. In just one blink, this utopia will be obliterated and it will be as if it never existed. The dark inky pools that are the reality of these eyes will devour this created world, erasing it just as readily as a black hole consuming a planet. Once again the darkness will take hold and annihilate the fabrication which you held so dear. Even when this happens you will go on searching though. You will stare deep into my eyes, trying to find this world again amidst the ink-black darkness. There is no light that can shine any longer which may just happen to illuminate where this world has gone to. The darkness is absolute because it is the darkness that is the reality. Not that it will stop you trying. You will keep looking and searching, trying to find the perfect world once again, hoping for it to emerge into the light once again. You will keep trying and that is why we show you the world in our eyes.

Sitting Target

You are a sitting target. You have no inkling of what awaits you. You can have no anticipation of what is going to happen to you. I chose you because I knew that you would fall prey to my overtures. I chose you because I knew that you would provide me with the fuel that I require. I chose you because I knew that you would be unable to resist my approach. I chose you because I knew that you would not be able to fathom out what would happen to you when I commenced my devaluation of you. Everything was already decided for you. Everything was mapped out and pre-destined. My kind and I stand by the adage that every battle is won before it is ever fought. You were conquered before I even spoke to you.

What part did you play in this? You never asked to me ensnared by me. You did not ask to be seduced by me. You ever asked to me devalued, degraded and denigrated by me. All you did was appear in my sights. That is all that it takes and once you do, once I have decided that you are what I want you do not stand a chance. You have no chance to evade me because you have no idea what I am. You have no understanding of the danger that wraps its tendrils around you. You have no comprehension of the total and utter blitzkrieg of affection that is coming your way and how it is built on an illusion. You have no chance to evade my reach, to escape my clutches or to avoid the toxic effect of being entangled with me. You are the complete victim, totally innocent and devoid of blame. You are a good person, a decent person and an honest person and it is those traits which draw me in, like a shark scenting blood, those valued traits which are what my kind always look for. The hallmarks of the empathic individual. Yes it is unjust. You never asked for this to happen, you never took any step to invite this treatment that has been meted out against you, but that does not matter. All that matters is you are who you are. Should you ever ascertain who we are and learn more of all of the other people who have been sucked into my world and then discarded, broken and spent; you will see so many similarities. All of the other victims are similar to you. The nasty and the selfish are of no interest to my kind. The types of wretched individuals who perhaps deserve the abuse that we dole out are of no interest to us. They do not provide us with what we need. The despicable and the disgusting are never targeted by us. It is people like you, straightforward, kind and loving people who really do deserve better but who are the classic victims of our kind. We do not respect the fact that you deserve to be treated better. We have no concern for the fact that you may have already been chewed up by one of our kind previously. In fact we welcome the fact that this may have happened as we regard this act as one whereby you have been tenderised in anticipation of our feeding frenzy.

We watched you from afar before we made our move. We observed you at work and at home, watching who you interacted with. We carefully created a picture of your world as we spoke to friends and family, gathering those all-important shards of information in preparation for our seduction of you. You sat in that bar talking with your friends, unaware of the person sat in the next booth that was noting what you drank and listening in to the conversations that you were having. Your social media output has been pored over, viewed and dissected as I gathered more and more information about you. You walked down the driveway from your house in the morning to collect your post, oblivious to the fact that I was sat in the car opposite observing you. I knew your routine as well as you did as I made careful notes about the places you visit, the people you socialise with and who your family are. All of this was added to my dossier as I constructed my intelligence ready to use it against you as I seduced you.

Once the love-bombing began and those manipulative missiles of pseudo-affection rained down on you, you had no chance. The sitting target that you are meant that within a short space of time you succumbed to the shock and awe campaign and you fell swiftly and easily into my grip. You were not the first and you will not be the last. There are targets everywhere, absolutely everywhere and all of them are just sitting, waiting anticipating nothing.

Piercing the Veil

Much of our effort in creating a false reality revolves around ensuring that everyone but you thinks well of us. We work hard to ensure that your friends like us, your family think highly of us and we are well regarded in the community. This provides us notably with fuel from a great array of different appliances. It also generates for us a whole range of manipulative methods to use against you from triangulation to lieutenants to character assassinations. It is a sweet sight indeed to watch you as you try to convince those who have become indoctrinated to how wonderful we are, to the contrary. Your attempts are futile and we derive such satisfaction from your frenzied attempts to persuade people that we are the devil incarnate when all you are doing is convincing people that you are exactly what we said you are. Crazy.

Occasionally, the astute amongst our victims realise that these attempts to persuade the indoctrinated merely provide us with more fuel and result in the victim digging themselves deeper and deeper into an unpleasant hole. These are rare occasions when the victim works out what we are whilst still attached to us. If the veil I pierced in this way it is usually the case that the lesser members of our brethren make good their departure. The effort that is required in maintaining the façade becomes too great and will not return the fuel that is necessary. The lesser type of our breed are quick to realise when they have been exposed in this way or worked out and in such circumstances they will jettison their victim and move straight on to whoever else has been lined-up as a contingency. The greater type of our kind however are never willing to give up the ghost so easily. You may have worked us out and punctured our supply of fuel but we will not let the matter rest there. Should you show an awareness of what we are and even more so act on that knowledge, then you can expect to be punished for your audacity in exposing us. We do not take kindly to those who seek to tarnish our reputations. You are inferior to us and you are not permitted to cause our standing to be reduced in the eyes of the world. Should you attempt to persuade others that we are not all that we seem we will unleash the full force of our ignited fury against you. We will embark on a sustained and vicious campaign that has one aim and one aim only. Your destruction. You will be hunted down, subjected to repeated abuse and your life will be made a living hell. Every conceivable method of harassment, bullying and intimidation will be rolled out against you. We will slander you to anyone who will listen, we will report you for non-existent crimes, and we will report you to the authorities for child neglect, breach of environmental codes and regulations. You can expect your employer to be made fully aware of all your non-normative behaviour. The sex tapes that we obtained from you will appear all over the internet. Your mobile number will be plastered across cyberspace so that you are bombarded with calls from pestering males. Your property will be defaced and destroyed, money taken from you, loans taken out in your name as we seek your financial obliteration. You will be assaulted, pestered, harassed and victimised. It will be incessant and it will be brutal. Of course it is your entire fault because it is never our fault. You brought this on yourself and you will pay the ultimate price for your treason and treachery. This onslaught will go on and on until either you to cease to exist or we are removed. It will take a dramatic and final outcome to bring an end to this campaign. You will need to move far away from us or ensure that we are imprisoned for a long time. Of course it is not beyond the realms of possibility that those who experience the most malign of our kind seek the ultimate way of escape.

Nothing's Impossible

There are times when even my charm is in limited supply and is refusing to stretch. This often happens when I have subjected a victim to a fierce period of devaluation so that they have been pushed to their limits and they are at breaking point. Something stirs inside of them which causes them to decide that they need to escape me. They may not fully understand why but they know that they need to depart. It may be the case that an external influence is interfering in my carefully laid plans of denigration and this meddling threatens to puncture of even sever my supply of delicious negative fuel. It is at these moments when I am staring at the potential loss of a succulent supply of fuel that I make a particular play in order to prevent the cessation of supply. In such circumstances I will ensure that there is only you and I and that the potential for external interference is at a minimum. I need to ensure that I have your undivided attention and there will not be somebody else seeking to throw a spanner into the works. I want them excluded and banished so that I can concentrate entirely on you and make my last throw of the dice.

"I know that this time I will have to change," I will begin as I fix you with my most earnest of looks. You stop what you are doing and look at me and already I can see the indecision in your eyes as I start with this sentence. It is always a good opening gambit. You and your like love to think that we can change, that there is some goodness deep within us that can be harnessed and used to get us back on track. You are great believers in redemption.

"I need a miracle to help me this time, " I continue as I underline the gravity of the task that I am faced with. By according such gravitas to your stated intention to depart, I demonstrate just how seriously I am taking your threat. Inside I am exploding with rage at your audacity in daring to even to suggest that you will leave me. Me, of all people, me who has done so much for you. It is everything I can do to contain the fury but I know I must do so for an explosion now will be what finally pushes you away.

"How did we come to be this far apart?" I ask fixing you with a pleading look. By underlining that we were once so close, nay inseparable, I am appealing to your desire to bring us back to that closeness once again. This also allows you a chance to talk and talk is something you like to do. I let you trot out all the perceived injustices that you have supposedly suffered at my hands. I hear little of it because I know that you are mistaken and this is all based on your incorrect perceptions of me. This time I just have to let it wash over me in order to allow my influence to exert itself over you. I cannot stand to be criticised and inside I am dying but I am taking this blow for the greater good, the greater good of ensuring this precious fuel supply remains intact.

"Just tell me what you need me to do and I will do it," I trot out next, conning you into thinking that you have some vestige of power and authority over me, when of course you have none. Again in order to serve my own purposes I am content to allow you to think that you can bring some influence to bear over me. Again this will give you a chance to detail all of the change and remedial behaviours you expect me to engage in. I will nod and make the appropriate noises as you ramble on about the changes you want me to effect. I pluck the lines which I have heard others use on so many occasions to enable me to continue my con. You are suckered by it on every occasion. I know it works and this is why I do it.

"I know we can get through this, nothing's impossible," I add as I take your hands and stare into your eyes. Invariably this line secures you giving me yet another chance and your relief eclipses my own as I know that I have you once again. Your joy at not parting provides me with even further fuel and I can allow you a brief golden period by way of reward. After all, you may as well enjoy it because it is not going to last for long is it?

Soaring

We derive such pleasure from seeing you climb high. We treasure the fact that you soar high into the sky, buoyed by the support and the perfect love that we bear for you. It gives us immeasurable delight to know that we are responsible for your ascendancy and that heady climb into the stratosphere is down to us. We watch with open-mouthed delight as like a graceful bird you take to the air and with minimal effort you fly higher and higher. You are floating on the sensation of being loved and adored and it is only us that can engender that feeling in you. It is only our kind that knows exactly how you tick and what it is that gives you that feeling of delight and invulnerability. We send you skywards, powered by waves of desire and love, each gesture and word helping you climb ever upwards. You swoop and dart, flitting across the beautiful sky, the sun blazing down, warming the air as you cut through the azure, carefree and untouchable. Nothing can hold you back. You are unfettered and unrestrained, free to climb ever upwards, following your uncluttered path into an ascendancy. Nothing can stand in your way and even if it did you would surmount it with absolute ease such is the all-conquering nature of our love for you. This perfect and complete love is the very thing that enables you to climb upwards, rising higher and higher, the world becoming smaller and more distant beneath you. It is a heady and intoxicating experience as you keep going upwards, the air thinning but having no appreciable effect on your upwards trajectory. It is a wonder to behold as you climb upwards into the sky, leaving all concerns, troubles and tribulations far behind. You are heaven bound, angels coaxing you into the firmament, urging you ever upwards, soaring to a zenith of happiness and delight. The world spins away beneath you, a dizzying array of concerns which no longer affect you. Every word we say and every act we perform is designed to help you keep going upwards. We want you to climb higher and higher moving through that rarefied atmosphere where nobody else has gone before you. That is why you are so special. That is why you and only you can climb this high, surging high above your peers, gaining height and stature over others and all of this borne on the tide of perfect love and desire that we generate. You know no limits and dare not even contemplate just how high you might climb as you continue to soar. You feel unstoppable, there is nothing that can pin you back, hold you down or prevent your inexorable rise. You are magnificent, the fiery glint of the sun reflecting from you, your angelic countenance now barely visible to the mere mortals which stare up at your from below. They watch, heads tilted and hands lifted across their eyes, struggling to maintain their gaze as you climb higher and higher. How far might you soar, all the way to heaven where you rightly belong? You feel free, uplifted and elated. Can this get any better? You power forward as you surge upwards once again and then we smile the smile we have smiled so many times before as we lift the rifle and focus the crosshairs on your soaring frame. You remain in our sights as we begin to squeeze the trigger.

Sooner or later you must always fall. Always.

Ringing You

I know this ring is expensive. It sparkles and it shines. It is ostentatious yet elegant and I know what some of you may be thinking, yes, just like the narcissist when he first arrives. It is all dazzling, shining, mesmerising and showing off. That much is true but that is not the purpose of this post. No. This ring is real. It is very real. This ring is a symbol of my intent. I want you to wear this ring and I am sure, no I know that you will wear it. You see this ring binds you to me. It will ensure that you admire and love me by reason of such a grand gesture. Do you see how much I adore you? Do you see how much you mean to me so that I would have such a ring of such expense fashioned just for you and you alone? Who else would do that for you? Nobody because there is not anyone who is as good to you as me is there? Nobody treats you the way I do, do they? This is a special ring for a special person.

You see this ring signifies so much. It is a demonstration of your commitment to me. It is there to bind you to me for now you have agreed to ensure that I am provided for at all times. By wearing this ring you have accepted your role. Your role is to furnish me with fuel. Sweet, potent fuel in vast quantities. You are duty bound to lavish me with admiration, awe, affection and love to ensure that my voracious appetite for fuel is met. Placing this ring on your finger amounts to a contract between us. A contract that is water-tight and can only be revoked by me. You must not breach this contract. You must strive each and every day to provide me that fuel.

Should you fail in your obligation to provide me with the best quality positive fuel then I reserve the right, without qualification or condition and without notice to shift the supply of fuel to that of the negative variety. Your wearing of this ring will mean that you will endure the torment and misery that I will put you through in order to extract this negative fuel. By brandishing this ring on your finger, you have agreed to be subjected to my vacillating will, my capricious nature and the violent fury that rages with me waiting to be ignited. The moment this ring slides onto your finger and you smile in delight, showing the large glinting diamond off, you have consented to all manipulative machinations at my disposal. The ring cannot be removed. It does not work like that. It shrinks to grip your finger and no amount of twisting and pulling will free you from it. In much the same way that no amount of pulling and twisting will free you from my grip. Once that ring has been worn then you and I have been joined together. You are my appliance and you will do as I say. You will pump out that fuel and provide me with the emotional reactions I seek from my incessant torture of you. You gladly placed the ring on your finger. You wanted to wear it. Did you not think that I would extract nothing in return for furnishing you with such a delight? In fact, I knew you would think like that, that naivety appealed to me and is why I chose you.

Each and every humiliation, beratement, denigration and lambasting has been agreed to by you wearing that ring. It is done and must be so in order to allow me to get what I want and need. You will consent. You will submit. You will be subjugated to my will. You shall not escape. You shall not defy me. You shall not deny me that which is rightfully mine. You put on the ring. You agreed to what was to come. You must pay the price.

This is what happens when you accept this ring when it is offered by my kind and me. This is the necessary consequence of accepting such a luxurious gift. You would do well in future to be aware of this ring and what it signifies.

Does this ring have a name?

Of course it does.

It is suffering.

Fuelling the Attraction

I remember when I was younger that I would fall in love so quickly with the objects of my desire. To me there was nothing untoward about this. I found someone who had so many attributes that I admired and loved that it was entirely conceivable that I would fall head over heels in love with them. People often speak about love at first sight. I was a great believer in that phrase as it happened to me time and time again. I could not help but feel that way. It would never last however and I soon found myself falling in love with somebody else. They appeared to me and instantly I wanted them. I was infatuated with making them mine. I wanted to please them so they would love me back in the same intense way that I love them. I would say the most wonderful things to them and they would thank me and tell me how talented I was at writing down poems for them or with the way I would convey how I felt about them. I loved to hear this praise. I would sit and think about new ways I could get this new love of mine to think highly of me. I would concoct fresh ways of impressing them. I regularly would invent stories about the things that I had done in order to produce that amazed look and then lap up the marvellous things that they would say to me.

After a while I found that they did not say the praise as often. It became harder and harder to think of new things to say and do to draw this reaction from them. I found this unfair. Surely they realised and recognised my talent and brilliance, I knew they did because they had remarked upon it, but why did they not continue to do so? Why did I sometimes even become tired of hearing them say the same thing to me? As soon as I found the effect was less I would be off to hunt down someone new. It was easy enough. At Sixth Form College and then university I was immersed in a pool of intelligent, engaging ladies by the hundreds and then thousands. I merely had to place my net in the water and in moments I would catch somebody from whom I could then gather this praise and admiration I needed. I found that it yielded results for me if I had more than one girlfriend on the go at once. There were a couple of close calls and sometimes the tearful questioning I was subjected to when they became suspicious of my evasiveness or other behaviour would take place. I felt no shame or guilt in doing this. I wanted the attention of two ladies (sometimes more). Indeed on certain nights out at university I would make it my mission to see how many I could 'pull' and then bask in the warmth of their admiration. When the tearful inquisitions took place I realised I was not bothered at all by their distress. I just did not care. In fact, I realised I enjoyed the fact that they were getting upset over me. I found the fact that I had made them react in this way rather edifying. I would then go out of my way to upset one girlfriend whilst adoring the other. A few times I did used to wonder if this was normal. A couple of my friends had long-term girlfriends and when we spoke they assured me they had always been faithful to them. I did not believe them. Surely they did as I did? That was part of being young and learning wasn't it? Trying out new partners to see who you fitted with best. I just had not found the 'one'. I often believed I had done so as when a new prospect came into view I found myself drawn to them by the most powerful force. I needed to ensure they felt the same way. I had to make them want me too. I found I was very able at doing this, my natural magnetism and charm enabling me to seduce these ladies with ease.

The more women I seduced the stronger I felt. I was all-conquering. I saw someone, felt an instant connection and went after them. It did not matter if I was seeing someone already, this new person was obviously a better fit for me, and otherwise why would I feel so strongly about them? It just happened to be the case that every time someone better was available and I went after them. Was it the case that my existing girlfriend was inferior or had I become bored of her? Perhaps it was a bit of both. Either way I did not ponder long on this state of affairs, there was too much to do. Too many women to bring into my life, too much admiration and praise to extract from them and the need, always the need to put them down as well, to show them who was in charge and have them weeping as I chastised them for the smallest of transgressions. No matter how much I punished them they still wanted to be with me. I had always been told I was special and this confirmed this to me. If I was not brilliant why on earth would someone who has just been called every name under the sun still want to be with me and be my girlfriend? They knew they were on to something good.

This through those early years of college and university I moved hither and zither as I gathered conquest after conquest. It was intoxicating. I was addicted to hunting these ladies down, drawing them into my world and then seeing how long they would hang around once I tired of them and began to put them down. I would keep a list of the names and the time periods, compiling this chart and seeing the list become longer and feeling powerful.

Of course back then I was no aware of what was really happening. To me this as all that mattered. This was what life was all about. The hedonism and admiration that came with it. I loved it. This was the beginning of my life-long attraction to fuel.

Perfect Scents

I have written previously about Ever Presence. This is a deliberate state that we create so that you repeatedly think about us. We weave into your lives a number of triggers that affect each and every sense. When we are not there then something will trigger and a memory of me will flood into your mind with the associated euphoria of that once wonderful moment. This serves a purpose in causing you to want to be with me and making you susceptible to the inevitable Hoover.

One of my trademark steps is to use a form of this Ever Presence at the outset of a relationship. I will select a particular fragrance applicable to the newly acquired target. A recent example was the use of Chanel Allure Homme Sport. When my bottle of fragrance is running low I do not use it all up but I go and buy another bottle. Then when I select a target I choose an applicable fragrance that is to be used in my seduction and ensnarement of them. Accordingly, I would always wear Chanel Allure which my target would naturally compliment me on and she would naturally associate with me. After three or so encounters at an opportune moment when she remarks on how good I smell I will give her the bottle with a little fragrance left in it.

"Here, take this," I offer, "you can spray it on a scarf so you can always smell it and feel near to me."

This gesture is always met with thanks and a warm smile. The target thinks that she is being granted admittance into part of my world with that small gift. Of course she is utterly unaware that I am sliding a tendril around her as I present this token. She goes away happy and I of course have created another connection. The sense of smell is a great evoker of memory and emotion. I know it will not be long before I receive that first text confirming that my use of this technique has proven successful. Sure enough that evening my 'phone alerts me to a text message.

"I am lying on my bed holding a scarf to my face and drinking in your scent. How I wish you were here with me."

Later still.

"It is dark. I cannot see you or hear you but I know you are here with me. All I do is drink deep of your scent and I can feel you next to me."

After a day or two of deliberate incommunicado.

"I miss you. I have the scarf pressed to my nose. You are here but you are not. I need you. Please call me."

In order to ensure that my target becomes subsumed into my world and is malleable to my manipulative wiles I need to ensure I am present as often as possible. Technology has made this task far easier than it used to be, but the seemingly thoughtful gesture of the provision of a near empty bottle of scent works wonder. It is a significant step towards conquest and victory. I have a further target in my sights so I need to allocate a sense to her. I think this time it will be Truth by Calvin Klein. That seems apt somehow.

The Language of Love

I have always used the love letter as a method of building my connections with my target. I first started at school when one would write a short note and pass it across the class to the object of one's affection. With a sideways glance I would watch as she would open the piece of paper up and smile before nudging her friend sat beside her and both would look my way with a smile and a giggle. Ah, from such acorns did my prowess with the billet-doux grow.

Those early 'romances' which in truth lasted little more than a month or so before we moved on to someone else gave way to the first proper girlfriend and then more meaningful correspondences sprang up. I remember during the Easter holidays in my penultimate year at school I engaged in an exchange of letters with a young lady who lived in a village a little way from where I lived. She would write a letter and I would receive it the next day. I immediately wrote a reply and she would receive it the next day. Back and forth our letters went. Of course we had no such thing as Instant Messenger or text messages. E-mail was in its infancy and was certainly not something that was used from home. I remember she wrote on light green paper placed inside a green envelope. It certainly stood our when it arrived on the doormat in the morning. I of course responded by writing (no use of typewriter or word processor back then) on crisp white paper of a decent thickness which would be folded into a third and inserted into an envelope. I still have her letters along with all of the others that I have received. Once in a while I will lift the box from on top of the wardrobe and sit and rifle through the contents. I have no real interest in the content or returning to those moments, I usually do it in front of my current partner in order to provoke a reaction from her.

Those early letters exchanged that Easter began as exchanges about what we had been doing each day, talking about other friends and then began a mild flirtation. We ended up as girlfriend and boyfriend after the letter writing. This earned me considerable kudos with my peers since the girl in question was held up as one of the most desirable in the year (although looking back I suspect much of that was to do with the fact that she arrived in our first year well-developed for her age). I recall when we went to watch Platoon at the cinema on of our dates she told me,

"You are not my usual type. I usually go for older boys but I loved what you wrote to me. Nobody has done that before."

Whilst I cannot of course lay claim to be the only person who has written a love letter, it became apparent that it had become something of a dying art. I do not mean silly notes in class or something that resembles little more than an extract from a diary. Instead I am referring to the sweeping, grand, romantic proclamations of love and desire. Vulgarity is not allowed in these poetic pieces of literature, instead should one wish to express a physical need for coupling then the application of euphemism and analogy came to the fore.

I honed my craft corresponding with girlfriends from university. Invariably we came from different parts of the country and therefore during holidays we wrote to one another. I used this as an opportunity to sharpen my skills and polish my prose. The upshot was that thereafter although there was no real need to write to one another (we lived in the same place or even together) the production of a love letter left on a pillow or placed by a prepared breakfast on the dining table worked magically as a method of seduction.

I had a template of about five differing types of letter and have used them on several different ladies. I would copy them word for word with suitable alterations mutatis mutandis to cater for differences in appearance or demeanour. These crafted missives were powerful indeed. They created strong connections between my target and I. The content was such the lady in question would always be swept off her feet and of course when those loving words became barbed and thorny, she would retreat to where she kept them and weep over the beauty contained in those first letters. Knowing that these letters would be clutched in a shaking hand as the tears rolled down her cheeks however weeks down the line was edifying indeed.

I still use them. In a world governed by technology, text speak and the immediacy of communication, the provision of a hand-written billet-doux has a tremendous effect.

Hair's To You

I have always been a fan of red-headed women. Oh and blonde-haired ones too. Of course I love brunettes as well. From deep auburn to fiery titian, platinum blonde to ash blonde, chestnut to raven black I love them all. Show me red-gold, mahogany, black brown, highlights or lowlights they all work for me. Long hair, short hair, cropped, bobbed, straight or curly. I love them all. I recall on one occasion talking with a female friend who I had designs on. We were sat in the café of an art gallery and the topic moved onto hair. She asked me what my favourite type of hair colour was.

"Oh raven black, most definitely, I shot back without even pausing to think."

She smiled and raised a hand to push it through her raven black locks. If the waitress had come over and asked the same question then I would have said blonde as I gazed at her short bobbed blonde hair. On other occasions I might get asked this by someone else and naturally I would tell them my favourite. Lo and behold it just happened to be the same as the one she had.

"You are just saying that because it is my colour," she responded.

"No, it is my absolute favourite. All of my previous girlfriends had strawberry blonde hair."

"Really? I thought the one before me was a brunette. I saw a picture of her."

"Oh her? No, no, she was not my girlfriend. Goodness me no, she was just a friend. Admittedly we did lock lips a couple of times, but it was nothing, she was a tad obsessed if you really must know."

"Was she? I am sure you referred to her as your girlfriend."

"You must have her confused with an earlier one maybe. No, always been ladies with strawberry blonde hair, it is a particular weakness of mine."

If she had green hair with blue dots in it I would have said the exact same thing. Sometimes these comments have been said so many times but with the appropriate alterations that I cannot help but say them. Occasionally, if my target has some awareness and has been listening, I might contradict myself but I have enough charm and evasiveness to get out of the situation.

Hair colours and hair styles are such a useful device for currying favour with a target or by contrast upsetting them. When all is well in the world and we are enjoying our golden period, then whatever you do to your hair I love it. You can colour it, put in extensions or even shave it all off. I will always tell you how beautiful you look because that is what you want to hear. With every visit to the hairdresser's a lady wants that compliment. I have seen you sashaying back from a visit to the salon and parading before me. I will be effusive in my praise, espousing how natural it looks, how the colour sets off your eyes and the shape frames your face magnificently. I have a whole list of suitably complimentary comments to churn out when you return with your new 'do'.

The stock that a lady places in the power of a new hair style of hair cut is such that it really makes it too easy to gather some negative fuel. I can tell you are really happy with this new style and you are just waiting for the compliments. Not today. Why should it be all about you and your new hairstyle? What about me? I look after my hair too and have it cut every twelve days so it always looks smart, but do you say anything? No. You regard a man and his hair as purely something of function. You on the other hand regard the colour and style as an opportunity to express yourself. Feel free because I am only too happy to rain on your parade and make that sleek do go frizzy. I will frown and peer at your new hairstyle.

"What's wrong?" you ask as your triumphant smile vanishes.

"It does not suit you."

"Why? How? Roger at the salon said it was very me."

"Well he would when you spend that ridiculous sum of money there. It does not suit you. It makes your face look too....severe."

"Are you serious?"

Damn right I am serious. This is about getting some lovely fuel from you and this is too good an opportunity to pass up. Whereas once I rolled out the barrage of compliments, I know issue my damning verdict on how wrong the colour is, it is too short, too long, and too voluminous. I will pick fault and soon have you running from the room to the bedroom to cry and try and alter it. You bring it on yourselves you know, you really do.

Seconds Out Round One

I know a number of you ask about my interactions with the good doctors, Dr E and Dr O so I thought I would take you back. Way back. My first involvement with these people of medicine was not with Dr E or Dr O but a fellow who I shall refer to as Dr M. I thought I would take you back to my first meeting with Dr M. It was a cold winter's day when I entered the elegant building where Dr M had his consulting rooms. They are in the same building as where I would later learn that Dr E and Dr O practise. I was shown into a drawing room which had an open fire but it was not lit. The room was warm nevertheless. Dr M was already sat in front of his expansive desk. He rose to greet me but I walked straight past him and sat in a chair. He tried not to look taken aback but I knew that he was. He sat down and adjusted his position as he placed his fingertips together creating a triangle and rested his hands on his chest. He was clearly trying to conjure up an image of intelligence. I was not impressed.

"Good morning Mr Tudor, I am Dr M. I will be working with you. Thank you for addressing the administrative details with my secretary, I appreciate it is a bit of a bind but the paperwork needs to be in place. I thought that today we could just have a general discussion rather than launch into specifics. A fireside chat if you will. I usually take notes but I am not going to do so today. So let me ask how are you?"

I said nothing. I looked at the doctor's shoes. I noticed he was wearing Chelsea boots which interested me but not enough to comment on it. The doctor waited and I could hear a clock ticking in the room. It was somewhere behind me. There was no other sound. The walls in this old building were thick, not like the tissue and spit of modern constructions. The door was solid as well. No noise would be heard from beyond and I reasoned nobody would hear what was said in here either.

"I asked how are you?" the doctor repeated after a moment of waiting. I shifted my gaze to look at him but I still said nothing. He seemed unfazed by my silence.

"Very well. Let's begin by discussing why you are with me today."

I waited but there was no question. I remained silent. I looked over at Dr M's desk. It was an antique partner's made from mahogany and was inset with maroon leather. It was one of those large desks which had draws on both sides so that a partner, in whatever business it might be, would sit on one side and an underling, some kind of clerk, would sit directly opposite him sharing the desk. There was a large leather chair on the other side of the desk. The top of the desk bore a couple of books although I could not read the titles from where I was sat and a neat pile of papers. I could see a pen lying on its side also.

"I appreciate you do not want to be here but you are now. In order for us to help one another we do need to have a conversation," said Dr M.

I flicked my gaze back at him and focussed on his suit. It was navy, heavy looking most likely wool. There was a pinstripe in the material. I wondered if he purchased two pairs of trousers with the suit. He looked like a man who spent a lot of time on his backside and this would mean the woollen crotch of his trousers would soon wear away. A second pair was a must. I glanced at Dr M's crotch to try and ascertain if I could see a whole forming. A small opening in the trousers through which his doubtless white underwear could be viewed. So far the wool was holding out.

"Very well. Why don't you tell me something about yourself?" he invited.

I was nonplussed earlier but now I was becoming bored. I let my eyes wander over to the fireplace. It was substantial and I thought it was a pity that there was no fire lit. I could see logs stacked up inside the fireplace but the flames were absent. No doubt it would contravene patient safety having a fire in here. I baulked at using the word patient. That was what he regarded me as. I was no patient. I was not some drooling imbecile wheeled in by white uniformed staff and followed by anxious relatives. I was no drink-addled half-wit whose brain had turned to mush through years of alcohol abuse so he would routinely soil himself. Those were the type of degenerates, admittedly well-looked after degenerates that normally came to these places.

"Whenever you are ready Mr Tudor," he gave me a short smile which I assume was meant to reassure me. I looked at him again and fixed him with a stare. Interestingly he met my gaze. His expression was not challenging nor was it threatening. He just looked at me as I looked at him. He glanced towards his desk and then moved slightly in his seat. Yes he was prone to fidgeting, that crotch would soon be worn away on that suit. His shirt was white which amused me. Only police officers and airline pilots wear white shirts. Even though I could see it was expensive it should not have been white. I did notice that it was double-cuffed so that was something at least. Single cuff would have generated scorn and heaven forbid he wore a short-sleeve shirt under a suit jacket I would have walked straight out.

"We have plenty of time, so just when you are comfortable."

Indeed we did have plenty of time. Two hours' worth thanks to the power of my parents' cheque book. So the pair of us sat in that grand drawing room with the absent fire and let two hours pass in complete silence. Dr M said nothing more as he waited for me to speak and I said nothing more as I had nothing to say to him. I concentrated on using my silence to make him feel uncomfortable. I could tell by the way he kept shifting in his seat he wanted to speak or listen. He made to speak on several occasions but something prevented him from doing so. I occupied my thoughts with planning the rest of my day and also how I might entice his frosty looking but obviously hugely efficient secretary into my world. I ran through a variety of scenarios which made the time pass rather quickly. I was almost taken by surprised when Dr M cleared his throat and spoke.

"Well our time is at end this week Mr Tudor. I shall see you again next week same day and the same time. Good day," he said pleasantly as he rose from his seat.

I said nothing. I walked past him and headed to the door as the surge began inside me.

Round one to HG.

But Why Does He Do This?

I have heard this said so many times, read about it from bewildered and perplexed people and know from experience the confusion accompanies this question.

"But how could he do this to me after everything else? He said he loved me.I know he loved me. How does someone love someone else in such a perfect way and then act as if he does not even know them?"

I have written about how the empath likes to know everything. This is not because you are big-headed or wish to boast. You like to know everything in order to allow you to help. You need to understand a situation. It has to make sense to you. You must be able to comprehend what has happened and find some logical reason for the occurrence. This is why you spend so long trying to work us out. This is why when we are doling out the silent treatment you need to ascertain why we are doing it (I think now you understand we do it because we need to not because there is a valid (according to your reality) reason for this behaviour). It is a natural empathic reaction. If you understand why something has happened you can then consider the ways in which it can be addressed, remedied and fixed. You want everything to be alright.

Accordingly, when our devaluation occurs to you it comes out of nowhere. Yesterday we held hands as we walked through the park together and kissed beneath the spreading oak. Today you have been subjected to a nasty period of name-calling and blaming. You are dumbfounded. Where on earth did that come from? In your reality it makes no sense at all. One minute everything is okay, nothing changes but then suddenly we are being horrible to you. It just does not add up. It makes no sense. It gets worse. Not only does it not follow in a logical sense since our response (viewed in your reality remember) seems random, how can a person who says he loves you then batter you with his fists, lock you out of your home, sleep rape you, smash up your car, spit on you and so on? Not only is it not a normal sequence of events if you love somebody then you just do not do that, do you?

This is what makes it so difficult for you to comprehend. We have conned you into thinking that we loved you. We gave you the huge seduction and dazzled you with the golden period. We know what you perceive love to be and we gave it to you in spade loads all manufactured by Narc Inc. Our production line went into overtime creating these false acts and hollow declarations of love but you fell for it. You always do. Accordingly, you were duped into thinking that we loved you so that when we begin to devalue you it flies completely in the face of what you understand to be the situation.

You will sit for hours with your close friends and recite example after example of all the wonderful things that we have said and done and then ask,

"How can he hurt me when he loves me so much?"

It is utterly perplexing. Naturally there is method in this madness. If it made sense, if there was a logical reason for this volte face you are more likely to accept it and walk away. This twisted and nonsensical logic is purposefully designed to keep you with us because:-

- You must know what has happened and make sense of it
- You want to make things rights
- You want the wonderful golden period again

All of this keeps you right besides us. Guess what? We dole out even more awful behaviour and it still does not make sense and you still do not go. We give you a glimpse of the golden period and your confusion increases. He does still love me I knew it. Then the door is slammed shut and you are left confused yet again but even worse this time, the brief return to the golden period has given you additional hope. You still do not go.

For once, rather than looking at it through your own eyes, consider it from our point of view. The devaluation does not come out of nowhere. It does to you but not to us. It happens because you are not giving us our fuel in the strength, quantity and frequency we demand. That is the logic behind our change in behaviour.

Why is it then that we are able to hurt you when we love you so much? Again, look at it through our eyes and the answer is straight forward. We never loved you. Accordingly, we are not affected by what appears (in your world) to be a hurtful and contradictory shift in our behaviour. Let me help you further. To us you are just an appliance. Initially because this appliance does what we want we look after it. We clean it, maintain it and take pride in it. Then it goes wrong. It is too much effort to try and repair it. We are horrible to you in order to make you work in a different way rather than trying to repair you to run as normal. Remember how people would slap the side of their television to make it work or give the washing machine a kick in the hope of causing it to run properly? You are just the same. You are an appliance and we give you a boot be it figurative or literal to make you provide us with fuel of a negative nature. We eventually get fed up that you are not working as we want you to so we chuck you on the scrap heap like so many discarded fridges, computers and washing machines. We have seen a new, shiny model which has attracted our attention instead.

So when you sit and wonder why this devaluation has happened, why our behaviour makes no sense and how can it be that someone who expresses such perfect love can be so hurtful, you know the answer. It makes no sense in your world but every sense in our world where you are just an appliance. Perhaps you had better start thinking about making some self-improvements and increasing your longevity yes?

A Missive From Mother

Do you remember Dr M? The fine suit wearing doctor with the soon to be worn away crotch? Of course you do. Well as you will recall the first consultation ended in a resounding victory to me as I kept him at bay with my silent treatment. I fair floated out of his consulting room and exited onto the cold street outside. Two days after this trouncing of Dr M I received a letter. I knew straight away who it was from. She always used 100gsm manila C5 envelopes. The quality and weight of the envelope was something she was fastidious about. She would often snort at personal letters which arrived in anything which was white and below the weight she preferred. I naturally recognised her immaculate copperplate handwriting as well. I knew what would be contained in the enclosed letter but I read it anyway.

"Dear HG

To sin by silence when they should protest makes cowards of men.

Speak up or suffer the consequences.

With fondness

Mother"

I tore the letter up. Her hypocrisy was evident once again. There she was chastising me for remaining silence with Dr M when all through her life (or at least that much that I could actually recall) she had used silence. Silence to convey her fury with anyone who had not given her what she wanted. Silence to let people know that they were in the wrong. Silence to hurt. Silence to control. Silence to compel. The High Priestess of Hush was admonishing me for saying nothing. She should be praising me but then I had come to expect this. I keenly observed her deportment. Impeccable manners, politeness, punctuality and high standards. Shoes must always be black for men; there is no brown in town. A Windsor knot in my tie (I had to learn at ten years old to do it myself. I can remember standing in the living room with the tears of frustration trickling down my face as I was scolded for getting it wrong once again). Never wear white shirts unless it is a funeral or you are an airline pilot. Oh or a police officer. At dinner remember to ask "Do you know the Bishop of Norwich?" and "Is your passport in order?" All her lectures I absorbed and obeyed and most of all I learned all about her use of silence. I had done exactly as I should when dealing with someone who was trying to undermine me. That Dr M was trying to unnerve me and make him the superior being in the room. He soon came undone when faced by the Tudor Icewall. I did precisely the right thing but there we are it was the wrong thing according to the Duchess of Disdain. I did not take kindly to the threat contained in the letter either but I could not ignore it. And she knew that. Of course she knew that. She fires off one of her standard howitzer quotations in order to gain the high ground. Typically she was economic with her writing too.

"No letter should ever be more than a page in length, anymore and you are waffling."

I can hear her saying that now. Mind you, she was right about that and was right about most things, I am like her in that respect, that much I will concede. Nevertheless I did not welcome this diktat and hurled the torn pieces of paper on the floor before I stormed out of my house. I felt wounded by this correspondence. She could always wound me so easily with her letters. Whenever she wanted to set me straight she would send me a letter. It was like a papal bull and it always made me feel crippled. Whenever I received one of these letters I could feel the scorching criticism tearing through me and I needed to douse it. I needed to find a salve for the affliction. It was no good confronting her. She would only make matters worse. No others would pay in order to ease my suffering and pay they did.

I lambasted the girl on reception at the office for not having her hair tied up and found three other petty reasons to tear a strip off her. She was soon in tears. I threw a report from a junior colleague back at him and told him to come back when he had learned how to do joined-up writing. I told my secretary her forthcoming extended weekend break was cancelled because there was too much work to do. I removed another colleague from leading a team and appointed one of his peers instead. I knew from her grateful smile and thankful gaze that I had credit to be used between her legs and I would readily do so by the end of the day. I wrote some disgusting graffiti about a head of department in one of the cubicles in the gentlemens' bathroom. I got my secretary to ring the restaurant where I did most of my entertaining and as I stood listening she was instructed to tell them that their sablefish was sub-standard and for that reason my expense account would be used at a competitor establishment. The manager of the restaurant rang four times to apologise and sent a bottle of champagne in order to try and in back my patronage. I called my sister and told her how useless she was and she was never to ring me ever again. I cancelled a meeting and spent two hours blitzing three fuel prospects with texts, ensuring the content became progressively filthier. I telephoned my then girlfriend and explained I had to take someone else out for dinner in the evening and put the phone down on her. I was a whirlwind of malice throughout the rest of the day until as 6pm approached I realised the horrible burning inside had ceased and I felt cleansed. I say at my desk and dragged my hand across my face relieved to have overcome the weakness that threatened to topple me as a consequence of that single sheet of paper with the minimum of words etched upon it.

I opened one of the drawers on my desk and selected a single heavy sheet of cream paper. I set it straight before me and taking up my fountain pen I began to write.

"Mother dearest,

The word listen contains the same letters as the word silent. Dr M will listen.

Yours

HG"

I slid the letter in the envelope and smiled. She would be proud of me this time, surely?

Tell Me What You Are Thinking

You may remember Sophie who was one of my ex-girlfriends. She was a happy-go-lucky kind of person and loved dashing from person to person wishing them well. She was like a machine spewing out good wishes, pleasantries and compliments.

"You look really well, you have lost weight."

"That skirt really suits you."

"I heard you recently got married, you must be really happy. That's really wonderful."

"Hey great news on that new job. I am really pleased for you."

"You look so content, I am really happy for you."

She was really, really good natured. Oh and she used really a lot. There was not a bad bone in Sophie's body and she always saw the good side of everything. I was by turns fascinated by how she managed it and also hugely attracted by her capacity to find victory from the jaws of defeat.

"He's grumpy because he is tired, he works very hard you know."

"I guess he didn't have time to speak to me today, he has really huge responsibilities. He really has."

"I don't mind that he forgot my birthday, I am just really pleased to be with him, that's a good enough present for me."

"I haven't heard from him so I guess he is out with his friends. It is really good to spend time with other people now and again, it keeps things really fresh."

She just skipped along merrily handing out kindness and warmth as if that was all she was programmed to do. I reached this conclusion because behind the permanent smile, the twinkling eyes and elated expression she wore there really was not a lot else. She had no interest in politics, current affairs, sport, history, literature and so on. She would listen patiently if I railed against the latest proposals concerning immigration nodding and smiling and when I asked her what she thought she would say,

"Oh all of that is for people really clever. It's not for me."

She was never dismissive in the sense of pouring scorn on it just because she was not interested or she did not understand. No, she just had no interest because she felt it was beyond her, not something she had to be concerned about. She was concerned with just one thing; skipping around like some modern day fairy sprinkling goodness everywhere. I do think she lacked much in the way of her own opinions and thoughts because she usually deflected any attempt to get her to critique something with a self-effacing comment like the one above. She never seemed to be caught in a moment of contemplation. She never seemed to pause for thought. She would just ask what I thought. She did this repeatedly. She was always concerned to know what I was thinking about.

"What's on your mind?"

"Penny for your thoughts?"

"What are you thinking?"

"Where is your mind today?"

"What's going on upstairs?"

Repeatedly throughout the day, as we sat watching television, after we had made love, during dinner, going for a walk, when I was shaving and so on. Always wanting to know what I was thinking. So I told her. From the mundane ("This shaving gel is not as good as the last lot I bought") through to the loving ("I was just thinking how wonderful it is being with you") to the scathing ("I was just wondering why on earth I am with such an empty-headed woman as you"). That was all she wanted to know. What was I thinking? On and on she would go, asking and asking and no matter what I said, be it compliment or nasty comment or ephemera she would smile and give a satisfied nod.

All of this made her very attractive to someone like me at the outset as she was a real high volume fuel generator but once that wore thin, it was rather difficult to denigrate her so she would react the way that I wanted. She put me in mind of that toy the Weeble. The catchphrase surrounding the Weeble was "Weebles wobble but they don't fall down. "Sophie was like that. I would be horrible to her and she maintained a smile (although I thought or at least hoped she was dying inside) and made an excuse and found a rationale for my unpleasantness. Insults just seemed to bounce off her. Smashing plates and ornaments caused her to stand and watch with a slightly perplexed look on her face before she tidied the pieces away. She did not cry or show fear. I would sit and flirt with other women online and comment to Sophie about how attractive they were. She would look over and agree with my comments and go on to compliment how white their teeth were or how she liked their hairstyle. If I wandered in during the middle of the morning she would just ask how my night had gone. I am sure she could smell other women on me but she did not seem to react. It was as if she was wrapped in this coating of pleasantness that was impervious to any nastiness thrown at her. She would either respond with a soothing comment, make an excuse for what I had said or done or just not react and get on with her day. I used to wonder if she had me worked out and this was her way of negating me. How had she done this? Who had put her on to this strategy?

One weekend she was staying with me at my house and I returned earlier than she expected. She had not heard me come in (it is often said that I manage to move around with a strange ability to be very quiet, popping up without warning) and I could hear her talking in the bedroom. I crept closer and through the slightly ajar door I realised she was talking to herself.

"Must not think, do not think Sophie. Just keep doing. Smile and shine, shine and smile. Keep going forward. Don't think about it. We know what happens when you think about it. Bad things happen but we don't do bad things do we? No. Only good things. I don't do the thinking, he does. I need to know what he is thinking and then I can make him happy, it is only fair, he deserves it doesn't he? Don't think Sophie, must not do that, come on, you can do this, you always do. Do it don't daydream."

I stole away and then realised what I needed to do to break her.

After that, whenever she asked me what I was thinking about, I would respond by saying "Nothing." She would look puzzled and ask again. I would repeat my answer. She then would look slightly anxious. I would turn to her and ask

"What are *you* thinking about?"

She would try and deflect my question by asking me again or changing the subject but now I knew how to get to her. I would never tell her what I was thinking and instead pursue her to tell me what was going on inside that sugary head of hers. It worked. She became upset, angry, frustrated and anxious so I kept it going and going and going. I have no idea why it troubled her so much. Her eyes filled with panic when I kept saying nothing and then she seemed to shrink, her light dimming as I asked her about what she was really thinking. She could not cope with it. I did not work out what it was about thinking that caused her so much consternation and I did not care, all that mattered to me was being able to provoke her into giving me that emotional reaction. It seemed that too much thinking on her part was a dangerous thing indeed.

New and Improved

You messed up. I gave you the world, I really did. I truly gave you everything you ever wanted from someone. I know I did because this is what I always do. I always deliver. You did not though and you let me down. Despite everything I said, everything that I did you failed. Oh I hear you bleat on about how you loved me like nobody else. You protest about all the things you sacrificed for me, all the things you did for me and how you put me ahead of everything else in order to please me, to make me happy. Stop going on about yourself will you? It is not very becoming. This hysteria surrounding how you pulled out all the stops, gave your all and did everything that I ever asked of you, even doing some things you did not like. Ah I see, you complain about it now, but you did not at the time did you, you charlatan? You disgust me.

I am well rid of you and in a way I suppose I must thank you because if you had not failed you would not have made me realise how we did not belong together. I did everything I could to make it work but you let me down. Thank goodness I woke up and saw it otherwise I would still be trapped by you. You at least enabled me to realise how flawed you actually are and I won't be making that mistake again. Not a chance of that happening. In fact, as testament to just how wonderful I am and how brilliantly I treat you I have someone else. What do you mean I wasted no time in moving on? Why should I? I am not going to sit around and bemoan how you let me down. That will not serve any purpose and besides I cannot help it if people want to be with me, it is only natural.

Yes I am with Lauren now. She is wonderful. She is everything I have ever wanted and I am her soul mate. I know that we are going to be very happy together now. She is the one. I know I thought that of you, but you misled me. Lauren is not like that. I am moving in with her next week. It makes perfect sense. I want to be with her all of the time. She is beautiful, just look at her, perfectly put together. She is so shiny and new. I am head over heels in love with her; I cannot be apart from her. Take a look. If you had been more like her then I would not have had to punish you the way I did. That is not going to happen with Lauren. No way. I can only see a bright and beautiful future for us. I hope she falls pregnant soon as our child will be such a wonder to behold. Thank God I did not have a child with you. Imagine that? Good God that would have been terrible having to share a child with a monster like you. Lauren will be a first class mother, we have already talked about it and I can tell that she is keen. She adores me and always will. Not like you. You had your chance but you messed it up. You only have yourself to blame. Oh I know what you are like, you will try and make out that it was me that was the problem but I know it was you. So do all my friends and yours. Yes I have already spoken to them and they agree that I am better off without you and that Lauren and I are the perfect couple. She always knows what to say you see. She understands me like nobody else does. She gets me. She is the only one. I bought a new 'phone with an increased megapixel camera because there will be so many photographs I have to take of Lauren and I. I want all those perfect moments captured so I can show the world how happy we are together. I know other relationships have not worked out but that is what happens when you get duped by harpies. Lauren is not like them. She is not like you. We have booked a holiday away already. Two weeks in the sunshine. We are going to have such a brilliant time being together in paradise. You can expect plenty of postings on Facebook so feel free to look in on them, I know you will. You can expect all my friends to be talking about us. We are the golden couple. Thank goodness I found her. This is it. This is the one for me. We just fit together. It is as if she knows what I am thinking. She listens and learns and then always knows the right thing to say and to do. It is marvellous and just shows why we belong together. I know you will need to know all of this because, well, I deserve to be happy after what you did to me.

You should be happy for me, you should, that is if you really do love me. You tell me you do but that does not matter now. I have a perfect love with Lauren and this is the one that will last. I imagine we will be married by the summer. It will be a glorious ceremony and she will look absolutely stunning, polished and gleaming, stood just the way I want and looking at me with rapturous adoration.

I could not be happier, I really could not. I have my soul mate, I am her angel sent from heaven to make her happy and I will do that because I am so good at doing that for people. Everything is going to be just wonderful and you had your chance but you blew it. I get so excited when I find someone new and when I know they will be better than you. Someone who puts me first rather than themselves. Someone who deserves me. Someone who is not you. Someone who is new and improved.

The Grass is Always Greener

I attended a consultation with Dr E. The view from his consulting room looks over the gardens to the rear of the building in which his room is situated. It is a well-tended garden and is immaculate all year around. I have yet to see anyone working in it or any sign of someone working there. There are never any tools left lying around or piles of leaves gathered together waiting to be burned. The lawn is especially verdant. A lush, green carpet which is devoid of daisies and dandelions. It has been cut and rolled so it appears pristine.

"Now," began Dr E from his seat across the room from me. I moved my eyes from the garden to the doctor.

"We had been discussing your thirst for fuel."

I nodded.

"You explained to me about how you draw that from those nearest to you and at first this comes in a positive fashion through admiration and adoration."

I nodded again.

"Unfortunately however this never seems to last and you need to then collect what we have established is negative fuel based on negative emotional responses from those around us."

I gave another nod.

"From our discussions I understand you have an unquenchable thirst for this fuel. I understand that. Accordingly, since you must always gather this fuel you are going to obtain it in both positive and negative forms. I wondered whether today we might look at why it should not always come from a positive form. How does that sound to you?"

"By all means."

"Good. Now, you have told me previously about the different way that people provide you with this positive fuel. It is based on praise, attention, love, adoration and admiration. The nature of the provider influences the quality of the effect it has for you and also the nature of the praise etc. has an influence on the quality. Now I understand how you draw this positive fuel from numerous sources but let us focus on it all coming from just one source, the most obvious being that person you are in an intimate relationship with."

I gave another nod.

"We all like praise. We all enjoy being liked. It matters more to some than others. People offer attention and praise when they choose but as we have discussed you find it necessary to behave in certain ways that causes this to be given as a matter of course and in some instances you actively manipulate a scenario in order to produce this adoration. You have told me how you do this repeatedly during a typical day. "

I nodded once more and wondered when he was actually going to ask me something.

"So, my question is this, how might you ensure you get this positive fuel from just one person? How might you go about drawing it from one person and not needing to draw it from other sources? They may provide it voluntarily, that is fair enough, but I want you to focus on applying your manipulations to just one person to gather this positive fuel and leave the rest alone. How might you do that?"

"I don't think that it can be done."

Dr E remained silent as he used the void to encourage me to expand.

"I live in hope that someone might be able to satisfy me and give me this positive fuel all of the time."

This time it was Dr E's opportunity to nod.

"If they did it would make my life a lot easier. I would not have to seek the additional fuel from these other sources. You know, the lady in the coffee shop, people in the street, my colleagues and so on. The fact is I am not with the primary provider of my fuel all of the time."

"I see. So you feel a need to be with them all of the time?"

"Well no I don't and that is precisely because I am able to draw my fuel from other sources. If you denied me those secondary sources then I would be in trouble."

"What would you do?" asked Dr E.

"Well, if the stipulation is that I am only allowed, for the purposes of this discussion, to draw my fuel from one source I would have to be with that source all of the time."

"Because you need to draw on it frequently?"

"Precisely. No matter how much fuel say a girlfriend provides me in the morning I will need more and soon."

"How soon?"

"A few hours, sometimes less."

"Why?"

"Because if I don't get it I feel weakened and then well you know, it starts to make itself known."

"It being the creature?"

I nodded quickly.

"Very well. But if your primary source remains with you all of the time pumping out positive fuel you would not feel weak?"

"Yes but that isn't practical is it? I have a job to do, she usually has one too. I have to go places where she won't be there and I cannot be in constant contact on the telephone even when we are apart, however much I might try."

"Sure, sure but I want to leave the practical to one side for now. I want to understand your mind set and attitude to this. I can then look at the practicalities later."

"If you say so."

"So if you could be with this one person, this intimate partner, this primary source of your positive fuel all of the time you would not feel weak because they are giving you the fuel you need. This would sustain you?" suggested Dr E.

"For a period of time."

"I see. How long that would be?"

"I don't know because it has never happened."

"But you don't feel it will last because you referred to it sustaining you for a period of time?"

"Yes."

"Why do you say that? Could it not sustain your permanently, leaving aside the practicalities for now, but if that primary source is there all the time giving you praise, admiration, love and attention, won't that be sufficient?"

"No."

"You said that straight away. Why are you so sure?"

"Because in the past they have let me down."

"Okay but this time the source is not going to go away, it is going to keep producing positive fuel just as you need."

"It still won't work."

"Tell me why."

I leant back in my chair and stretched.

"Where do I start? They stop trying. They do not give me the level of admiration I need. I don't know why this is. It is not as if I stop being good to them. They always do this first. They don't look at me the same way that they used to. That shining in their eyes has dulled. I have seen it happen and I don't understand why. I am still the same, I still shower them with affection and make them feel wanted but they change. They don't praise me as often as they once did, notwithstanding how often I tell them of my achievements. It's them doctor, it as if they become bored of me but still want to be around me. I don't get it. I don't get it all. How can they be bored by someone like me? I hope they won't do this but they do. That's why I have to prepare my contingencies and have others waiting in the wings in anticipation of this happening. They make it happen. Not me. Experience has taught me that I have to have these reserves. Plus as well doctor there is so much fuel out there to be gathered and I know it wants to be supplied to me. A monk would be hard pressed to resist the lure of all this fuel. I am always wondering whether it will be sweeter and stronger than what I am getting already and guess what? When I go and get it I find out that it is. It is fresh and invigorating and it is all because the current supply is not doing what it should."

Dr E was scribbling energetically as I turned back to the window and looked out into the garden again.

"You see the grass is always greener doctor and I have to go and lie on it."

A few days ago I was recounting my consultation with Dr E. He and I were discussing whether I could be sustained from the provision of solely positive fuel from just one source, namely an intimate partner. I pointed out that this could not work, leaving aside how practical this really was, because the source always goes stale and I am forced to look upon the greener grass around me. The consultation continued.

"So you think that your intimate partner will always let you down because the fuel they will supply drops off in terms of quantity and quality?"

"I don't think it, I know it. It always happens."

"Understood. Why do you think this happens?"

"Because they let it happen."

"Do they let it happen or is it not the natural consequence of being with someone for a longer period of time."

"Familiarity breeds contempt?"

"Perhaps at the very least it might be less dazzling and less exciting."

"Well yes, that is what happens."

"Indeed and if this keeps happening could it not be the fact that this is normal, this is what happens when you get to know somebody for a period of time. The honeymoon period when everything is fresh, new and exciting ends and matters become more deep-seated and solid. The razzle dazzle gives way to something more substantial and long lasting."

"If that is the case then that is no good for me doctor."

"Because it makes you feel weakened?"

"Yes. I need my fuel to be potent and fulsome. I understand what you are saying that it might be just the way a relationship goes but I don't buy that. They do it on purpose. They have got what they want from me and believe me do I go overboard in making them happy and then once they are embedded they start to turn off the taps. I don't know why, what on earth have I done to them to deserve this? They start it so I have to fight back and that means I have to punish and hurt them to get the new invigorating negative fuel."

"I understand. Tell me, when you have a new car does it not become familiar over time. Does it feel less exciting to drive it?"

"Yes I agree with that."

"So what do you do about that situation then?"

"Buy a new car."

"Okay. What about your house then. How long have you lived there?"

"Which one, I have two."

"The one here in this city."

"Five years."

"Does it feel new and exciting?"

"It's a house doctor, houses aren't exciting. Am I bored of it? If you are asking that then no, I am not."

"Why?"

"I don't know, I like it. I like where I live and I like the house."

"Okay why did you move house from your last property?"

"I wanted a larger one."

"Why when you live alone?"

"I wanted to impress people with it."

"Very well and are they impressed?"

"Of course they are," I smiled.

"My point is this; whenever we get used to something over a period of time the heightened interest and excitement we had fades. It is a natural consequence of the effluxion of time. It always happens. It happens with everything and especially with relationships."

"Well, I still think they do it on purpose but I am a reasonable man, so let's say you are correct about this doctor and this is just the way it goes, it still is of no use to me. This is what you don't seem to understand. Whether they turn off the taps or whether it just happens because that is what happens, that is no good to me. I cannot survive if the fuel is lessened in strength and quantity. I need the fresh, edifying fuel and that means change has to be effected. Change in supplier and change in the method of delivery. That is why I cannot be with one person forever, it just will not work. It may work for you but not for me because I am different. I am special."

Dr E continued to write. I wonder if he is starting to understand what it is like now. They try and enforce their world onto me but they cannot. That will not work. They need to understand my world because that is where I reside. You need to as well.

Those of you who are among my longer-term readers or those who have gorged on all my writings may remember Karen. Karen was my ex-girlfriend who I tested from the start. She enjoyed the challenge that I presented to her. At first I charmed her in the usual way but I did not go all out with my weapons of mass seduction. I ascertained that I would draw her in much more readily through the application of challenging behaviour. This behaviour did not belittle or demean her (that, as it always does, comes later). No, instead this behaviour was designed to make her go the extra mile in order to please me. One of the particular ways that I would do this was by appealing to the nurse inside of her.

Karen was not a trained nurse although if she had opted for such a vocation it would have suited her considerably but she was an expert at caring for others and mopping their fevered brows. I used this to my advantage by repeatedly playing the sickness card. I have never done this with anyone else because generally I like to maintain the impression of being fit and healthy but with her I knew it would grab her and it was another method of presenting a challenge. I would feign stomach pains, a sore throat, a bad back, stabbing pains in my feet, headache, blurred vision and such like. If I did not want Karen going out all I had to do was call her and make groans down the telephone and she would come over and embark on her nursing routine. She would take my temperature, gently check the affected area with her fingers, peer into my mouth, place her hand against my brow and so on in respect of whatever affliction I had dreamt up. I would lie in the bed moaning and groaning and asking her to stay and look after me. She always did. She would sit in the chair in the bedroom and watch over me, shuttling back and forth with food (if of course I felt up to eating) hot drinks, cold drinks, medicinal drinks and whatever else I could think of to have her running around after me. She would make soothing noises, massage where it hurt and kiss it all better. She revelled in this role and of course the very next day I was fully recovered and able to go and play golf despite her advising me not to.

Nonsense," I would reply as she urged me to stay in bed, "the fresh air will do me good. It was one of those 24 hour things wasn't it? You can't keep me down for long, not with you looking after me."

She would smile and hug me, delighted at my recognition of her nursing of me.

Karen enjoyed ski-ing. She was a real ski nut and massively enthusiastic about it. I less so. I don't really get it You ski down a slope once and there you are you have done it. Why go up and around again? Why keep going over and over the same thing repeatedly? Makes no sense to me. She had booked a ski holiday for us both at Val Thorens and we had an impressive chalet (which of course meant chalet maid) to look forward to. As the holiday neared I made repeated comment about how my right knee was giving me trouble. I had injured it when playing football when I was younger and repeated matches thereafter took their toll on it so that occasionally I would wear a brace when playing but it was not anything which ever stopped me from playing my favourite sport. I naturally made reference to the injury as causing me considerable pain and concern as the departure date neared.

Should we not go?" asked Karen.

Oh no, I would not want to spoil the holiday. I am sure I will be fine." I answered.

"Well only if you are sure."

We flew out and once there I explained that my knee was giving me real trouble and I had decided I was not going to risk any exacerbation of the condition by ski-ing. The friends we went with were suitable sympathetic.

"But please don't let me stop you, you carry on I will be okay, Karen will look after me." I announced showing how much of a trooper I was.

"I will just read outside the nearest bar and admire the view with Karen."

I looked at Karen. She made to say something but did not do so and gave a small nod. Thus Karen did not ski once that holiday but instead she sat with me outside the Bar Hibou and we read, talked and drank beer until our friends returned from their day on their slopes. If she had any complaint she never articulated it but continued to ensure I was looked after. She would walk slowly alongside me to make sure I did not slip as we walked from the chalet to the bar. She would place me in a chair and then allow me to stay there all day, wrapped up with the sun on my face and whatever I needed to hand. She once again showed she was up to the task and would readily put my needs well ahead of her own. She took great care of me. I cannot say I did the same for her however.

Knowing the Narcissist

The Bridge

You are at a fork in the road. Your destination is utopia. You have heard of this place from many people but you never thought you would be in a position to be able to reach it. This place is everything that you have ever wanted. It is elation, contentment, passion and a perfect love. It is a place where you are made to feel like a king or queen. Everything is made of gold in utopia. It shines and it gleams and you want it. Everybody wants it. Everybody wants to feel that love which is legendary in utopia.

It is usually the case that most people have to follow the left-hand road to utopia. It is a long, long road which winds and twists and meanders. There are some signposts but many are missing and as a consequence many people who travel this lengthy toad never reach their destination of utopia. They make a wrong turning and head off to Obscurity. They may miss a slip road and end up heading on a direct route to Mediocrity. These travellers may find themselves reaching places such as Momentary, As Good As It Gets or This Will Do. Nobody really wants to travel to those places but those who take the lengthy road find they end up in these places and they never manage to escape them. The road to Utopia passes through some Badlands where there are people waiting to derail them, hijack their vehicle and leave them stranded. There are some good Samaritans who roam this hinterland acting as guides as they try to send people along back on track after giving them a lift. There are some fascinating sights along this route any of which captivate the travellers so that they actually forget where they are heading. The destinations of Money, Career, Family and Friends often manage to distract travellers and cause them to halt their journey towards Utopia. Occasionally the storms which rage over this road obscure the way ahead and those lost souls who drive onwards end up in remote places such as Addiction Despair, Loneliness and

Penury. It is a hazardous and fascinating road which goes through the bane and the beautiful as it wends its way towards Utopia. Many take this route and with good intentions. They prepare themselves in a fastidious fashion and swear dedication to their quest but there is much to hamper and distract them on this route. One does not embark upon this lengthy road to Utopia with a faint heart.

You however have a choice. You are not forced like so many others to run the risks on the elongated route. You do not have to gamble and be subjected to the vagaries that come with driving that way. You can turn right and avail yourself of my bridge. Look at that super structure, isn't it magnificent? Look how it soars into the sky, a spectacular edifice of concrete, steel cables and that unmarked pristine tarmac. There is no congestion on this bridge. No waiting for the traffic to clear before you can progress. It is a swift and direct route to Utopia. You do not have to go the long way round. You are not forced to run the gauntlet of risks and potential mishaps like so many other people. You have been chosen to have access to this super-fast and direct route into the Promised Land. All you need to do is make that right turn and drive onto the bridge. You need not have any concerns about it as it carries you over the abyss below. This bridge has been constructed from the strongest materials and built by the most qualified engineers in the world. It is a testament to the ability of man to conquer that which was once thought of as insurmountable. You will cruise across the bridge, the tarmac designed to muffle any noise from your car as you transported promptly and safely to Utopia. Once you are on the bridge of course you cannot turn back as that would cause a problem but you need not be concerned about that because I know you want to carry on straight to Utopia taken there by my bridge. I can see you nodding. That's right; indicate to the right and away you go. Amazing isn't it? Breathtaking in its dominance as you drive towards it and before you know it you are on my bridge and racing across it. Can you see that golden light of Utopia now? Yes I thought you could. You are not far away at all. The abyss is wide and deep but it is no obstacle to my bridge and before you know it you have crossed the halfway point and you are nearing the other side. You can see the booths and the barriers ahead. You slow your car down as you approach. Oh yes, I forget to mention there was a toll to pay for using my bridge. Well, you surely did not expect to be transported to magnificently to Utopia without paying a price did you? It's okay, you can put your wallet or purse away I am not going to take money on this occasion. What's the price you have to pay? It is straightforward. Just give me your life as you know it and in return I will give you a husk and passage through the barriers. Deal?

With the brief injunction from my mother to ensure I spoke up or suffer the consequences I returned to the consulting room of Dr M. We took our seats and he smiled before adjusting his suit trousers, pulling them up at the thigh. I cast a quick glance to his nether regions but no hole had yet emerged.

"Now Mr Tudor, we did not make much progress last week. It is of no concern. I wondered if you perhaps felt more amenable to speaking with me on this occasion?"

I started to nod and then spoke.

"Very well."

"Excellent. What would you like to talk about?" he asked.

"Why am I here as in why am I sat in your consulting room," I clarified before he started providing me with some smart alec response as to the meaning of my existence. I knew why my family had insisted that I see Dr M and more recently underline the necessity of speaking to him, but I wanted to know what he thought. That way I would be better prepared to deflect him.

"Why do you think you are here with me?" he answered casually. Marvellous. He was one of those people who answered a question with another question.

"I asked first," I pointed out. He nodded.

"Your family are concerned about you." I snorted which seemed to take him by surprise.

"Those bastards only care about themselves."

"Why do you say that?" asked Dr M seizing on my remark.

"It does not matter, go on, you were saying."

"Your family are concerned about you. I met with them and they provided me with background information. I am aware that you are a high achiever and have always been so. Your family are concerned however that you stop at nothing to get what you want, that you have disdain for most people and you leave a trail of carnage in your wake. I think that is a succinct way of putting it. They want me to discuss this with you and to receive my opinion." he explained.

"It's bullshit all of it," I remarked. My voice was low but the venom was tangible. Dr M remained silent.

"I have no idea what they are talking about. I stop at nothing to get what I want? They have never complained about my achievements before. They don't like it that I am outshining them. That is the problem here. They always do this. Try and make their problems my problems, I am sick and tired of it. I have forged my own path and done bloody well too and all they want to do is bring me down. It is jealousy. That's why I have little to do with them. Did they tell you that? I bet they tried to make out that I am aloof and never attend family gatherings didn't they? They never invite me to them. I keep in touch most with my younger brother and he tells me about these gatherings and I always find out after the event. Did my younger brother speak to you?"

Dr M nodded.

"Who else?" I asked.

"Both your parents, your sister, your younger brother and your cousin, Charlotte."

"Huh, the usual cabal. All of them are liars. Do you have any idea what it is like having to put up with all of them? My god it is a wonder that I am a success. My mother is always trying to pin the blame for her shortcomings on me. She would love to plant a microchip in my head and control me. That would be ideal for her. She has controlled my father for years. He isn't a bad fellow really but he fell under her spell and believes anything she says and if he dares not to well let's just say he has suffered the consequences too many times before so he has learned his lesson. It's weak of him and I hate him for being like that. He should stand up to her rather than be her metaphorical punching bag. Always tries to keep the peace at first and then takes her side. He is brainwashed and my sister is just as bad. Jesus she always defers to my mother, but then she could never make a decision for herself. So Charlie has weighed in as well has she? Do you know why doctor M? It is because she wants me for herself and I won't let that happen. Bet they did not tell you that did they? She is totally in love with me and because I have rejected her, this is how she goes about paying me back by making up lies about me. I would not put it past that harpy to try and section me you know. You don't want to believe anything that lot say to you."

Dr M was jotting down the odd note as I spoke. Yes, make some notes Dr M and you can tell them what I think of them. How dare they? How bastard dare they make out like I am the one with the problem? I should be used to it by now but it still infuriates me. I stood up, agitated at this unwarranted attack on me.

"This is what they always do doctor. I am the one who was suffered at their hands. Years of it but they twist it around and try to pin the blame on me. I have made the best of a bad hand and they cannot stand to see me doing well so they conjure up this. Liars the lot of them."

I was pacing up and down in front of the fireplace and fighting to resist the urge to grab one of the logs and hurl it at the large mirror which hung above the fireplace.

"I wish they were all dead doctor, you have no idea. The times I have wished that they would get wiped out in some car accident or a building falls on them when they are inside. They have made my life hell and just as I am pulling free of them they pull this stunt. I hate them. I am surprised at my brother joining in with this as well, I thought he had some sense."

"Your brother expressed considerable concern about you and wants to help you," offered Dr M.

"I don't need any help. I suggest you fill your sessions with them. You will have plenty of material for your shrink times or whatever publication you write for. My mother is a control freak with a drink problem, my father is spineless, my sister is a professional victim oh yes, ask her about her failed marriage but make sure you have the bleeding heart and violins to hand. My cousin, well as I said, she is a lecherous nymphomaniac and as for my brother, he has gone down in my estimation joining this cabal of perfidy."

I spat the words out as I waved my arms around, wind milling through the air. I felt a little better for this explosion of annoyance and I returned to my seat and sat down. Dr M was still writing.

"So Dr M there really is nothing to see here. I know you will want to make some money from us and I respect that, you are like me, you see an opportunity and exploit it. Nothing wrong with that. Let me give you a tip. You need to suggest working with those liars and parking your involvement with me. You have nothing to achieve here but as for them, well you will make a fortune sorting out the quagmire that is their lives."

I sat back and smiled as Dr M continued to write. I had spoken up just as she had urged. I had done as I was told. Again. This time though I was fighting back.

Ticking Over

A few days ago I was recounting my consultation with Dr E. He and I were discussing whether I could be sustained from the provision of solely positive fuel from just one source, namely an intimate partner. I pointed out that this could not work, leaving aside how practical this really was, because the source always goes stale and I am forced to look upon the greener grass around me. The consultation continued.

"So you think that your intimate partner will always let you down because the fuel they will supply drops off in terms of quantity and quality?"

"I don't think it, I know it. It always happens."

"Understood. Why do you think this happens?"

"Because they let it happen."

"Do they let it happen or is it not the natural consequence of being with someone for a longer period of time."

"Familiarity breeds contempt?"

"Perhaps at the very least it might be less dazzling and less exciting."

"Well yes, that is what happens."

"Indeed and if this keeps happening could it not be the fact that this is normal, this is what happens when you get to know somebody for a period of time. The honeymoon period when everything is fresh, new and exciting ends and matters become more deep-seated and solid. The razzle dazzle gives way to something more substantial and long lasting."

"If that is the case then that is no good for me doctor."

"Because it makes you feel weakened?"

"Yes. I need my fuel to be potent and fulsome. I understand what you are saying that it might be just the way a relationship goes but I don't buy that. They do it on purpose. They have got what they want from me and believe me do I go overboard in making them happy and then once they are embedded they start to turn off the taps. I don't know why, what on earth have I done to them to deserve this? They start it so I have to fight back and that means I have to punish and hurt them to get the new invigorating negative fuel."

"I understand. Tell me, when you have a new car does it not become familiar over time. Does it feel less exciting to drive it?"

"Yes I agree with that."

"So what do you do about that situation then?"

"Buy a new car."

"Okay. What about your house then. How long have you lived there?"

"Which one, I have two."

"The one here in this city."

"Five years."

"Does it feel new and exciting?"

"It's a house doctor, houses aren't exciting. Am I bored of it? If you are asking that then no, I am not."

"Why?"

"I don't know, I like it. I like where I live and I like the house."

"Okay why did you move house from your last property?"

"I wanted a larger one."

"Why when you live alone?"

"I wanted to impress people with it."

"Very well and are they impressed?"

"Of course they are," I smiled.

"My point is this; whenever we get used to something over a period of time the heightened interest and excitement we had fades. It is a natural consequence of the effluxion of time. It always happens. It happens with everything and especially with relationships."

"Well, I still think they do it on purpose but I am a reasonable man, so let's say you are correct about this doctor and this is just the way it goes, it still is of no use to me. This is what you don't seem to understand. Whether they turn off the taps or whether it just happens because that is what happens, that is no good to me. I cannot survive if the fuel is lessened in strength and quantity. I need the fresh, edifying fuel and that means change has to be effected. Change in supplier and change in the method of delivery. That is why I cannot be with one person forever, it just will not work. It may work for you but not for me because I am different. I am special."

Dr E continued to write. I wonder if he is starting to understand what it is like now. They try and enforce their world onto me but they cannot. That will not work. They need to understand my world because that is where I reside. You need to as well.

Tractor Beam

I recently received an e-mail which was a pleasant surprise and immediately attracted my interest. It was from Lesley. You may remember that Lesley is a former girlfriend of mine and I used to call her 'it' which really got to her. When I devalued her I would conduct a running commentary on her as if she was not there and would always call her 'it'. It really got to her. She would become frustrated, cry and beg me to stop it. If I then called her by her name she was so relieved she became so easy to control. I always enjoyed this verbal method of manipulation. Her e-mail read as follows:-

'Hi HG

I hope you are well. I am sure you are. I am in the city next Friday and I wonder if you would be free for lunch. Nothing more mind I know what you are like! It would be lovely to have a catch up and see how you are doing.

Lesley xx'

I reflected on the e-mail before I replied. Of course I would be happy to meet for lunch. I had not seen Lesley in almost three years since she moved to a different city a few hundred miles away. I toyed with her for a while afterwards sending her text messages and e-mails and they drew a response at first but eventually she changed those details and vanished from Facebook so she was put on ice as I busied myself with my other appliances. I knew she would get in touch with me at some point, you just cannot help but want to know what I am doing, who I am with and most of all to try and find out if I am sorry for what I did to you. I regarded this as an opportunity to remind Lesley of how brilliant I am and I would treat her to lunch at a decent restaurant, one where I was well known and bound to be well looked after by the staff which would impress her no doubt. I responded to Lesley in the following manner

Hello dearest Lesley,

How lovely to receive a missive from you. You still often invade my consciousness and only last week I was remembering the time we went to Nice for that break. I was thinking about going again and we had such a super time didn't we Lesley? Anyway I would be delighted to meet up for lunch. I will book somewhere fabulous and it is on me, it is the least I can do. Let me know your number Lesley and I will text you time and place.

Fond regards

HG xxx

I flicked on my tractor beam as Lesley the It Girl came within my orbit once again. We traded a few e-mails which I kept pleasant, light and flirty, always making reference to her name. She sent me her mobile number which of course had altered from the one that I once had. I stored that and used it just the once to text her the details of the booking.

Friday came and I arranged for two of my lieutenants to be in the restaurant. One male and one female. I arranged for them to wander over once Lesley and I were in situ. Lieutenant One was to congratulate me on a recent deal and comment how I was making waves in the industry. Lieutenant Two was to thank me for dinner the other evening and ask me to call her when I had chance. I picked a restaurant which served Thai food as this was a favourite of Lesley's and I decided I would give her a little gift by way of acknowledging that I had not always treated her as well as I ought to have done. I made sure I was ten minutes early and waiting in the bar area for Lesley so she would not have to wait. She arrived on time and looked very well. Her face lit up when she saw me waiting and my tractor beam grew ever stronger as she walked over to me embracing me on the cheek.

Lunch was most pleasant. I ensured I kept using her name, saying Lesley after most of my comments to her. I was polite, charming and good company. My lieutenants acquitted their assigned roles and I could see that Lesley was impressed from the admiring glances that she sent me and the questions she asked afterwards. I responded in a modest fashion brushing away her compliments. I ensured I asked plenty of questions about her, where she was now working, whether she had a boyfriend (she was dating), how her family was, what she did at weekends and so on and so forth. I ensured I referred to events from our golden period with fondness and affection and she totally engaged with my stance. She offered no resistance and kept the compliments and admiration coming my way. Even when she moved on to the topic of my treatment of her I apologised and nodded as I allowed her to express her hurt and pain. Her eyes welled with tears and the emotion pouring from her obscured the inherent criticism in her comments as I drank deep of the fuel and my fury remained in check. I explained how my immaturity had the better of me then and I had changed from those grasping days.

I was flirtatious throughout but did not press her in anyway so she felt that she had a vestige of control over our situation even though she was very much in the grip of my tractor beam. Our lunch lasted for two and a half hours and as I settled the bill I looked at Lesley.

"Well, that was most enjoyable Lesley. We must do it again. I really enjoyed hearing how you have been getting on and I have to say I am really proud of you."

She smiled and looked at the table and back up at me. The admiration shining in her eyes was immense.

"Thank you. I have enjoyed it too. I would like to keep in touch HG and you have my number."

"Yes and you have mine. Feel free to call me whenever you like."

"I will. I have to say you are doing really well. You seem more settled, not as restless and it suits you."

I smiled and nodded and then waved to the waiter who I had secreted the gift with.

"Well I had better return to the office Lesley and see if hell has broken out without me there, but before I do, I wanted you to have this."

The waiter arrived and handed the small package to Lesley.

"What's this?" she smiled taking the present.

"Oh just a small gift by way of apology."

"You didn't need to do that," she added but continued smiling as the waiter walked away.

"Of course I did Lesley. You are worth it."

She folded back the expensive wrapping paper and pulled the slender rectangular item free from its packaging. She gave a slight frown and then turned it around. Her eyes fell on the front of the Blu-ray box and she gave a short cry as if startled. Her expression of delight immediately broke and a tear trickled from her right eye. I just sat smiling at her, my chin resting on my triangulated fingers as she slowly lowered the Blu-ray to the table, sobs now coming from her each one becoming louder. She dropped the Blu-ray and clasped her hands to her mouth as if to stifle a scream but her watering eyes remained fixed on the title of the Blue-ray.

Stephen King's It.

Working It Out

Welcome to the seat of power. This is the command headquarters from which my work-based machinations take place. I do enjoy the work place. It is a playground where I have access to all manner of different appliances to keep those important fuel levels topped up. Naturally when I am at work I am not with my primary source of fuel although I keep her plugged in by reason of text messages, e-mails and the telephone. This certainly helps get me through the day but I am not able to turn up, perform my job and then go home. If I did that I would be starved of fuel and consequently in trouble. I regard work as a place to acquire fuel first and secondly the place where I perform my role in the business. A number of our kind do not bother with work. These low level narcs occupy their days in a different way by obtaining fuel in the home environment. They do not know what they are missing but they are at the low end of functioning and therefore would not be as effective in a dynamic environment like me. Then there are the mid-level narcs who do work but they forgo the medium-term fuel gains for short-term acquisitions. These members of Narc Club will never climb high as they tend to move from job to job. Usually this is because when their fuel is ignited they lack the discipline to withdraw or use it as a shield and instead go on the warpath. They are not as high up as someone like me and therefore they are at risk of being fired. It is a temporary set-back because they have the guile and manipulative charm to secure another position soon after but they disappoint me. Securing a new position of employment takes time and energy, time and energy which could be far better applied to securing fuel.

Now, with my kind and me in the upper echelons of Narc Club the workplace is a huge fuel refinery. Lots of different people. Lots of different clients and suppliers. Repeatedly changing and therefore it is like being sat with a conveyor belt of appliances drifting past ready for me to hook up to me when I see fit. Work is a marvellous environment for gathering fuel. There are so many opportunities to shine and gain admiration. Post great results - fuel. Win new work - fuel. Deliver a report on time and within budget - fuel. Close the deal - fuel. Make savings to maximise profit - fuel. Dangle a promotion in front an ambitious associate - fuel. It does not stop there. So many delicious ladies to flirt with and draw into my influence. They are elegant and smart, wearing pencil skirts and blouses, hair tied up and high heels worn. I shower the compliments around and they always respond - fuel. Praise someone for working long hours - fuel. Praise my secretary (who is in love with me) for her output - fuel. It is a wonder I do not explode. You would think this would be enough with all the opportunities to show off my success and so many different people to expose to my brilliance but it gets even better. I know, it is fantastic isn't it? Supplier not come up to scratch? Time to let them know with a blast from the furnace of fury and harvest more fuel. Sub-ordinate slacking? Berate them and in flows the fuel. Set unachievable targets for the pool of associates and watch them tear their hair out in anguish - fuel. Make that secretary cry because she created too many typographical errors - fuel. Ignore that sexy junior who I took into the disabled toilet for some special attention and see her perplexed expression as I close the door in her face - fuel. Everywhere I go there are fuel lines it is a wonder I do not trip over them. I have my own personal fiefdom where I arrange the players as I see fit. The secretaries, the juniors and the associates are all organised to do as I please. I set them against one another and the fuel just flows. They fawn over me seeking my largesse and there is yet more fuel.

I am no fool however. The job must still be done and thanks to my manipulative charm, lack of remorse and mind set of the end always justifies the means my team always delivers. That is all the higher-ups care about. Anybody who is stupid enough and I mean they really are stupid if they try and cross me at work by running squealing to the higher-ups results in the end of their career. My boss Julia (who secretly fancies me) always backs me up because she knows I could do her job tomorrow and she is grateful that I have not plunged the knife into her back. I have not done so because I know she is blowing a board director and he has her back. She in turn has mine. So long as we deliver I can do whatever I want in my personal fiefdom. This means I can give the drudgery to others, make them toil whilst I focus on gathering my fuel and collecting the glory. I maintain a coterie within the workplace and they are so hungry for success they will turn on anyone I wish to character assassinate. Oh I do enjoy work, the wheels within wheels. What is it that I actually do you might wonder ? Well I will leave you to work it out.

You Said We'd Always Be Together

You told me that we would always be together. Do you remember that? I certainly do. We did so much together didn't we? I would call on you or you would call on me and just the two of us would fill our days together. Nothing concerned us. We had one another. We liked the same things and the same things made us laugh. We used to laugh a lot didn't we? Great big laughs which shook our bodies and made it hard to breathe. We would set one another off and the more you laughed the more you made me laugh and vice versa. We would collapse to the ground pointing and laughing as the tears rolled down our faces. People used to look at us and wonder what has got into those two again? We found humour in so many things and whatever one pointed out the other understood straight away. We worked together too we were a true team. Each knew what the other wanted and we never argued about it. You had your role and I had mine and together we got along just fine. I did not want anyone else apart from you. I did not need anyone other than you. Every day I would wonder what it would have in store for us as we explored and investigated the world together. There was never any disagreement about what we wanted to do. I made a suggestion and you agreed with it. You came up with an idea and I liked it.

The summer was the best time. Those long days. We would be up and away as the first rind of dawn broke on the horizon as the world was not even waking up. How we enjoyed the silence as we made our way to seek out the day's adventure. We would explore and find something new even if we had been down that path on a previous occasion. Sometimes there would be a scrape and we would have that moment of panic, that sudden uncertainty until we helped one another and then we would halt, free of the danger and stand panting until the laughter took us.

"You should have seen your face," you would laugh.

"You should have seen yours," I would respond.

We would break into paroxysms of laughter once again but this time there would be nobody to hear us. Many times we would follow the old rutted and meandering path into the forest to spend time at that lake. The water cool and inviting, an ideal antidote to the heat of the day. The clearing would echo to our shouts as we embarked on some new escapade but there was only ever us there. Nobody knew about this place or if they did, they never chose to visit it. It was a secret place. It was our secret place. Although we loved it most during the summer for it offered so many possibilities for excitement, we did not abandon our haven in the other seasons. Autumn would see us attend there amidst the blustery wind and the swirling leaves to collect and forage. Winter would be a spectacular vision of sparkling whites. The lake frozen and unyielding, a beautiful yet deadly spectacle out before us. Spring brought the smell of life and rejuvenation as the pouring rain woke the forest once again. We loved it all but best of all we loved it together.

We were inseparable and even though the march of time had cast others asunder it had not even shown the first inkling of doing the same to us. We had something different, something that was forever, something real. It was something forged from such similarity that we really were two halves of the same thing. We often looked at one another stood beside that silent pool, the birds silent, too tired from the heat to fly or sing. We stared at our reflections in the tranquil water and without speaking recognised our similarities. It might not have ever come to happen. I sometimes made reference to this serendipity that we had enjoyed but you preferred not to talk about it. I did not mind. It was admittedly easier that way. Sometimes as we crouched beneath the shielding canopy of a tree as the rain lashed down around us, the drumming noise so great that it filled our ears with sound, I would ask if this would always be the way it would be. Without fail you always reassured me.

"We will always be together, I promise."

You would tell me and I knew you meant it. I knew you stood by your promises.

I know you did not choose to break that promise. Somebody else did. They broke it and then you were gone. It was not the only thing that broke that day.

Gamechanger

I love playing games. As I have written before, the games are always being played. I only ever play to win otherwise there is no point. I cannot lose and sit back and smile and accept it was nevertheless an enjoyable experience because if I was to lose then it could not be enjoyable. I would be accepting that you or someone else is better than me. You are not. He is not. They are not. I always have to win. In order to achieve this I operate by a particular set of rules. You think you know what those rules are because when we first come together I deign to play by your rules; I agree to operate by the systems and conventions of your reality. That is easy for me to do because everything is going swimmingly. I am seducing you and therefore you are letting me win because it feels good. I am content to go along with the pretence of agreeing that these are the rules of engagement. You think you are winning because you are getting this wonderful, generous and loving person. In reality, I am winning because I am receiving plenty of positive fuel from you.

It is thereafter that the rules alter because I decide (and it is always my decision) that we will now abide by the rules in my reality. You are not given a rulebook and you have to guess what those rules are. As soon as you think that you have grasped them and got a handle on them, they will suddenly change. It is akin to playing a game of football and I am winning three nil. You score two more goals and you are in the ascendancy and likely to equalise. There would normally be fifteen minutes to go but suddenly I change the rules so there is just one minute left. You fail to score and I win. You protest stating that is not the correct time but it does not matter because here I am the referee, the assistants and the fourth official and what I say goes. If you do not like it, tough. I will just pick up the ball and go home with it. It is like a game of darts where you have to start from 501 and end with a double. I on the other hand start from 51 and do not need a double. You claim it is not fair but why should I care about it? I have to win. Thus, you may realise that I enjoy a lie-in on a Sunday morning so you do not disturb me. I will purposefully set the alarm early and get up waking you early. Or if I do have a lie in, I will concoct some mystery appointment that I have missed because you let me lie in. When you wake me early the following Sunday I will erupt at you for being so selfish and not letting me sleep.

When you think have ascertained what the rules are they will alter. You will do your best to try and keep up but it is exhausting and frustrating. Yet, this manipulation of the rules to allow our kind to win does not end there. Goodness me no. Our driven desire to always be the winner means that not only will we sucker you by pretending to play by your rules and then change them; we will then change the game. One moment you think you are playing Monopoly and then I am telling you it was Professor Plum in the Study with the Candlestick.

"But that is Cluedo," you will declare rather puzzled.

"I know," I will smile in return.

"But we are playing monopoly.

"No we are not."

"Yes we are, look this board has streets from New York on it."

"No it doesn't, those are rooms in the stately home."

"What are you talking about? See here and here, street names."

"Are you blind? Those are snakes and ladders."

"What? You've changed it again."

"No I haven't. You are just making a fuss because you are losing."

"What are you on about? I am not losing, I was winning."

"Not at all. Check mate."

"What?"

Our phenomenal capabilities for lying, blame-shifting, denial and reflection all mean that the game will change. You are wrong footed, unsure of yourself, confused and we keep on doing it. We must win, always and you have to lose, at your cost. We will apply all our methods of manipulation to ensure we are victorious and you lie sprawled in the dirt, broken and defeated. Our success has to be at everything and I mean everything, from the trivial to the substantial, Defeat is never an option for our kind and we will bend, twist and snap the rules and alter the game in order to achieve this. Now, let's play a game. It is my favourite. You may know it. It is called Guess Who? You have no chance.

A Bowl of Cherries

I have an Inner Circle Friend. He is what people would generally regard as a 'good man'. He is older than me, not old enough to be a father. More of the younger uncle who is solid but enjoys a little spice to his life. He tackles fraud in government organisations, enjoys a beer, loves his sport, a keen family man, devout and plays a part in his local church, plays musical instruments, writes poetry and every Saturday he picks up the shopping and spends an hour chatting with a housebound friend of his. He and I enjoy Italian food and a good debate as we set the world to rights. He enjoys a fierce discussion and it is all good fuel but there is never any grudge afterwards, even when I have twisted and spun in order to avoid conceding a particular point. Every time we meet up he always begins by reminding me that my life is a bowl of cherries.

"Yes HG it is bowl of cherries. Look at you. An educated man with many friends, good job, well-read, able to do as he pleases and you travel. You organise your time so you can spend time with lots of people and most of all the girls. Holy Toledo, the girls. You get through them and no mistake but you are never troubled by it are you? Sometimes I wish I was single and younger so I could join you in these adventures. You are a man comfortable in his own skin. I can see that and this means you are able to have a life which is a bowl of cherries."

I always enjoy this little speech of his. It is important to people to recognise my elevated position and the rewards that come with it. He never displays any jealousy nor does he judge what I do (albeit of course he does not know it all). He regards my behaviours as 'hi-jinks' and ' capers' . The preserve of the younger man with the world at his feet. I will relay the latest tale of my activities as he sips from his rioja. He laughs and shakes his head as I detail to him what I have been doing, but he is never alarmed by what I tell him. He is a big believer in living life to the full, seizing opportunities and setting the world alight. All of which I naturally do. There is only topic where he passes comment in a slightly adverse way. Children.

"So HG," he will begin before swallowing more of his wine and lighting yet another cigarette if we are dining at his house, "when can we expect some children? All these ladies and you cannot tell me that they do not want a little HG to share the cherries with?"

"Maybe one day," I lie since I have no intention of having any children. He is unaware I took care of that some time ago.

"Well you are in your prime so those cherries will keep on appearing, juicy and ripe, but seriously, a man should have children. I have four. Two by each wife. Children are a great comfort. Tells you that someone can bear you if they want to carry your offspring, they give you something to strive for, something to live for and then you have a legacy as you see them go into the world making their own way."

I smile and allow him to say all of this. I hear it each time that we meet up.

"You must have met the right lady by now, surely? You have no problem attracting them with your big bowl of cherries now do you?"

"True enough but there is so much to do and sharing those cherries isn't really on the agenda."

"Come now," he smiles, "you have more than enough and you should share. You should be showering your gifts on someone special and your offspring. It is the right thing to do. You have no need to worry, my lad, about sharing those cherries you know. You always have a bowl full and if you share a few around then you will always be able to pick some more won't you?"

"There is never enough though and I have to be careful you know, there are too many who would steal my cherries from me and leave me with nothing."

"No there isn't, I have told you before, the cherries are there to share, not to hoard. You need to listen to me. Share and keep picking."

I smile and let him continue with his monologue about cherries and children. He is right though I am the cherry picker. I am up on high, elevated above everything else around me and I reach those places that the little people can never reach. I can move from side to side, up and down and ensure that I always obtain the tastiest and most succulent cherries before anybody else. I can see them dark red and with that polished lustre just waiting to be picked by me and me alone. So many out there to collect in order to try and fill my bowl. If only I could figure out some way to plug the hole in my bowl, maybe then I might just be tempted to share.

Do You Feel the Darkness

Do you feel the darkness as it coils about you? Do you see those midnight black tendrils as they slither towards you? Do you recognise that encroaching cloak of nothingness as it begins to wrap around you? Do you see how the inky murk blots out parts of your life as your friends become obscured by the gathering darkness? Have you any idea what is waiting for you in the shade as the pools of despair begin to form at your feet? Can you feel the icy embrace as the levels of gloom start to rise, swallowing you up bit by bit? Are you aware of the advancing chasm as it swallows up your family, wrenching them away from you consigning them to oblivion? The engulfing darkness causes them to vanish and even their desperate cries and shouts become muffled and then extinguished. Do you remember what held your interest before this fog arrived? Can you recall those hobbies and past times that entertained you and gave you a sense of who you were as you enjoyed engaging in them and with other people? Can you or is the fog too thick so that you doubt if you ever did undertake them at all? Have you noticed how the air has become thicker and cloyed with poison or do you breathe it in oblivious to the toxicity that comes with it? Are you aware how the twilight has percolated into your ears so that everything you hear has become twisted and distorted? Do you recognise what is patently before you or do the shadowy shapes and figures make little sense when they once did? Have you realised that your words have become dust in your mouth as the fur of the darkness fills your mouth and slides down your throat, strangling the sounds you try to make? Do you feel the icy embrace of this impenetrable wall of darkness which advances to you and over you? Do you recognise this glacier of despair as it slides over you, subsuming you and sucking you deep inside, preserving you in a dark, icy tomb? Do you even see your reflection in the mirror anymore or has that become masked in darkness too, the glass dulled so that everything becomes obscured and shows something else entirely? Do you see those shades which come and torment you, their sinewy fingers pulling at you as they strip you piece by piece of what you are? Do you observe these wraiths as they devour you, sucking what you are into their dark maws? How does it feel as this corrupting night brings permanent darkness to your world? Do you see how nothing grows anymore when touched by the gloomy taint? Do you smell that foul stench which accompanies this unending blanket of murk? The acrid fumes which waft into your nostrils and eradicate anything sweet and pleasant. Do you notice how your tongue lies flat and useless in your mouth, little more than a cold slab? Do you even acknowledge how everything tastes like ash? Do you feel the leaden weight of this darkness pulling at you, slowing you and seeking to engulf you? Do you recognise how it prevents you from breaking free, this glue-like morass which has fastened on to you and will not yield? Do you notice the fatigue that now wraps around you, leeching at your energy and vitality? Do you hear anything other than the whispers of malevolent control that rattle about your beleaguered brain? Do you know who you are or has this vast amorphous darkness eradicated your sense of being? Do you remember what it was to feel uplifted, joyous and happy or have you become accustomed to the flat, perilous embrace of this total darkness? Do you even feel anything anymore other or has the cosseting black cloud anaesthetised you, numbing and freezing? Do you feel the darkness? No, you ever do. You never see the darkness until you have seen the light.

Hack the Quack

It is an acknowledged fact that you never see us coming. We are creatures that are insidious and pervasive. It is astonishing that we are not seen because we hardly arrive quietly. We appear with great fanfare, fireworks, flashing lights and symphonic sounds. You cannot miss us but of course all of that obscures what we really are. Even when our true intentions begin to manifest you still do not recognise what we are. There are those of you who meet us once and then fall prey a second or even a third time, such is the manner in which we inveigle our way into your lives. You never ever know who we are when we first enter your life and often you do not realise until years afterwards what has happened to you. Some never even achieve enlightenment. Everything we do is designed to deceive. We are shrouded in deceit, it oozes from us and taints everything around us but you rarely see all of that. We are masters of deception, masked and cloaked, our true intentions hidden behind a sheen of flattery and a wall of manipulation. We know you blame yourselves when you finally realise who you have danced with. We are aware that you see it all too clearly after the event and you blame yourself repeatedly. You really ought not to be so harsh on yourselves, you never stood a chance. It is not just you who cannot penetrate our veil of secrecy; the so-called professionals often fail as well. If they cannot see us then you can be forgiven for doing so can't you?

There is an army of therapists, doctors, counsellors, life-coaches and so on. Call them what you will and for all their academic brilliance, their soothing words and supposed insight there are many (although not all admittedly) who are unable to detect us either. They have not experienced what you have and therefore they can only speak from a position of learned, rather than experienced, knowledge. Many of our kind never have any interaction with these people since we refuse to acknowledge there is anything wrong with us much less see any need to be subjected to this scrutiny. This diminishes the prospects of these professionals from gaining a proper understanding. Moreover on the occasions when they might just happen to have one of our kind inside their consulting rooms we do everything in our expansive charismatic power to persuade them that not only is there nothing wrong with us but we are the victims of vile behaviour from the very person who forced us to attend on this shrink. Accordingly, their opportunities to understand us and learn from us are limited and this in turn allows us to continue unhindered in our machinations.

Prior to the good doctors who at least appear to know what they are doing, I merrily attended sessions with therapists and their ilk on five occasions. How could I pass up such a succulent opportunity to gather more fuel from this new arrival and also from you? I would resist any attempt to move into this arena of psychoanalysis at first, purely in order to heighten your woe, hurt and frustration. Eventually and often when perceiving a risk that you would voluntarily threaten my supply of fuel I would agree to attend. I prepared in advance as I selected all of the instruments of charm and flattery from my Devil's Toolkit. Oh how I enjoyed those sessions. My other half would always pay for them so there was a blast of fuel from the off and I relished the opportunity to demonstrate my amenable and charming nature to them. In these sessions with therapists and the like I always adopted a twin strategy. Charm on the one hand and plausible deniability on the other.

I would present at the appropriate place, early, relaxed and looking forward to the chance to tell someone all about me for an hour and paid for by you. I would be pleasant, engaging and treat the time as a fireside chat as I spoke well of my other half, my friends, my job and my achievements. I talked about some of my interests, film in particular and would always ask the other person about their favourite films. They never refused me an answer. The first session was always a breeze as I filly busted until the time had elapsed. I would continue to do this in each session and often they would allow me to talk and talk. They might try and steer the conversation onto something relevant to my behaviour and I would steer it back on to something else. The first counsellor I saw admitted after five sessions that there was nothing to discuss much to my delight and the girlfriend at the time's dismay.

It became a challenge whenever the issue of help, therapy or treatment arose. I would go along and draw the positive fuel from the therapist and then draw negative fuel from whoever had insisted on me attending.

"Yes it is going well; we just have a chat really. It is all very amicable."

"She clearly likes me as she always laughs at my jokes."

"Did you know he supports the same football team as me? He even sits in the same stand."

"I am not allowed to tell you about it."

The last one is a favourite as the pseudo-confidentiality that I apply to the scenario frustrates and irritates you because after all, you need to know because you want to help and by not telling you anything on the basis of instruction from the therapist your bewilderment and frustration increases.

Where my opponent has pressed the issue and asked me and kept on asking me about the alleged behaviours that you have detailed to them beforehand I am always able to drive such doubt into the conversation that it dilutes any attempt to identify what I truly am. It is laughable. When I first ensnare you I do not show you my true colours so do you think that I would behave any different with someone who is trying to trap me and pin me down? Of course not. The catalogue of behaviour outside of normative engagements is fed back to me and I am able to deal with it all. I am an astute enough person to realise that a bare-faced denial will seem evasive and may alert my examiner. Instead, I explain away the perceived problem.

"Yes I admit I do sometimes lose my temper but who doesn't? I work long hours and I do get a little irritable at times, I know I shouldn't but I am only human aren't I?"

"She is rather sensitive so she does tend to exaggerate. She had a bad time of it with her last boyfriend you see. I try and am supportive but it can be difficult because she sees so much in the same way as when she was with him. I don't blame her it just becomes hard to deal with at times, I am sure you know what I mean, for example there was this one time....."

"We have a passionate relationship so there are break-ups and make-ups. There is a lot of passionate energy between us and sometimes it does get a little out of hand, on both sides, but that's the way we are. I recognise my part in this, that after all is why I am here and I would really appreciate it if you could help me to help her. What do you suggest?"

Events are watered down, instances diluted and happenings blurred. Plausible deniability is rolled out and allied with charm results in me walking away with another admirer to my collection and you bemused as to how I have seemingly got away with it again. You really ought not to (although I am pleased you do) get so upset by it since they really do have little chance to uncover what we truly are. What of Dr E and Dr O I hear you ask? Yes well it took two of them in a pincer movement and only because I had to yield to them but that war is still ongoing and there is much fuel to obtain yet.

By the Fading Light

When we commence our devaluation of you it always comes out of nowhere. By now you should be acquainted with the fact that our modus operandi is that we strike from out of the blue. We arrive full of noise, colour and light although you never saw us coming. We turn on our manipulative abuse from out of nothing and then we open the door to the golden period seemingly at a moment's notice. Our devaluation just appears and of course it has to be this way to keep you spinning around and unsettled. We unleash our array of dizzying and destructive words and actions in order to throw you from that pedestal and have you sprawling in the dirt. It is rare for our victims to submit immediately. It takes a period of time to get them where we want them and that does not cause us concern because plenty of fuel will be spilled towards us in the meanwhile. Initially you are bewildered, puzzled and confused. Yesterday we were so loving towards you and today so cold. It really is the archetypal Jekyll and Hyde behaviour. The shutters have been lowered, the drawbridge raised and the door slammed shut. It leaves you perplexed. You have a few days of asking us what is wrong, asking us to talk to you and explain, you rack your brains trying to work out was is going on. You may ask your friends and receive supportive yet ultimately unhelpful responses as they do not know either what you are dealing with. You move to try and resurrect the golden period. You make our favourite meals, suggest trips out, buy us gifts, lavish us with attention and offer your body as you dress up to entice us. This all worked before and as you sit frowning and worrying, you wonder who took away that person you loved and replaced him with this doppelganger. He looks the same but it is not him. You double your efforts to try to return to our golden period, you beg and plead, you ask and cajole but it seems as if we have been cast from stone. Your optimistic entreaties give way to anger and frustration as you demand that we tell you what has changed, you rant and shout as your capacity for understanding becomes overloaded. You feel at your wits' end as your boil over with frustration. You begin to suggest there is something wrong with us and this ignites our fury. We may allow a short return to the golden period just to confuse you further and raise your hopes. Back and forth we will vacillate as we engage in this push and pull. Round and round we go, dragging you along as we take you back through puzzlement then to endeavour once again. Anger and frustration are familiar stops once again on this circular journey and you begin to feel dizzy. Confusion, charisma, consternation and anger. Each day brings a different emotion and all the while you are being ground down, drained and leeched from. This incessant dance we force you to endure seems never-ending even though the tempo and steps alter. All through this you are haemorrhaging emotion which we gladly drink as our fuel. It is all intentional. It is all deliberate. We will look into your eyes and see the confusion that reigns. Good. Time to make you work for the golden period again. We see that flicker of optimism and hope as you try to win us back; you try to bring us back from wherever it is we have gone. We never went anywhere of course. We have been in the same place all along, but you never noticed because of the illusion we created. Now we want to see your frustration. Now we want to see your anger. Push, pull, prod and twist. We stare into your eyes drinking deep of the emotion that we find there. Over and over we do this, making you run the gauntlet of differing emotions as you pour fuel in our direction We use your eyes as a gauge to see how our treatment is affecting you. There in your eyes we see the fuel. We keep watching until eventually, after everything you have endured we see the light in your eyes begin to fade. It is then we know that we are gods.

I Spy A Private Eye

I have often mentioned the empath's need to know. Initially this is borne out of your desire to know and to understand for the purpose of enabling you to discharge your caring and nurturing abilities. Only by understanding and knowing what is wrong, what is going through someone's mind or understanding their situation are you able to assist and help. Some people like to know because they are inquisitive. Some people like to know because they are downright nosey. We like to know so we can use if against you or to further our own schemes. You like to know so you can help. This is a core trait of the empathic individual and it is not something that you are ever able to let go. Even when we are subjecting you to the devaluation you are unable to accept that it is happening without being able to understand why. You need to know. We know you need to know and we exploit this. This is why we engage in denial, deflection and circular arguments because we are entirely aware this inability to allow you to know and to understand draws fuel from you but also keeps you doing this. Even when we discard you, you still want to make sense of what has happened. You need and want to know why did we treat in the way we did, why did we do all those awful things to you and why were you not enough? By tapping into this trait of yours we also ensure that you have to know what we are doing once we have flung you to one side.

You will ask our friends what we are doing and pose similar questions to our family in a bid to ascertain what we are now doing without you. You ask your friends to spy on your behalf, gathering information about the places that we have been to and the people we have fraternised with. You see, if you try to escape from us then you cannot get rid of us as we appear with Hoover in hand ready to suck you back. However, if we have decided that we have extracted as much fuel as we possibly can from you (at least for now) we will do our utmost to remain invisible and keep you guessing. We want you wondering what we are doing? We want you to be sat contemplating where we are and who we are with? Are we happy? Are we thinking of you? This need to know becomes overwhelming and you then embark on your role as private eye. You will stalk our Facebook page in order to gather information. We will block you in order to increase the work for you but you will use a friend's profile to look or create a false one. You will drive past the places you know we might be, home, work and recreational and social places hoping to catch a glimpse of what we are doing so you can satiate that need to know. You will create a new profile and follow us on Twitter, checking each day to see what we have written. Is there a new girlfriend? What is she like? Are we taking her to the places we took you? Who are these people in the photographs and where are they taken? We know you will be spying and the more you try and learn the more questions will arise. We use obsessing as a method of manipulation and this continues in this mould. Our ever presence will keep reminding you and you do not help yourself as you repeatedly reinforce our presence in your mind by searching, checking and spying. You will search our name on Google, examine our work website for any changes, and check on Facebook, Twitter, Instagram and LinkedIn. Like a detective hunting for clues you will keep at it each day. You create a habit in order to feed the addiction which is the need to know. We know you will do this, we engineer and we encourage this behaviour in you. The knowledge that you are engaged in these practices gives us fuel. We cannot see you or hear you yet we know you are spying on us. We know what you are like and we can picture you earnestly hunched over your keyboard as you stare at your monitor. Don't deny it because when we do Hoover you it is one of the first things we tease from you. How many times a day did you check our Facebook profile? You will admit you did it at least three times a day and and tell us how much you missed us. You will ask about the new person we were with and who you saw posts referring to and all the photographs that we displayed. Did we miss you too? You always ask this as well. Why? Because you always need to know.

Catfish

To catfish is to create false identities for use on-line and in particular for the purpose of carrying on deceptive online romances. The term was invited for our kind. The creation of false dating profiles, false Facebook profiles and the like is a standard tool of the narcissist as it allows for the gathering of fuel from multiple individuals on a regular basis. From being sat in a study one can reach out around the world and portray whatever we want to a vast array of individuals. Many people who are not of our kind engage in this behaviour as they seek to flirt with someone, to coerce them to send them nude pictures and videos or just to engage in some filthy chat with someone. Those individuals will do this to avoid detection from their current partner or perhaps friends and family who might inadvertently stumble upon their clumsy overtures. We go further than this as we look to ensnare our unwitting victims. Naturally since we are invariably excellent wordsmiths our ability to sit hidden, obscured by the internet allows the focus to be on words so that we can lure people in. I do it from time to time, making full use of the connectivity that arises from being able to access the internet from virtually anywhere and also the various platforms and applications which facilitate this kind of behaviour. I recall a particularly effective profile which I used on Facebook some time ago and which every so often I will roll out. I found a picture of an educated and handsome-looking fellow on the internet. It looked like a work profile picture which was just what I was looking for. I created a false name and then embellished the profile with various interests. I then began the hunt for some friends. I know that nearly everyone has friends on their Facebook profile who they do not know. Accordingly, it is not going to be difficult to begin to generate a coterie of supposed friends. After all, who is going to turn down a request from the erudite and attractive gentleman with the refined name? Very few as it transpires. Once the profile started to take on the look of one which had a base in reality then it was over to certain applications on Facebook to start the fun. At the time there was one called Social Me. It was very straight forward. A picture appeared and you could choose a compliment from a selection (sexy, crazy, hot, beautiful and so on - it was hardly taxing) or you could choose your own. Of course I am not from the herd so I embarked on my own descriptions using my well-known ability to flatter and describe. This soon grabbed the attention of many ladies and the comments went back and forth as they lavished me with their own comments. The fuel came flowing from scores of women as they locked on to me. They then sent the friend requests having been reeled in through Social Me. Messages would pass backwards and forwards and it was not long before they offered mobile telephone numbers. From there the conversations ranged from me talking about an entirely fictitious career (after all I am not going to tell them my real profession) to engaging in filthy chat was they masturbated down the telephone. All delicious fuel. I would be sat with my computer lighting up from Social Me comments, friend requests and messages as the mobile buzzed and pinged. I have a voice which many have commented on as alluring, the baritone of British received pronunciation proving a particular draw. With many I maintained the façade but with a handful I eventually admitted to being someone else, the person I actually was. This privileged group was allowed into knowing my real name and such additional information because they wanted to meet me and who was I to deny them that opportunity. This coterie consisted of a dominatrix from a city in the north-east of England, a nurse from the midlands, a chain-smoking charity worker from a city in the north-west of England, a long-nailed administrator from the south coast and most entertaining of all a police officer from the midlands. Not one of them challenged me about the artifice that I had created. Why? Because throughout I had created something plausible and their desire for me, created on the basis of electronic exchanges with a complete stranger and then late night telephone calls had proven too attractive to pass up. If ever questions were asked I always had an answer.

"Why are most of your friends on FB women?"

"Many of my male friends are not on FB and those that are I see them often. I use FB to keep in touch with long-distance friends and make new ones, just like you."

"Why aren't there more pictures on FB of you?"

"My job (which I was always amorphous about mentioning words such as 'finance', 'developing nations' and 'war-torn' means if I provide clues as to where I am I could place myself at risk."

Similar questions were always deflected with a plausible answer and they always accepted the explanation. Why? Because they liked the attention. They liked being able to have a conversation with someone who is intelligent and erudite rather than someone who writes, "Fancy a shag" as his opening gambit. I have mentioned before the poor standards of male engagement over the internet provides vast opportunities for those of us who exhibit skill. Those that I allowed beyond the false persona accepted my explanation of its use. I was engaged in tracking a fraud suspect online for a major bank and then befriending her. She knew what I looked life in real life so a false persona had to be adopted in order to draw her in. It gave the ruse credibility by interacting with lots of other people and it also allowed me to meet you. Not one of those admitted to the inner sanctum rejected this explanation or felt any annoyance at the subterfuge. They wanted something so they believed in it, whatever was said. I must admit even I was taken aback at times by how readily they had accepted it. I met all of them, some on numerous occasions and it was evident that they had considerable feelings for me and that was all good fuel. They have no idea what I am and nor would they. Some have been cast to one side whilst others are still used as pipelines as and when the need arises. Just like the catfish my barbels were attuned to sniffing out prey, but beyond that I have no likeness to such a creature. All we share in common is our ability to swim along and detect prey. The catfish combs the water whilst I cruise through cyberspace.

How many times have you declared that you have had enough? How many times have you vowed that you are no longer putting up with this behaviour and making a fresh start? How often have you put in place steps to depart and leave this confusing and twisted reality behind? We hear these assertive comments from time to time. We have subjected you to a sustained devaluation, provoked so many heightened emotional responses from you which has given us fuel. At times you did not know whether you were coming or going, your head swam and that dull ache in the centre of your forehead never seemed to diminish. You wondered who you could trust as you fought to establish what you believed was right against a backdrop of contradictions. From somewhere you mustered some strength, a bolt of fortitude sprang from the maelstrom and in that moment of clarity you knew it was time to go. This situation is not right surely? Nobody should be treated in this manner. Yes, it was the moment to depart.

Of course you could not do so without your parting speech. It was not borne out of spite or venom. Those are not watchwords that apply to you. Notwithstanding the horrendous treatment meted out against you, the repeated abuse and the incessant put downs, you still behaved with dignity and grace. There was little doubt that you wanted to lash out. You wanted to flail us with stinging words and some home truths, just in the same way we had used our acidic tongues and savage words to berate you, yet despite how much you wanted to speak to us in this manner you did not do so. Instead, demonstrating the empathy which attracted us to you all that time ago you explained how you still loved us. You fought back the tears as you explained that you loved us more than you did when we first became a couple and despite everything that has happened you still love us. You ought to have torn strips of us, levelling a lengthy charge sheet against us but you did not behave in this way. That is not who you are. You talked about all the wonderful traits we have and how you miss them, you continued to praise us even after everything that we had done to you. You stood there bearing the emotional and physical bruises and rather than lambast us for putting you in such a state you preferred to talk about the magical times we had together. You clearly had committed each of those occasions to your memory as you brought up each event and occurrence as the tears trickled down your cheeks. You explained how wonderful we made you feel, how you had never experienced anything like that before and you consequently truly believed you had found the one. You work through the golden period, talking about the trips we took, the days we spent together and the glittering and scintillating moments we created. We can see this is hurting you all the more yet still your selflessness continues. You are exhausted after the tortuous time you have been put through and yet still you only try to remember the good and thank us for those wonderful times. You tell us that although they lasted a few months, the memories of that time are seared into your mind and you will always treasure them. You explain that you will reflect on those memories and not what came to pass afterwards as you still prefer to think the best of us, despite everything we have subjected you to. Your nobility in behaving in this manner is most impressive and your admirable words continue to fuel us. You explain between sobs that you do not want to go but you have to. You do not want to leave everything that we have built up behind but if you do not do so then you will be destroyed. You apologise, yes you actually apologise that you have not been able to help us, to steer us away from the destructive and malevolent behaviour that has marred the latter months together. You explain how hard you have tried but admit you have been defeated. You express your desire for us to change and to seek help because you truly believe that we are a good person who just needs to seize on that goodness and allow it to shine. You tell us you have seen what we can do and achieve and you still want what is best for us. You stand there staring at us; some of your possessions already packed in the two suitcases which are waiting in the hallway. You tell us you will make arrangements with us to collect the remainder of your belongings once you have had a chance to think and breathe.

We rise from our seat and walk towards you. You are quietly sobbing and we take your hands in our hands and hold them in that tender manner you recall so well. The vicious squeezing that one day arrived out of nowhere is not in existence. Instead, we hold your hands and look you straight in the eye as we summon up a look we have practised before with others in the situation. The look begins as sorrow and then morphs into hope as we search your eyes looking for that flicker of flame once again through the tears. You hold our gaze as we keep searching and then we speak, our words soft and gentle, just as they were when we whispered into your ear as we lay next to you holding you late at night.

"I am sorry, I know this time I have to change. Please help me be the good person I know I can be, that I want to be. Something is wrong with me and I do not know what it is, but you can save me, you are the only one. Please do not leave me. I cannot survive without you. I need you. I want to make you happy again because someone as wonderful and as loving as you deserves it. I will get help but I know I can only do it with you at my side. Please, please stay."

The short speech is delivered with true brilliance as I gather the right inflection in tone coupled with suitable contrite looks and mannerisms. I continue to look into your eyes as you let my words sink in. The moments pass and then the light flickers, that flame of hope sparks into life and I know your next words before you have even spoken them and I begin to give you that enticing and winning smile again. I know that you will stay. Again.

Power Drain

Power. Everywhere you look you will see power at work. One company takes over another because of the former's greater financial power. A boxer knocks out his opponent since he has a more powerful punch. A car accelerates faster than a competing model owing to it having a more powerful. Power is all around us and dictate and governs all our interactions. In the home so much of what we rely on, cookers, fridges, television sets, hair dryers, blenders and heating rely on power. Power is central to a happier existence. By contrast, when power is absent so much goes wrong. If there is a storm and the electricity supply has been interrupted there is massive inconvenience. There is no heating with the risk to the health of the elderly, young and infirm. Lighting reverts to primitive methods such as illumination by candle. The younger generation experiences frustration as the wifi network fails and the multiplicity of devices which they have connected to the internet are useless. Witness the agitation of a teenage who has forgotten to charge his or her 'phone and they realise they only have 8% power showing on the batter icon. The necessity of power is absolute and the absence of power is abhorred. We are no different.

You are far more powerful than you may actually realise. You are our walking battery or cell. You yield fuel which powers us. We want you providing us with high quality fuel repeatedly as we rely on this for the preservation of ourselves. Your fuel grants us power to allow us to do what we need to. Look around your home and consider that if every heating element was switched on, every light shone and every household appliance was operating, the amount of power used is considerable. In the same way, when we enter your world we appear in a blaze of light, loud and unmissable. We give our warmth, we shine brightly and we are a spinning, whirling dervish of activity. All of this uses up power in the same way that your household appliances do. The drain to the energy network is substantial. If you want something as brilliant as us then there is a power cost associated with us and that is where you come in. In order to enable us to charm and seduce multiple targets, to allow us to roll out or campaign of love bombing with our arsenal of desire takes a tremendous amount of power. Thereafter, the denigration and devaluation all takes up energy and power. We like to conserve out power as you well know. Instead we want to take your power.

Consider how you once were at the outset of our relationship. You were confident, independent, happy and bright. Yes, you may have experienced some problems and they lurked beneath a fragile surface but you had survived what had happened in the past. You got on with things, supported by your own power networks of friends and family. We come along and sever some of those networks or if we can, we uncouple them from you and attach them to us instead in order to seize their power for our own use. At this time you felt stronger, more vibrant and energetic as you motored through life, taking care of yourself and others. Then we come along. The dazzling sound and light show which sweeps you off your feet is impressive but it has to be powered somehow. We provide that power at first, regarding it as an investment in order to ensnare you. We cannot however deplete our power reserves and that is why once we have you connected to us that we begin to leech your power, your fuel, for ourselves. Not only does this sequestration of your energy bolster us, making us powerful and more able to carry out our wicked machinations against you and others, it drains you.

Each day, our demands for your fuel to power us, means that there is less and less for you. You find that your power source becomes depleted. Your defences become weakened, just like the loss of shields on the Enterprise in Star Trek when they suffer a power failure. You have no energy, you feel listless and weak. You have little interest in anything anymore. Your bright and vivacious personality has become muted and dulled. We keep draining you of your power, feeding on your fuel as you become systematically weaker and weaker. Soon your loss of power results in your doing less and less. You have not the energy or functionality to do those things you once did. You forgo friends, you forget about family and you let your interests fray. This reduces your power further as you attempt, in vain, to conserve enough power to enable you to function at the most basic level. Yet we are not content. We continue to suck the life, the energy and the power from you, in order to sustain ourselves with no concern at all for the impact it has on you. You become a shell, a dud battery, a drained cell as all that power is taken for us. You have no interest in your appearance, you do very little, you no longer speak up for yourself or indeed have anything much to say. You switch to auto-pilot as the last traces of power continue to be sucked from you. You carry out only the most rudimentary of tasks until even they begin to be too much. You stop washing, you stop eating and you stop taking medication. On we go leeching this power from you until the warning lights that had been shining for some time about your low levels of power eventually flicker and go out. It is then you stop, broken and unable to function any longer. It is now that when you are utterly drained that we will uncouple from you and push you to one side, allowing you to crash into the dust. Our power lines are now attached to someone else as you lay there a malfunctioned, powerless appliance. You have been drained and ended up going down the drain, no longer of any use to us, that is until you start to recover and regain your power. Then we will be back. You can guarantee that.

Do Your Homework!

How often did you hear this refrain when you were a child? The command to get on with your homework and not to leave it until Sunday evening or even worse on the bus to school the following day. Homework is seen as an integral part of a student's academic progress. I was a diligent student. I could not be any other since I was trapped between the rock of a headmaster for a father and a hard face; I mean a hard place in the form of my driving and ambitious mother. From time to time she would place me in her car and drive to a run down and dilapidated area of the nearest city.

"Take a look, HG," she would announce as she drove along a street with boarded up windows, graffiti-sprayed walls and broken roofs, "these are the type of places you end up if you do not study hard at school. You do not want that do you?"

"No mother," I would dutifully respond as I watched the derelict houses speed by. Thus I was always reminded of the value of positive application across my various academic disciplines. It was reinforced repeatedly that I had to study hard, complete my essays and assignments and always do my homework. I am sure you can recall the temptation posed by your friends calling round to ask if you were coming out, or you had a new computer game you would much rather play or there was something on television that you would rather watch. The allure of something shiny and attractive always proved a distraction. We would all much rather do the exciting things rather than attend to the humdrum even if the humdrum is what is required to enable us to benefit in the long term. That naturally requires discipline. It is difficult isn't it to focus on something that is not especially exciting or is mundane? We would all much rather choose to the things which are new, fresh and exciting.

This is precisely what we rely on when we come blazing into your life. We distract you with our flattery and our charm. We turn your heads with the compliments and the excitement. Our whirlwind of desire is so difficult to resist. There may be one or two voices struggling to make themselves heard above the noise of our incessant flattering chatter. Those voices may know what we are or they at the very least are concerned by what they are witnessing and they urge you to consider carefully what you are doing. They see certain behaviours and they are not caught up in the excitement and razzle dazzle. They have some objectivity and quite possibly more life experience than you. They may recognise these behaviours having seen them with other people and they are trying to guide you to avoid making the mistakes that they have. Theirs is the voice of reason, akin to that parent who reminds you to get that homework done. It is never a popular suggestion and one that is always too readily ignored. I am sure you know people who now as adults perhaps have not made the best of themselves and they rue the fact that they should have tried harder at school or they should have listened to their parents but now it is too late for them. They did not listen and they chose the excitement of hanging out with their friends and larking about at McDonald's or on street corners to getting their head down and doing their homework. They have failed to heed the advice that was given by those who have more experience and wisdom. Just like them you were too absorbed with the excitement we brought into your world, it was far easier and far more attractive to become engrossed in what we offered than to sit and reflect, heed advice and do the homework. I have heard it many times,

"If only I had listened to my mother, she kept saying something was not right."

"My friends kept trying to tell me but I thought I knew best."

"I wish I had done some due diligence now, but I guess it is too late."

When we arrive promising you the world and telling you that you do not need to do your homework because you have us now, you might just want to re-consider that and get out some books and do some studying. By reading and learning you will protect yourself and achieve more. You will go further. Just like I did.

Taking the Empath to Victory

The predatory lion will watch from the grass at the wildebeest gathered at the edge of the river of the watering hole. He is waiting for his moment to strike, to pick off one of the herd which has foolishly strayed from the protection of the herd. Once that beast has ventured into the range of the waiting lion its fate has been sealed. Much like the empathic individual who has recklessly wandered back into the sphere of influence of the waiting narcissist who is ready to perform a Hoover, the wildebeest is just moments away from being captured and meeting a grisly fate. The narcissist and the hunting lion share several similarities. We are predators, kings of our environments and noble. We have the edge on the lion however. He may be able to sit unnoticed amidst the dried out grassland, his coat blending in with the sun-scorched yellows, ochres and browns, but once he makes his move and breaks cover, his intended target has a chance. It may only be a slim window of opportunity to escape this savage beast but there is an opportunity nevertheless. I am sure the proud feline would welcome being able to stroll right into that pack of waiting wildebeest, mingle with them, move about them and then strike without any of the creatures noticing that one of their number has been taken down. He can wander freely around as he takes his prey and never break cover. That is where we hold the advantage over the lion. We are able to move amongst our prey, unnoticed and even welcomed as we study and observe, choosing our moment to strike again and again and again.

With such a spectacular cloaking ability we are able to choose the choicest environments in order to ensnare an empath, super-empath or co-dependent. Just like the wildebeest that congregate at a watering hole, providing a target-rich environment for the lion, we seek out those places where we know that we will find plenty of empathic individuals and thus our quest for prime, potent fuel meets with victory. Accordingly as an empathic individual you will be well aware of the places where there are many of your kind. Those environments which require those who care, protect and nurture are prime locations for us to infiltrate and gorge on the victims that mill around us. Charities, hospitals, schools, animal rescue shelters, homeless shelters and domestic violence refuges are just some examples of the places where we will worm our way in. We have little difficulty in doing this. As you know, we are masters of mimicry with our unrivalled ability to take on the traits and abilities of others. Although empathy is an alien feeling to us we are easily able to exhibit the ways of the empath. We spend so much time amongst your kind that we know what to say, how to look and what to do so that we pass unchallenged amongst your ranks. Moreover, the thrusting dynamism that we bring, our charismatic leadership and motivational skills are highly prized in such caring places. The hard-hearted captain of industry may see finance, law, accountancy, technology and the like as 'sexier' environments in which to prosper but all of the above places I have mentioned where one finds a higher proportion of empathic individuals than usual have their rewards. The executives of charities are well remunerated, the leaders of hospital trusts invariably have flittering CVs and various honours attached to their names. These sectors need thrusting individuals alongside the care givers in order to ensure that the organisation is effective. This suits us perfectly. Our driven natures, our sense of entitlement and grandiose behaviour is just what is required for those top roles. Couple this with our chameleon like ability to feign that we care and that we are empathic means we ease into the charitable and caring sectors with unchallenged ease.

These environments not only provide us with plenty of succulent empaths to feast on but they present us with opportunities for easy wins. We can dazzle and shine, using our ambition to progress where others are more concerned about the delivery of care as opposed to clambering up the career ladder. These organisations need a dynamic hand on the tiller (us) combined with the delivery of caring services (you). The fact that there are empaths on tap for us to hunt down is serendipity indeed. Thus, next time you look around the management at your hospital or you are sat in a meeting with a committee of trustees for your charity there is every chance that one of our kind is sat there, lurking in the grassland, sliding a forked-tongue across those sharp, sharp teeth.

Further required reading from H G Tudor

Evil

Narcissist: Seduction

Narcissist: Ensnared

Manipulated

Confessions of a Narcissist

More Confessions of a Narcissist

Further Confessions of a Narcissist

From the Mouth of a Narcissist

Escape: How to Beat the Narcissist

Danger: 50 Things You Should Not Do with a Narcissist

Departure Imminent: Preparing for No Contact to beat the

Narcissist

Fuel

Chained: The Narcissist's Co-Dependent

A Delinquent Mind

Fury

Beautiful and Barbaric

The Devil's Toolkit

Sex and the Narcissist

Treasured and Tormented

No Contact: How to Beat the Narcissist

Revenge: How to Beat the Narcissist

Adored and Abhorred

Sitting Target: How and Why the Narcissist Chooses You

Black Hole: The Narcissistic Hoover

A Grimoire of Narcissism

Cherished and Chastised

Red Flag: 50 Warning Signs of Narcissistic Seduction

Ask the Narcissist: The Answers to Your Questions

Darlings and Demons

Black Flag: 50 Warning Signs of Abuse

Your Fault: Blame and the Narcissist

Elated and Eroded

Outnumber Not Outgunned

Deciphered: What the Narcissist Really Means

Feted and Feared

Smeared: Knowing and Beating the Narcissist's Campaign

Ghosted and Gilded

Why? Understanding the Narcissist's Behaviour

Exorcism : Purging the Narcissist from Heart and Soul

All available on Amazon

Further interaction with H G Tudor

Knowing the Narcissist

@narcissist_me

Facebook

Narcsite.wordpress.com

Further interaction

Knowing the Narcissist

Facebook

@narcissist_me

narcsite.wordpress.com

www.ingramcontent.com/pod-product-compliance
Lightning Source LLC
Chambersburg PA
CBHW060612290526
45793CB00001B/11